TRANSFORMING SOCIAL REPRESENTATIONS

Common sense, by definition, is familiar to us all. Science, for some of us, is more remote, yet it is not always clear what the connections are between these two ways of seeing the world. In *Transforming Social Representations*, S. Caroline Purkhardt explores several related themes in social psychology to elucidate the way we understand the social construction of knowledge and the means by which we change social reality.

From the perspective of a critique of social representations theory, S. Caroline Purkhardt argues that this necessitates a change of viewpoint from the individualistic and mechanistic assumptions of Cartesian science to the social and evolutionary perspective of a Hegelian framework. This not only emphasizes the cultural and historical dimensions of social phenomena but also illuminates the social and dynamic nature of individuals. As a consequence, the discipline of social psychology must itself be transformed, recognizing the active participation of scientists in the social construction of scientific knowledge.

Transforming Social Representations will be essential reading to those working in social psychology, history and philosophy of science, and sociology.

S. Caroline Purkhardt completed the work for this book while at the London School of Economics, has been involved in research projects at Surrey University, and is currently a freelance research scientist.

TRANSFORMING SOCIAL REPRESENTATIONS

A social psychology of common sense and science

S. Caroline Purkhardt

London and New York

First published 1993
by Routledge
11 New Fetter Lane, London EC4P 4EE

Simultaneously published in the USA and Canada
by Routledge
29 West 35th Street, New York, NY 10001

Typeset in Bembo by LaserScript, Mitcham, Surrey
Printed and bound in Great Britain by
T.J. Press (Padstow) Ltd, Padstow, Cornwall

British Library Cataloguing in Publication Data
A catalogue record for this book is available from the British Library.

Library of Congress Cataloging in Publication Data
Purkhardt, S. Caroline (Susan Caroline), 1961–
Transforming social representations: a social psychology of
common sense and science/S. Caroline Purkhardt.
p. cm.
Simultaneously published in the USA and Canada.
Includes bibliographical references and index.
1. Social psychology. I. Title.
HM251.P89   1993
302 – dc20   92-47076
CIP

ISBN 0–415–07960–8

TO MY MOTHER

CONTENTS

vii

CONTENTS

viii

CONTENTS

PREFACE

Being awarded my PhD in 1991 gave me a sense of achievement and relief, but my task was still not complete. I felt that the issues raised in my thesis needed to be addressed publicly and the ideas that I had developed could make a valid and worthwhile contribution to the debate on social representations, common sense and science. It was important not to leave them collecting dust on the library shelves. Unfortunately, the thesis did not lend itself to division into journal articles so I decided to dedicate the next year to expressing my ideas in a book. This required considerably more work and rewriting than I had anticipated. My only hope is that you, the reader, will find it fruitful.

I would like to thank a number of people who have contributed to the contents and completion of this book. Rob Farr stimulated my interest in social representations and I owe much to our many discussions and his constructive comments on my ideas and research. Similarly, I am indebted to Jan Stockdale for her invaluable encouragement and support. I would also like to thank my fellow students at the London School of Economics with whom I learned to express and clarify my thoughts. More recently, a research group with colleagues at the University of Surrey has helped me develop ideas relating social representations with identity. I am grateful to Howard Gruber for his permission to reprint a diagram illustrating Darwin's changing world view. I would also like to acknowledge the Economic and Social Research Council's award No. A00428624145.

INTRODUCTION

Over the past two decades our common-sense understandings of nature have changed dramatically. Terms such as the global environment or the greenhouse effect, once only heard in specialized circles, have become common currency. Similarly, virtually everyone knows that a good diet and moderate exercise are an integral part of healthy living, but this would not have been common knowledge a generation ago. Yet more striking is the rapidity with which we have absorbed a general knowledge of AIDS (Acquired Immune Deficiency Syndrome) into our belief and value systems.

What these examples illustrate is that, far from being static and mundane, common sense is continually evolving and changing, as it adapts to our activities in everyday life. We live in a thinking society and a changing reality. As Serge Moscovici (1982, 1984b, 1987) proclaims, one of the distinguishing characteristics of modern society is the dynamic nature of our beliefs, values and activities. As a consequence, one of the priorities of the social sciences must be to understand social change and examine 'society in the making'. Furthermore, as social scientists, we must participate in the dynamics of social knowledge and direct social change. In particular, social psychology itself must be transformed so as to recognize the actions and thinking of individuals and, simultaneously, their cultural or societal context.

Such a perspective would go beyond cognitive approaches that dominate contemporary social psychology. Rather than focusing on the individual's ability to process information about social objects we would be concerned with the social nature of thought and the creative ability of people together to change society. It would also go beyond traditional sociological approaches that use concepts such as collective representations or ideology as explanatory devices without reference to the creative participation of individuals. Social or societal psychology would be an anthropology of modern society: a study of culture, the evolution of common sense and its impact on social life (Moscovici, 1981, 1984b). As such, it could develop links with sociology, anthropology, linguistics and history, suggesting alternative approaches to research and theory building. Instead of bowing to an overriding concern for a methodology that makes spurious demands for accuracy we would use sources and methods that do justice to the complexities of cultural phenomena, acknowledging both their social and historical dimensions.

One of the most exciting and promising developments in this area is the theory of social representations, which focuses on the dynamics of common sense in everyday communication and social interaction. In its earliest form the theory identified science as a prominent force in modern society, transforming the very nature of common sense. In *La Psychanalyse: son image et son public*, Moscovici (1961) examined the diffusion of scientific knowledge and the influence of psychoanalysis on French culture and common-sense understandings. Since then, an ever-increasing number of European social psychologists and social scientists more generally have shown an interest in social representations, both in their research and in their theoretical debates. Social representations of such diverse topics as health and illness, cities, children and inequalities in gender, class and intelligence have been studied. The theory has been applied to various fields including social cognition, intergroup relations and child development. In addition, there have been comments and critiques from psychologists, philosophers, sociologists, anthropologists and historians alike. What is missing, however, is a comprehensive view that attempts to develop social representations theory and make explicit its perspective in the social sciences. The purpose of this book is to fill that gap while simultaneously applying the theory to a new area of study.

The point of departure for this book is the claim that, far from being exclusive to common sense, social representations theory also applies to science itself. This claim demands the interdependent development of social representations theory on the one hand and our understanding of science on the other. As it stands, the theory makes a sharp distinction between science and common sense. It suggests that, while an objectivist view of reality may be appropriate for the sciences, a different approach is required for the study of common sense: an approach that recognizes the consensual and constructive nature of everyday thought and interaction. I contend that this social perspective is also instrumental in the study of science. Like common sense, science is a social activity involving the active participation and collaboration of scientists in their particular cultural and historical contexts.

The application of social representations theory to the dynamics of scientific knowledge not only challenges some of the theory's presuppositions but also highlights a number of problematic issues. These include the relationship between common sense and science, between individuals and culture, between knowledge and environment and between stability and change. These dichotomies are transcended by elaborating and restructuring the theory of social representations within a cultural and evolutionary framework. The study of science using social representations theory facilitates the development of a social psychology of science. This provides a social constructionist perspective that addresses both the growth of scientific knowledge and the transformation of social reality.

This perspective evolves in the course of the book as central themes relating to the nature of individuals, of reality and of knowledge are explored. In Part I (Chapters 1–3) I focus on the theory of social representations and related research, highlighting the central problems that face psychologists using this framework. In particular, there are contradictions, both between individuals and society in the dynamics of social representations and also in the domain of the theory's application.

In Part II (Chapters 4 and 5) I broaden the scope of the book to the discipline of social psychology as a whole, examining the contrasting conception of the individual, of reality and of science within the dominant Cartesian paradigm and the alternative Hegelian (social constructionist) paradigm. I argue that the latter provides a more suitable framework for the study of evolving social phenomena.

In Part III (Chapters 6–8) I consider, in depth, the distinction between science and common sense. Drawing on the philosophy and sociology of science, I contend that social representations theory and the Hegelian paradigm are applicable both to common sense and to science itself. I argue that science (as well as common sense) is an historical and cultural endeavour that involves the social construction of reality through people's interactions with and communication about their environment.

Finally, in Part IV (Sections I–VII of Chapter 9) I elaborate and vivify the arguments presented in this book with reference to a case study on the transformation of social representations in social psychology. This illuminates the interdependence between social individuals and their society; the mutual relations among organisms, their environment and their culture; and the transformation of social representations in the social construction of social reality.

Chapter 1 familiarizes the reader with social representations theory, providing a structured presentation of their nature, their functions in social life and the processes by which they are transformed. It also gives me the opportunity to raise a number of significant issues that are addressed in subsequent chapters of the book. These converge on the conception of the relationship between individuals and society and the processes of transformation in the social construction of reality.

As it stands, the theory fails to create a societal psychology that integrates the psychological, cultural and historical dimensions of social reality. In Chapter 2 I focus on the manifest contradictions and confusions, both in the theory and in related research, regarding the role of individuals and of society in the dynamics of social representations. While the collective or supra-individual nature of social representations is emphasized, some of the theoretical principles and much of the research suggest that social representations can ultimately be reduced to the cognition of individuals. I propose that this dichotomy (between the individual and culture) can be overcome by reinterpreting the prescriptive nature of social representations as a dynamic process; by denying their autonomous nature; and by acknowledging the significance of conflict as well as consensus. This is reflected in research that emphasizes the interdependence of people's identities, their social interactions and communications, and their representations in an evolutionary dialectics that both sustains and transforms social reality.

In Chapter 3 I consider the theory's domain of application. Moscovici developed social representations theory in order to describe and explain how the innovations and discoveries of science diffuse into and transform common-sense understandings in modern societies. However, both the theoretical principles and the variety of research suggest a wider domain of application, embracing social representations that emerge within common sense as well as those relating to developments in science. Much of the research has investigated social representations that are only indirectly associated with science, if at all. Furthermore, the balance between tradition and innovation, the forms of communication and interaction and the processes of transformation suggest that such a distinction is unfounded. While Chapter 2 prepares the ground for our discussions on the appropriate paradigm for social psychology in Part II, Chapter 3 provides the foundations for Part III in which I re-examine the relationship between science and common sense.

The implicit difficulties presented by the theory and research are not exclusive to the field of social representations. Rather, they are expressions of the fundamental problems that have confronted psychology and social psychology throughout their history. In Chapter 4 I argue that a commitment to the individualistic and mechanistic principles of the

Cartesian paradigm and to a positive-empiricist representation of science has perpetuated a division between the individual and culture. In contrast, the Hegelian paradigm propounds an evolutionary and constructionist perspective in which the individual is both the product and the producer of culture. This perspective is expressed in recent developments since the 'crisis' in social psychology. Furthermore, it conjoins with an alternative methodology that favours theory construction over data collection, adopting an evolutionary and comparative approach to the qualitative examination of relational systems in multi-method research programmes.

Representations of the individual and of reality that are commensurate with the Hegelian paradigm are elaborated in Chapter 5. Drawing on the writings of Dewey, Mead and Vygotsky, I propound a representation of the individual as a social being within an organism–environment–culture system. This conceptual framework supports my claim that social representations exist not only in our minds but also in our interactions and in the cultural environment. It is unified with a social realist definition of reality that avoids both a positive empiricist view, locating reality in the external world, and an extreme social constructionist view, locating reality in the heads of individuals. As a consequence it is possible to reassess the role of individuals in the dynamics of social representations. Both the perpetuation and the transformation of social representations is interdependent with people's identities.

The social conception of individuals, reality and science elaborated in Part II plays an important part in re-evaluating the distinction between science and common sense in Part III. While the distinction between the reified universe of science and the consensual universe of common sense serves to demarcate social representations as the public understanding of science, it also creates substantial problems for the theory as a whole. These are examined in Chapter 6, with reference both to the definition of the reified universe and the interaction between science and common sense. Ultimately, the reified universe enshrines a positive-empiricist epistemology that is antithetical to the social constructionist epistemology of the theory.

In Chapter 7 I show that the depiction of the reified universe reflects the received tradition in the philosophy of science. This was challenged by significant developments in science in the early part of the twentieth century that gave rise to alternative philosophies. In particular, I compare Kuhn's description of paradigms with the notion of social representations, propounding a historical, cultural and social-psychological approach to the growth of scientific knowledge. This view is strengthened by parallel developments in the sociology of scientific knowledge, corroborating my contention that social representations theory is applicable to science as well as to common sense.

This position is developed further in Chapter 8, in which I present the foundations for a social psychology of science, offering a social constructionist account of the transformation of scientific knowledge. Firstly, it is necessary to reconsider the processes of transformation described within the theory of social representations. I propose that the transformation of social representations involves not only the assimilation of the unfamiliar, but also the social construction of the unfamiliar and the accommodation of the familiar. These processes must be conceived in relation to dynamic systems of social representations rather than any single social representation. Secondly, we are now in a position to reconsider the dynamics and transformation of science. Science itself must be conceived as a human endeavour in which knowledge is socially constructed within the organism–environment–culture system. I elaborate this perspective with reference to more recent developments in the philosophy of science that illuminate the processes of science within an evolutionary and constructionist paradigm. Finally, I illustrate these contentions about the social construction of science and its relation to common sense by presenting an outline of the origins and diffusion of Darwin's theory of evolution. This prepares the ground for the in-depth case study on the transformation of social representations in science presented in Part IV (Chapter 9).

Chapter 9 commences with an introduction, outlining the theoretical and methodological rationale for selecting Henri Tajfel's contribution to the science of psychology as the object of study. The research programme investigated the dynamics of social representations in the social psychology of groups, analysing the origins of change and the process of transformation in the organism–environment–culture system. It will be seen that assimilation and accommodation in the evolution of social representations systems involves not only generalization, particularization and naming but also discovery, inclusion and integration. Furthermore, it will be seen that these processes occur only in relation to an individual's identity, their immediate environment, both physical and social, and the cultural and societal milieux in which they are immersed.

Chapter 9 consists of seven consecutive sections or phases, providing both a description and analysis of an evolving social representations system in the social construction of science. Section I deals with the earliest phase of Tajfel's career in psychology, from the psychophysics of perceptual overestimation to the study of stereotypes. The conflicts and similarities within his own and others' research led to Tajfel's distinctive contribution, involving particularization, generalization and naming in the transformation of the relevant social representations system.

In section II we see that the psychology proffered by Tajfel at this time was dependent upon his socialization into the conventions of the discipline. Despite his interest in social and cultural phenomena the prescriptive force of social representations led him to adopt a reductionist approach to the problems of stereotypes and prejudice, constructing explanations in terms of individual cognition. This process of socialization is effected through personal interactions with other psychologists, communication through journals or books and involvement in research practice. Furthermore, Tajfel's contribution plays an important part in establishing his identity as a psychologist.

In section III Tajfel breaks with conventional reductionism to consider both assimilation of social values about groups and the causal attributions people make about social relations in his explanation of prejudice. This preliminary transition from individualistic to social levels of explanation was directed by his own and others' experience of prejudice as well as others' research, involving inclusion, differentiation and accommodation within the social representations system.

In section IV we turn our attention to European research on the development of national attitudes in children. This presented anomalies with regard to cultural influences on the assimilation of social values. A combination of conducting this research and reading social science literature on nationalism led Tajfel to challenge explicitly the conventions of social psychology. He propounded an approach that integrated the psychological and sociological aspects of large-scale intergroup relations, differentiating it both from traditional social psychology and from other social sciences. These transformations did not occur in a social vacuum. Rather, they were interdependent with his participation in collaborative research, his involvement with the emerging crisis in social psychology and his central role in establishing a European community of social psychologists.

By contrast, in section V Tajfel returns to the laboratory, conducting a series of experimental investigations with his colleagues, with the aim of establishing the minimal conditions for intergroup behaviour. Designing the 'minimal group paradigm' – a methodological innovation – they unexpectedly discovered that social categorization alone led respondents to discriminate between their own group and another group. Surprisingly, they did not attempt to employ the social representations system that had been developed previously. Challenging alternative explanations through argument, debate and further experimental research, Tajfel and his colleagues explained these findings in well-established terms of cognition and social norms. However, the research, both in national attitudes and in intergroup behaviour, had created many anomalies with regard to the role of social values, the impact of the cultural context and the psychological processes involved in intergroup conflict. An understanding of these issues was constructed gradually through the painstaking transformation and elaboration of the social representations system.

By the inception of section VI Tajfel's career was well established, having been rewarded with a professorship at Bristol University. Here he attracted a group of scientists who were all interested in the same issues. Their collaboration over a period of several years culminated in the construction of a theory of intergroup relations (social identity theory), which was to become a burgeoning field of study, and the emergence of a new perspective in social psychology. The experimental research of John Turner directed the specification of the psychological processes involved in intergroup discrimination. Elements within the social representations system were restructured, integrated and differentiated in order to explain the research findings. Further developments were interdependent with discussion within the growing European Association as to the future of social psychology.

Tajfel's commitment to understanding and resolving the devastating intergroup conflicts that he had experienced himself and that persisted in modern society led him, among others, to rethink the place of society and culture in social psychology. Understanding the psychological processes alone was insufficient to explain relations among groups extant in society. It was also necessary to consider the structure of society. This was not only included, but also integrated into the social representations system by transposing psychological to societal differentiations. The distinction between intragroup and intergroup relations, matched with personal and social identities respectively, is extrapolated to society, differentiating consensual beliefs about the structure of society in terms of social mobility and social change. While there still remained questions outstanding about power and status relations between groups and the creation or maintenance of consensual belief systems, this theoretical framework constituted a comprehensive, elaborate and integrated account of intergroup relations.

In subsequent years (section VII) intergroup relations became an established field of research and social identity theory was applied to various social psychological issues including intragroup relations and the study of language use. This involved not only a process of diffusion through various modes of communication within the sciences but also the further transformation and reconstruction of the social representations system through assimilation and accommodation. As we have seen, this is interdependent with the identities of the scientists involved, their research activities, their immediate community and their cultural or societal milieux.

In the course of this book I hope to have achieved three complementary aims. Firstly, while social representations theory offered a critique of dominant approaches in social psychology a number of substantive problems persisted. These are overcome by redefining the social individual and social reality in terms of an integrative organism–environment–culture system. Furthermore, it is through this dynamic and interdependent system that we transform social knowledge and change the social world.

Secondly, the book presents an alternative paradigm for social psychology. This emphasizes the societal and historical dimensions of the discipline's object of study. Furthermore, by adopting a self-reflexive stance, the same principles are applied to the conduct of social psychology, suggesting a methodology that recognizes the scientist's participation in research and theory construction.

Thirdly, by incorporating the insights of philosophy, sociology and social psychology, the book advances a science of science. This develops a social constructionist account of scientific progress within the Hegelian paradigm. In so doing, it demystifies science and encourages the greater participation of science in society.

Part I

SOCIAL REPRESENTATIONS AND COMMON SENSE

1

BUILDING CASTLES IN THE AIR

The nature, functions and processes of social representations

(Social representations are) 'theories' or 'branches of thought' in their own right, for the discovery and organization of reality.

(Moscovici, 1973: xiii)

(Social representations are) systems of values, ideas and practices with a two-fold function: first to establish an order which will enable individuals to orient themselves in and master their material world and second, to facilitate communication among members of a community by providing them with a code for naming and classifying the various aspects of their world and their individual and group history.

(Moscovici, 1973: xiii)

Social representations are 'systems' of preconceptions, images and values which have their own cultural meaning and persist independently of individual experience.

(Moscovici, 1982: 122)

Social representations (are) a set of concepts and explanations originating in daily life in the course of inter-individual communications. They are the equivalent, in our society, of the myths and belief systems in traditional societies; they might even be said to be the contemporary version of common sense.

(Moscovici, 1981: 181)

Since I commenced working with the theory of social representations, people have frequently asked me 'What is a social representation?' and, more specifically, 'What is social about social representations?' 'What do they do?' 'How do they work?' and 'Where does one find a social representation?' These questions have never been easy to answer. Moscovici's writings are expansive and eloquent but they tend to give a nebulous impression of his general approach rather than a clear idea of any theoretical postulates or empirical concerns. Other writers have tended to focus on particular aspects of the theory in relation to their own theoretical preoccupations or research interests. As a consequence, the literature available to the English-speaking community lacks a structured presentation of the theory as a whole. This chapter attempts to fill this gap, explicating the fundamental principles of the theory in terms of the nature, functions and processes of social representations.

The contents of this chapter serve as an introduction to social representations theory for the uninitiated reader, going beyond the frequent quotations and all too brief synopses that might have sparked their interest. For those who are already familiar with the general approach it will serve to clarify particular aspects of concern. However, it should be borne in mind that this is not a definitive, state-of-the-art presentation of social representations theory. Rather, it provides the groundwork on which I build the arguments that are presented in subsequent chapters. I draw together the ideas expressed in a selection of Moscovici's and Jodelet's articles (Moscovici, 1973, 1982, 1984a, b, 1987, 1988; Moscovici and Hewstone, 1983; Jodelet, 1984a, b). This familiarizes the reader with the social representations approach; its assumptions, its theoretical propositions and its scope. At the same time, it is possible to identify contradictions and points of confusion which create substantial problems for the coherence and integrity of the theory. In this way, this chapter both introduces the ideas to be elaborated and raises the issues to be dealt with in the course of this book.

THE NATURE OF SOCIAL REPRESENTATIONS: WHAT ARE THEY?

Social representations are the constituents of reality

Social representations describe a social reality that is constructed through our interactions with and communications about the social and physical world. At the same time, social representations form an 'environment of thought' that determines our perceptions or conceptions of reality and directs our actions. Social representations at once determine the way we see the world and how we act but are simultaneously determined by our interactions and communications. This notion of social reality can be difficult to grasp, not least because it breaks with conventional ways of thinking in social psychology. Firstly, we must break with the language of cause and effect which insists upon the independence of entities as

4

opposed to the integral relatedness of phenomena. Secondly, we must understand that priority is given to the social and cultural aspects of reality, that is the relational and supra-individual nature of social life.

To elaborate further, the nature of representations obviates the distinction which is typically made between a stimulus and a response or between a person's perception of an object and the object itself. A person sees or understands a physical or social object in a particular way only because that person has a representation of that object. The object and the person act together in the construction and expression of a representation. In other words, it is not the nature of the object that determines our construction of it but our relationship with that object. This representation, once formed, sustains these relations. Furthermore, it is not simply the relationship between an individual and an object that shapes a representation but also the individual's relations with others and others' relations with the object. A social representation is constructed through the processes of interaction and communication with other people, while those interactions and conversations are shaped themselves by people's social representations. This does not occur within an objective reality, rather it is conducted within a socially constructed reality. Reality is social through and through: we live in a thinking society and construct a social reality.

While the notion of social reality and its construction in social life lies at the heart of social representations theory it is still not entirely clear what this entails. Social representations are said to constitute our reality. From this we can surmise that social reality neither exists purely in the heads of independent individuals nor in an objective reality independent from individuals. But it still remains to explicate the role of individuals' beliefs and actions, the role of culture and the role of the physical environment in the construction of this social world.

Social representations are symbolic in nature

The symbolic nature of social representations embraces the social, cultural and historical aspects of social representations. It refers to the social significance of objects and events that is dependent upon the common meanings in verbal and non-verbal gestures by members of a community. These common meanings are, in turn, dependent upon a community's social norms and values and their common history. Firstly, an object or event is simultaneously and immediately perceived and conceived in terms of a symbolic or meaningful reality. This is expressed in terms of the two facets of a representation: the iconic facet or image and the

5

symbolic facet or concept. The object or event is not first seen and then interpreted. Rather the concrete image and the symbolic meaning go hand-in-hand. In this way representations embrace percepts, which reproduce the world in a meaningful way, and concepts, which abstract meaning from the world. The psychological activity of individuals is located in the social activity of a community; in the language, experience and knowledge shared within a particular culture; in the communications and interactions of social groups; and in the traditions and conventions of a collective history. Secondly, representations are always of something and of someone or some collective. Symbolic knowledge (unlike cognitive information) acknowledges the person who knows something and the perspective from which he or she knows it. Thus, there is always an interdependence between the social representations, the social groups and their expressive functions.

It is the symbolic that distinguishes purely cognitive representations from social representations. Cognitive psychology and information-processing approaches offer an individualistic and separatist account of representations. A representation is conceived as an internal construct in the mind of an individual that stands in place of something existing independently of that individual. The individual is isolated both from other people and from the world that is being represented. A 'social' representation would simply be an individual's representation of a social object. The process of representation and the representation itself maintains the individual character. The mental processes or psychological mechanisms are severed from their social context and their social functions.

This stands in stark contrast to social representations which are essentially social, cultural and historical phenomena. We have seen that their symbolic nature is expressed both in the process of representing something and in the functions of representations in social life. The symbolic nature of social representations also supports the construction of social reality. The act of representing something is always constructive. A representation, once constructed, exists in some sense independently of that which is being represented. The representation becomes an object in its own right. This applies not only to representations shared in the minds of individuals and groups but also to representations in the products and cultural artifacts of a society. Representations exist in the media, in books, in films, in drawings, to mention but a few, as much as in the minds of people. Once a representation is constructed it acquires a force of its own.

In that representations are symbolic reconstructions as opposed to a simple reproduction they are also creative. This creative force gives social representations a highly significant role to play in maintaining the social order and in bringing about social change. Thus, it is in the symbolic nature of social representations that the emphasis on meaning and social significance becomes apparent. It is here that the supra-individual or social character of representations is established. And it is here that the dynamic and constructive power of social representations is founded.

Social representations are both form and content

An acknowledgement of the symbolic nature of social representations with all its concomitants – social, cultural and historical – implies that, as long as we are studying common sense and everyday thought, it is not possible to distinguish the form of representations from their content. The content will vary between social groups, cultures and historical epochs and it is not possible to separate the regularities in representations from the processes that create them.

Once again, this contrasts with cognitive psychology. The latter has focused on the processes of representations which are considered to be universal, irrespective of the specific content of the representation. But representations are always of something, they take the place of and signify aspects of the world. This content cannot be ignored. It cannot be assumed that thought processes are general and invariant, that is, universal. Rather, as the content of a representation differs across cultures or changes over time, so does its form. The form and content of thinking are closely related to the form and content of communications and interactions; to the discussion and agreements between people; and to the relations of social groups. In other words, the manner of thinking, as well as what we think, depends upon the cultural context.

Looking at our own discipline Moscovici argues that it is inappropriate and misleading to apply the positivistic, scientific rules of thought to social, consensual knowledge, as the logic or form underlying these different contents is also different. The 'psychological laws' are related to the contents of the social representations and, hence, to their cultural and historical context. This has far-reaching implications for social psychology which are reflected in the research approach adopted by some scholars studying social representations. However, the implications for the conduct of socio-psychological investigations and our understanding of social reality need to be made explicit.

Social representations are conventional and prescriptive

Bearing in mind the social nature of reality and the symbolic nature of representations we are now in a position to understand the conventional and prescriptive nature of social representations. Firstly, social representations conventionalize the objects, persons and events that we encounter in daily life. They act on any previously established social object, or any new object entering into our awareness, constraining them so that they 'fit' into the categories and systems of relationships that we already possess. Thus, any object is understood in terms of a symbolic system that is conditioned by our social representations and, hence, by our cultural conditions. Secondly, social representations are prescriptive, imposing themselves upon us with an irresistible force. We cannot escape from the conventions of representation, language and culture. We experience and understand the present only in terms of the past, in terms of tradition and culture.

Social representations are thus fundamentally historical in nature. All the systems of perception and conception, of description and understanding which circulate within a society are linked to previous systems. They are reproduced by the continuity of human cultural and social life, and by the language and actions by which they are expressed. This historical, pre-scriptive thesis is potentially problematic. It presents a sociological thesis in which social representations become as coercive as Durkheim's collective representations or social facts. The past prevails over the present and the present remains powerless in the face of convention.

Social representations are dynamic

Social representations are not only conventional and prescriptive, they are also dynamic. As they circulate and diffuse throughout society their plasticity becomes apparent. Our perceptions and conceptions, our com-munications and actions and their meaning and relations are continually reconstructed and reconstituted. Our social reality is transformed as new social representations emerge and old ones disappear, along with the concomitant social objects and relations.

While the dynamic nature of social representations is a fundamental aspect of the theory it appears to portray an uneasy tension with the prescriptive nature of social representations. This returns us to our initial difficulty in understanding a social reality that both determines the way in which we understand, perceive and relate to the world and, simul-taneously, evolves and transforms through these same relations. In other words, if the past prevails over the present how can the present transform the ever-present past?

Social representations are autonomous

Social representations are also said to be autonomous. In characterizing social representations as the constituents of social reality *sui generis* Moscovici emphasizes their cultural or supra-individual quality. Their autonomy is reflected in the description of their dynamic nature. Not only do they communicate between themselves, but as they circulate and diffuse through society they merge, attract and repel each other, influencing the form and content of each other, changing in harmony with the course of social life. Their autonomy is also reflected in their conventional and prescriptive nature. Priority is given to the consensual aspects of social representations, being shared and strengthened by tradition, over and above their social or collective origins.

Their autonomous nature makes it obvious that, as socio-psychological phenomena, social representations cannot be reduced to the social psychology of individuals. However, this is in danger of leaving out the individual from the analysis altogether. It is in danger of presenting a sociological, rather than a social psychological thesis. It denies the role of individuals in transforming and changing our social representations. By giving so much power to culture and tradition the individual becomes impotent.

THE FUNCTIONS OF SOCIAL REPRESENTATIONS: WHAT DO THEY DO?

Social representations construct and shape reality

We have already seen that social representations are the constituents of our reality, forming a symbolic environment of thought. As such, they play an essential role in constructing and shaping reality, determining the meaning or significance of objects and events. Social representations provided an established order in which people can interpret and understand their material and social worlds and can become effective actors or participants in social life. Social representations embody and define the experience of reality, determining its boundaries, its significance and its relationships. In this way, reality is both continuous and stable. The ambiguity and diversity of life is reduced and the meanings of actions are made unequivocal. Social representations achieve this by indicating where to find the effects and how to choose the causes; by indicating what must be explained and what constitutes an explanation; and by setting an event in the context of a system of relations with other events.

Social representations enable communication and social interaction

The role of social representations in structuring and coordinating communication and social interaction also ensues from their symbolic nature and the construction of social reality. Individuals and groups communicate and interact with each other through the shared representations and conventional meanings of language and action. Language provides the medium for verbal communication which embodies the conventional meanings and contents of our social representations. Similarly, social representations imbue our actions and non-verbal gestures with meaning and significance.

We should also remember that social representations originate in communication and social interaction. They evolve in order to support the purposes and interests of individuals and groups, oriented towards communication, understanding and control. When individuals or groups share the same social representations, actions are understood in the same way. The action has the same significance or meaning for both the actor and the perceiver, giving rise to an exchange of gestures which is coordinated. The social representation both guides the social actions of an individual or group and allows these actions to be understood by others. However, where social representations are not shared, for example, between members of two different cultures or conflicting groups, the misinterpretation of actions is likely to occur.

Once again, we are confronted with the dilemma that there is a two-way influence between social representations and social action. On the one hand, the structure and content of social representations determine our social actions. On the other hand, communication and social interaction determine our social representations. We need to develop an understanding of social representations, not only as phenomena but also as an ongoing and dynamic process. In turn, we must also develop an understanding of communications and social interactions that goes beyond conversations and interpersonal relations.

Social representations demarcate and consolidate groups

The relationship between social representations and social actions has implications for our understanding of groups. Social representations form an environment of thought for communication and interaction within and between groups. They provide a stock of images and ideas that are taken for granted and mutually accepted by associated individuals. The shared meanings of objects and events serve to consolidate the group, providing a shared reality within which binding relations are formed with other people. They also serve to demarcate groups from each other through divergences in meaning incorporated in the social representations. In other words, they identify the groups which express them as well as the contents being represented. Furthermore, social representations themselves are rooted in the life of groups, being constructed in accordance with the group's purposes and the flow of interactions among social groups. Thus, they regulate, anticipate and justify the social relations that are established between groups.

Social representations direct socialization

The way in which social representations structure our social reality is most clearly seen in the socialization of an infant. Infants interact with their parents who are impregnated with the social representations derived from their early and adult experiences, from their conversations, and their social interactions. The parents interact with the infants in terms of these social representations, indicating the symbolic significance of the infants' various behaviours. Thus it is the meanings or symbolic significance of behaviours which are internalized by the infants. They become an integral part of the individual and of their interactions with others. Communications, through various forms of social interaction, and the meanings which they express, are thus interpersonal before they are internalized to become intrapersonal. In this way, the individual is absorbed into society and into the collective environment of thoughts. This applies to the socialization of an individual or group moving into a new environment as much as to the socialization of infants. Social representations draw the individual into the cultural traditions of a group and the group's representations are impressed upon the individual such that they become a part of the individual's personality.

While it is clear that social representations play an important role in the demarcation and consolidation of groups and in the process of socialization, these aspects of the theory need considerable development. In particular, little is said about the role of groups, people's identities and the processes of socialization in the evolution and transformation of social representations.

Social representations make the unfamiliar familiar

One of the most important functions of social representations is to make the unfamiliar familiar. We have seen that social representations order and stabilize our social reality and how communication and social inter-actions are directed and understood through them. Objects, individuals and events are perceived and understood in relation to our social representations. This is as true for those events with which we are familiar as it is for those events which seem strange.

Moscovici characterizes the unfamiliar as that which is threatening due to its discontinuity with the past and its meaninglessness in terms of our current representations. This would occur, for example, when conventions disappear, when distinctions between the abstract and the concrete become blurred, or when an atypical behaviour prevents a normal continuation of social interaction. That is, something is un-familiar when it does not conform to our expectations, resulting in a sense of incompleteness or randomness. This may occur when we enter a new culture or group, or when we are presented with a new object, event or concept. We are aware of unfamiliar objects, events or concepts, only in as far as they are visible, similar and accessible but they are unfamiliar and disturbing to the degree in which they are invisible, different and inaccessible. What is unfamiliar worries, threatens and preoccupies us as it breaks our sense of continuity and stability and it also acts as a barrier to mutual understanding.

The unfamiliar is transformed into the familiar by re-presenting it within the context of relations and meanings that comprise our social representations. The form and content of the social representation will determine the direction and means by which a group comes to terms with the unfamiliar. This occurs through the processes of social inter-action and communication: that is, the unfamiliar becomes familiar through its use in conversation and eventually in social interaction between members of the group. In this way its relation to the receiving social representation becomes defined and stabilized: as the unfamiliar is given meaning and value it enters into the realm of our social relations and becomes part of our social reality.

The example used by Moscovici is drawn from his study of psycho-analysis in France (Moscovici, 1961). Within the social representation of medicine and of medical treatment the psychoanalyst does not fulfil our expectations and is thus unfamiliar. He or she does not prescribe drugs or tell us what to do, as would an 'ordinary' doctor. Rather, the client is expected to do most of the talking and to take an active part in the therapeutic treatment. As such the psychoanalyst is unfamiliar. However, some people, such as Catholics, compared psychoanalysis to the con-fessional and the psychoanalyst to the priest. In this way, the psychoanalyst is made usual and familiar. The unfamiliar becomes meaningful and significant in our social reality and in our relations with others.

Despite the fact that 'the unfamiliar' plays an essential role in the dynamics of social representations it is still not very clear how we are to conceive or define the unfamiliar within the theoretical framework. Social representations are the constituents of our reality and it is difficult to see how the unfamiliar, or anything else for that matter, can lie outside that reality. Furthermore, although we are told that the unfamiliar is assimilated into our social representations and made familiar we are not told how this affects the structure of relations and the contents of those social representations. It will be essential to elaborate both aspects if we are to understand the evolution and transformation of social representation.

THE PROCESSES OF SOCIAL REPRESENTATIONS: HOW DO THEY WORK?

Anchoring: making the meaningless meaningful

Anchoring is the process by which all material and social objects and all events and actions are situated within our social representations. The very nature of social reality means that there cannot be meaningful percepts or ideas that are not anchored in a social representation. Furthermore, anchoring is the process by which unfamiliar objects and events enter into our social reality, making them meaningful and significant in our social relations. This process underlies the dynamic nature of social representations, at once transforming the newly integrated percept or idea while simultaneously transforming the content and structure of the social representation.

The process of anchoring involves two inextricably linked sub-processes; classification and naming. Those objects for which there is neither a category nor a name, although we have an awareness of them, remain meaningless and incommunicable. It cannot be described, either to ourselves or to others, nor can it be evaluated or judged. It is, therefore, unable to enter into our discourse or to play any significant part in our interactions. In such respects it is not part of our social reality. By classifying and naming objects within the context of prevalent social representations the unfamiliar becomes familiar, its identification specifying its meaning or significance in relation to the conventional meanings of the material and social objects or events.

13

Classification involves comparing the unfamiliar object to prototypes that represent a given class. This occurs in one of two ways, either by generalization or by particularization. If we wish to emphasize the similarity or the typicality of the objects we will generalize and reduce the differences between the unfamiliar object and the prototype. If we wish to emphasize the difference or the abnormality we will particularize the characteristics of the unfamiliar object. This will depend, not only on the similarities and differences *per se*, but also on the purposes of the group and the values associated with the social representation and the unfamiliar object or event involved.

Once it is classified those features which coincide with the prototypes are emphasized. This gives precedence to memory, to the conventional features of prototypes held within our social representations. It is the social representation, rather than the object itself, which is predominant. This reflects their symbolic nature, whereby the response is prior to the stimulus: we do not cognize the object, rather we recognize it. In this way classifying something simultaneously constrains it. The prescriptive force of classification stipulates which sets of behaviour and rules of action are permissible in relation to both people and material objects. Through interactions, the newly classified person or object itself will be transformed, being constrained by the meaning or significance imposed by the social representation.

Once classified, the object is subsequently named. This not only provides a label by which the object can be tagged but also defines its set of relations with other objects and events in accordance with the relation the name has with other linguistic categories. The name places the classified object in a complex system of related words; it is given an identity in as far as a consensus is established, which is communicable. Naming 'precipitates' the object such that there are three consequences: firstly, once named, the object can be described and acquires characteristics in accordance with the relations the name has with other words; secondly, the named object becomes distinct from other objects through its designated characteristics and tendencies; thirdly, the object becomes conventional for those who adopt and employ the same name.

These processes do not take place in the minds of individuals; representations are not the creations of individuals in isolation. Rather, it is a public activity in which individuals and groups create representations in the course of their conversations about and interactions with the relevant objects or events. In this way, unfamiliar phenomena become established within our social representations and enter into our social reality.

14

Objectification: making the abstract real

Objectification is the process by which abstract concepts, attributes or relationships are transformed into and replaced by concrete images or things. For Moscovici, we are 'under a constant compulsion' to give abstract concepts an equivalent concrete existence. By the process of objectification we create social objects and we objectify abstract concepts precisely in order to forget that they are a product of our own activity. We perceive our own creations but, rather than being a product of our imagination, the object becomes something in reality. Objectification or de-subjectification is thus an active and creative process by which social representations are transformed such that the unfamiliar in one generation becomes familiar and natural in the next.

Not all concepts can be objectified. There are limits to our imagination, constrained as it is by the prescriptive nature of social representations and the taboos these entail. Objectification occurs for those concepts which can merge with a complex of images or the 'figurative nucleus' of a social representation – for example, concepts within psychoanalysis, such as the unconscious and the conscious, are merged with our social representations of the body. The processes of the mind are transformed into the organs of the psychic system. In this way, the psychological is merged and assimilated into the biological and the concepts of the unconscious and the conscious are transformed into objects.

Once transfiguration or naturalization from a concept to an image has taken place, the image is indistinguishable from reality. It no longer has the status of a sign but becomes a part of our symbolic reality. It acquires an almost physical, independent existence which is perceived as being of the world and acquires efficacy, being something which can cause effects. This process is evidenced in the transformations of language. Verbs, adverbs and adjectives, which refer to relationships or processes, are frequently transformed into nouns. What was once a concept is transformed into an object. These nouns do not merely represent things, they also create them, investing them not only with meaning or significance but also with all the force of physical reality.

Thus anchoring makes the unfamiliar meaningful and objectification transforms the intangible into something real. However, these two processes alone do not provide a sufficient explanation for understanding the transformation of social representations. Firstly, we need to describe the reverse processes by which familiar objects and events become unfamiliar and how physical objects are imbued with abstract qualities. Secondly, we need to specify, not only the processes of assimilation, by

15

which the unfamiliar is located within our social representations and made real, but also the processes of accommodation, by which the conventional and prescriptive social representations themselves are transformed.

SUMMARY

At the beginning of this chapter, I suggested that it would serve two purposes. Firstly, it familiarizes the reader with the social representations approach, elaborating the nature, functions and processes of social representations. We can see that social representations are shared bodies of knowledge that constitute the social reality in which we live. They are the symbolic products of social thinking, communication and interaction among groups and individuals. Their conventional and prescriptive nature give precedence to the cultural traditions of society that largely determine the way in which we see and understand the world. At the same time, they are dynamic, their form and content transforming and evolving in harmony with social life. Everyone born into society is born into a culture and history such that our social representations form the environment of socialization within which we become part of cohesive groups. The particular function of social representations, however, is to transform unfamiliar concepts, objects and events into familiar aspects of our social reality, through the social processes of anchoring and objectification.

While I have devoted separate sections to different aspects of the theory it should be borne in mind that these aspects are interrelated and interdependent: the divisions in this chapter are artificial and have been adopted only for the sake of clarity. The nature of social representations supports, and is simultaneously supported by, their functions in social life. These functions, in their turn, are inseparable from the processes by which they evolve. A full understanding of social representations theory can only be gained by an appreciation of all three aspects.

Secondly, within the course of this chapter we have been able to identify points of confusion and potential contradictions which create substantial problems for the coherence and integrity of the theory. The most challenging task is to elaborate and understand the social construction of social reality: to develop our understanding of communication and social interaction so that it embraces the efficacy of individuals, culture and the environment in the maintenance and transformation of social representations. This has implications for social psychology that need to be explored and developed. Not only must we study social representations as both phenomena and processes but also we must consider the implications for the conduct of social psychological investigation and theory construction.

A related task is to transform our understanding of individuals and culture so that they are complementary rather than antagonistic. Within social representations theory there remains an uneasy tension between their autonomous and prescriptive nature on the one hand (emphasizing their cultural and historical aspects) and their dynamic nature on the other (emphasizing their transformation through people's social interactions and communications). This is epitomized in the vagueness surrounding the relationships between social representations, the process of socialization, and people's group memberships or identities.

Finally, a further area for concern relates to the processes by which social representations are transformed. Although the notion of the unfamiliar and the processes of anchoring and objectification go some way towards describing the transformation of social representations these, in themselves, are not sufficient. We need to look also at the social construction of the unfamiliar and the means by which social representations themselves are accommodated to the unfamiliar.

In sum, this chapter has provided the groundwork for the remainder of this book. It presents the ideas and raises the issues that will be elaborated and dealt with in the course of the subsequent chapters.

2

ANSWERING UNANSWERED QUESTIONS

The individual and society in the dynamics of social representations

Social representations theory has been criticized for its conceptual vagueness giving rise to both theoretical and methodological problems that, it is claimed, preclude any substantial progress (Potter and Litton, 1985; Eiser, 1986; McGuire, 1986; McKinlay and Potter, 1987). On a number of occasions, Moscovici (1984a, 1985b, 1987) has argued that the 'vagueness' of social representations is a virtue and that it arises by design. He suggests that precise definitions would be premature and are a requirement of predictive theories, concerning isolated mechanisms and the testing of hypotheses by the use of limiting experimental procedures. Social psychology should remain true to its subject-matter as opposed to the scientific and methodological principles associated with the natural sciences.

I would claim that the initial vagueness of the social representation concept has been a virtue not only because it has avoided premature and necessarily restrictive definitions but also because it has allowed a variety of theorists and researchers working from different perspectives and employing different methods to explore the usefulness and possible applications of social representations. This is not without its problems but the development of a theory, within which a central concept such as social representations finds its definition, is dependent on the community of scientists which take an interest in that theory. As Billig (1987a) argues in his rhetorical approach we progress as much through negation and conflict as through agreement and consensus.

I would go on to propose that there now exists a substantial body of research and theoretical discussion on social representations which provides ground for theoretical clarification. Rather than dismissing the theory because of its ambiguities or contradictions, these can be used constructively in the development of a novel and revolutionary approach in social psychology. It is not my intention to compare social representations with other concepts such as attitudes, widespread beliefs,

18

public opinion, linguistic repertoires and ideology. This has been done admirably both by social representation theorists and specialists in their respective fields (Jaspars and Fraser, 1984; Farr, 1987b; Roiser, 1987; Fraser and Gaskell, 1990). Rather, I shall focus on the issues and problems raised by the theory itself and on the theoretical implications of research in order to illuminate what we are dealing with when we talk about social representations.

It will be seen that the major difficulties arise as Moscovici attempts to convert a sociological concept into a social–psychological phenomenon; as he tries to integrate the cultural with the psychological to construct a societal psychology. Moscovici establishes the supra–individual nature of social representations by borrowing Durkheim's sociological concept of collective representations and by emphasizing their prescriptive and autonomous character. Simultaneously, he asserts the potency of the individual in the dynamics and transformation of social representations. However, in itself, this does not provide a synthesis of cognition and social structure.

The dualism between the individual and society which has bedeviled social psychology is perpetuated in the theory of social representations. Indeed, it is made even more apparent by a theory that attempts to reintroduce cultural phenomena into mainstream social psychology. This confusion is reflected in the diversity of research and the possible meanings of 'social'. The social nature of representations has been diversely defined with reference to the object being represented; the social context in which representations are expressed; the consensus or shared aspects of representations; their origins in social interaction and communication; and their relations to the social system and to the social reality of cultural phenomena such as language, books and other human products that have existence outside the heads of individuals.

The tension between the psychological and the cultural aspects of social representations is brought to the centre of the debate when we consider their dynamic nature; that is, their perpetual re-creation and transformation in social life. In order to overcome the contradictions between the force of society and the potency of the individual we need to modify and develop the theory. Firstly, social representations are both prescriptive and dynamic. This requires a reinterpretation of their pre-scriptive nature; a recognition of the significance of conflict as well as consensus; and a denial of their autonomous nature. Secondly, the cultural phenomenon of social representations is not divorced from individuals. This requires a greater understanding of the psycho-sociological processes involved in maintaining and transforming social representations. By taking the historical, genetic or evolutionary dimension seriously it is possible to recognize the role of the individual and elaborate the socio-psychological aspects involved without denying the supra-individual or collective character of social representations.

THESIS AND ANTITHESIS: THE FORCE OF SOCIETY VERSUS THE POTENCY OF THE INDIVIDUAL

The distinctively European character of social representations theory owes much to the cultural traditions of European society and to European thinkers including Marx, Durkheim, Weber, Freud, Levy-Strauss, Foucault and Piaget (Deutscher, 1984). In particular, Durkheim's (Durkheim, 1915; Thompson, 1985) sociological concepts of collective representations and social facts form an important part of the theory's intellectual history.

Durkheim introduced the concept of collective representations into his sociology in order to describe 'the system of symbols by means of which society becomes conscious of itself' including religion, law, morals, customs and political institutions. This 'conscience collective' is embedded in our language, tradition and customs, as well as in our institutions. These collective representations constitute a social reality *sui generis* that exists independently of individuals, in people's relations and associations within society. The well-known adage 'the total is greater than the sum of its parts' is as good as any; it is not the understanding in the mind of any one individual but rather it is the understanding provided by the collective, for the collective. Moscovici (1961) refers to the notion of collective representations as a neglected and forgotten concept which failed to have any great impact on research in sociology, anthropology or psychology. Furthermore, his aim, in part, is to re-establish this forgotten concept as a legitimate object of study essential to a truly social psychology. He sees the explicit task of social psychology to be the study of the nature and genesis of belief systems which shape our social reality. However, despite proclaiming Durkheim as an intellectual ancestor, there are a number of important distinctions to be made between Durkheim's collective representations and the current use of the term social representations (Moscovici, 1984b).

One of the fundamental differences is the conceptualization of the relationship between the individual and society. Durkheim conceptualized collective representations and individual representations as two distinct and opposing forms of knowledge. Collective representations were explanatory devices in his sociology which were irreducible by further analysis. He was concerned to establish sociology as a distinct discipline from psychology with its own object of study which was irreducible to individual psychology. In so doing, Durkheim separated individual and collective consciousness as the subject-matter of two distinct disciplines, psychology and sociology. For example, in his study of suicide he explicates how collective representations remain in opposition to individual representations. As the latter proliferate, the former break down, losing their cohesive and stabilizing power, resulting in a state of anomie and an increase in the number of suicides. Individual representations, for Durkheim, led to the disintegration of society and of moral values, isolating individuals from social purposes and social regulation. In contrast, social representations theory abandons this opposition between individual and collective representations in an attempt to provide a continuous description and integration of the individual and society. Social representations are a phenomenon to be studied, elucidating their structure, their content and their dynamics in a way that is pertinent both to the individual and to the collective level.

This is closely related to a second distinction which can be made between Durkheim's collective representations and social representations, and is one which is emphasized by Moscovici (1984b). Whereas Durkheim presented a structural sociology in which collective representations are relatively static and exist in a stable society, social representations are dynamic structures which evolve and transform in an ever-changing society. Hence, whereas collective representations constitute a sociological concept and are seen in opposition to individual representations, social representations constitute a social psychological phenomenon which is intimately related to individual representations. Individual and social representations do not function in opposition but have a dynamic interrelationship essential to the transformation of social representations and, in fact, to all aspects of individual and social life.

However, the integration of the individual and the collective in the dynamics of social representations is no easy task. In Durkheim's sociology, collective representations are characterized by their constraining and coercive power on the members of a given society. Social facts current in a stable society determine human behaviour. Furthermore, collective representations, being distinct from and acting in opposition to individual representations, are autonomous and independent of individuals and groups. Moscovici wishes to maintain this characteristic of collective representations in order to avoid the individual reductionism which has been prevalent in psychology for many decades. He states that although individuals and groups create social representations 'once

21

created, however, they lead a life of their own, circulate, merge, attract and repel each other and give birth to new representations while old ones die out' (Moscovici, 1984b: 13). However, he also wishes to distance the theory of social representations from such a restricting and coercive characterization. This is done with reference to the dynamic inter-relationship between an individual's representations and the representations shared within their group.

> we should not be led to underestimate . . . the contribution each member of a given society makes in creating and maintaining beliefs and behaviours shared by all. In other words, what counts is not the separateness of individual representations but the transformation each individual imposes on group representations and the converse.
>
> (Moscovici, 1984a: 950)

This poses a substantial problem for social representations' theorists. On the one hand, social representations are prescriptive, imposing themselves on us with irresistible force. The weight of tradition, of collective memory, the images and words embedded in language 'exerts a force against which our mind and conscience is powerless' (Moscovici, 1984a: 950). The past, it is claimed, prevails over the present. On the other hand, we are told not to underestimate 'the autonomy of the present'. Individuals are active in the creation and maintenance of social representations and play an essential role in the transformation and dynamic nature of social representations.

The theory is, paradoxically, in danger of both sociological and individualistic reductionism. At one extreme, in attempting to overcome the individualistic bias in social psychology, Moscovici has borrowed the concept of collective representations from Durkheim, almost by direct quotations. Social representations are autonomous social facts which are independent from individuals; they are external realities which lie outside the individual. By emphasizing the prescriptive and conventional nature of social representations which act as constraints on the perceptions, conceptions and behaviour of individuals and groups, Moscovici is in danger of presenting a sociological thesis which has little or no regard for the role of individuals. McKinlay and Potter (1987), in their conceptual critique of social representations theory, suggest that Moscovici's historical prescriptive thesis is so strong that it is totally inconsistent with and denies the possibility of change and individual involvement.

At the other extreme, the theory can be conceived as presenting an individualistic thesis. This has been an argument presented by a number of critics. According to Harré (1984, 1985), the French School fails to achieve a truly collective social psychology that recognizes the group as a supra-individual entity with attributes which cannot be reduced to the attributes of its individual members. For Harré, social representations theory continues to present a version of individualism whereby 'social' denotes distributed or aggregated individual representations. Similarly, McKinlay and Potter (1987) argue that the social aspects of the theory are in principle reducible to individual cognition. They build their argument on particular features of Moscovici's exposition of social representations. Firstly, although lay men and women inhabit the consensual universe which is constituted by social representations, scientists, who occupy the reified universe, are able to deliver non-social, objective knowledge of the world independently of social representations. Secondly, unfamiliar objects must be perceived by individuals in some way before they are anchored to a social representation. That is, individuals, in some instances, are able to perceive the world independently of social representations. In both instances the acquisition of knowledge is reducible to the cognitive activity of individuals and there is no reason to accept Moscovici's thesis that social representations are in some way essentially social.

These critics claim that in the last analysis the theory is restricted to the influence of social situations on the minds of individual human actors and, as such, makes little advance on traditional forms of social psychology. I believe that these critiques are indicative of a more substantial problem which, as yet, remains unresolved. The problem to which I refer is the dualism between the individual and culture; a dualism which must be overcome if the theory of social representations is to provide a revolutionary alternative to traditional social psychology. As Parker (1987, 1989) suggests, social representations theory does not provide a resolution of thesis and antithesis. Rather it constitutes the problem in that it attempts to deal with both the individual and the cultural but, in effect, reinforces the dualism inherent in the divide between psychology and sociology.

SOCIETY AND THE INDIVIDUAL IN RESEARCH ON SOCIAL REPRESENTATIONS

Much of the research on social representations reflects this persistent dualism between individuals and society. Both the experimental investigations and at least some of the field studies fail to construct a viable integration of the psychological with the cultural. The experimental studies have approached this problem from the direction of the individual. They tend to focus on the psychological or cognitive processes involved in the dynamics of social representations while failing to realize the significance of language and culture. The field studies, in contrast, tend to approach the individual/culture interface from the direction of society. In order to counteract the highly individualistic Anglo-American social psychology, many of the French researchers have stressed the sociological and Durkheimian aspects of social representations. Paradoxically, in as far as the sociological aspects of this research are conceived in terms of large-scale consensus, they can be reduced to the level of individual cognition. At the same time, with the emphasis on collective phenomena, the role of the individual in the dynamics of social representations remains largely unexamined and is assumed to be unimportant.

The experimental research

Moscovici has argued that although laboratory experimentation may be suitable for studying simple phenomena that can be taken out of context and operationally defined, it is unsuitable for the exploration of social representations, being a complex social phenomenon stored in our language and created in a dynamic human milieu. Despite this, there is a considerable body of experimental research on social representations, much of which has been conducted by the Aix-en-Provence group in France (Faucheux and Moscovici, 1968; Abric, 1971, 1984; Abric and Kahan, 1972; Codol, 1974, 1975, 1984; Flament, 1984). This research was originally conceived as a critique of Anglo-American social psychology on group dynamics, conflict studies and games theory. The latter failed to consider the genesis of groups in their own activity and the phenomenological and social aspects involved. In order to address these issues a series of experiments were conducted and only subsequently interpreted within the framework of social representations. These studies illuminate the relationship between social representations and behaviour and, more specifically, the relationship between the individual's system of representations and their interactions and communications within specific group structures. While they do not directly address the cultural and historical aspects of social representations they do address their subjective, phenomenological and cognitive aspects.

On closer examination, however, it can be seen that these studies focus on intra-individual cognitive activity: on the individual's attempt to organize and structure the so-called 'objective' features of an experimental social situation. For example, Abric (1984) employed the

'Prisoner's Dilemma' in a number of experimental studies exploring functional relationships between social representations and behaviour. The 'Prisoner's Dilemma' is a game situation in which two individuals are confronted by conflicting play strategies; one which achieves maximum gain for both players and the other which has the possibility of increasing differential gain, depending on the choice of the other player. The behaviour of subjects was found to be dependent on their representations of themselves, others, the task and the context. This individualistic orientation is justified by the researchers on the grounds that social representations are incontrovertibly cognitive phenomena. Although they are social forms of knowledge belonging to cultures and groups, in the final analysis, it is always individuals who convey and articulate them (e.g. Abric, 1971, 1984; Codol, 1984). This appears to perpetuate what Moscovici has termed a 'private' social psychology which ignores the distinctive features of genuine collective phenomena. Collective phenomena have their own structure which is not definable in terms of the cognitions or characteristics of individuals. They are related to the processes of production and consumption, to the rituals, symbols, institutions, norms and values of our society or group. They are phenomena with their own history and dynamics which cannot be derived from individuals alone (Moscovici, 1972). In the last analysis the experimental studies still portray an individual psychology of cognition as opposed to a social psychology of symbolic representation.

The limitations of this research are acknowledged by the experimenters themselves and is reflected in a general ambivalence towards the experimental studies (Herzlich, 1972; Farr, 1984; Moscovici, 1984b). In my opinion, as a single research method, it is certainly unable to deal with social representations in all their complexity. Having said this, experimentation is not totally devoid of culture. Rather, culture enters the laboratory through the back door. Codol (1984) emphasizes that the aim of the experimental studies is to examine the social processes of interaction, communication and influence involved in the creation of social representations. But it is not clear that these experiments do actually study the social processes involved in the origins of a system of representations. The laboratory research on social representations succeeds only because the wider culture enters into the laboratory which is still a part of the wider society. Subjects do not come to the laboratory as empty-headed, naïve individuals. They bring with them ideas, values and ideologies which they have assimilated from their culture and from their social groups. These include representations of social relations, of cooperative and competitive interactions, of social identities and of problem situations. These representations do not originate within the experimental context but rather are primed by the experimenter's instructions or by attributes of the experimental situation. Differences in the behaviour (dependent variable) of subjects are shown to be greatly influenced by the subjects' representations (independent variable). However, manipulation of these representations is dependent on the culture outside the laboratory, shared by both experimenter and research subjects. For example, representations of the task are manipulated by presenting the same task as either a 'problem-solving' or a 'creative' task (Abric, 1971). Representations of the group are manipulated by providing feedback such as 'this is a very collective group' or 'this is a very individualistic group' (Codol, 1974). Similarly, representations of opponents in a game situation are manipulated by presenting them as a 'machine' or as 'another student like yourself' (Abric, 1987).

Once it is recognized that culture enters into the laboratory then experimental methods can be used to investigate not only how social representations direct behaviour but also the social mechanisms by which pre-established representations are evoked, agreed upon and transformed within particular social contexts. In order to achieve this, the problems addressed, the experimental design and the interpretation of results must be a direct consequence of a theoretical framework that has constructed a viable integration of the psychological and the cultural.

Attribution research

The divide between the individual and culture is also perpetuated in the social extensions of attribution theory (Moscovici and Hewstone, 1983; Hewstone and Jaspars, 1984; Hewstone, 1989; Jaspars and Hewstone, 1990). Here, the emphasis lies on the consensual nature of social representations, i.e. the socially shared knowledge base which underlies the process and content of attribution and causal explanations. In order to understand how, when and why individuals make attributions, and where these attributions come from, it is necessary to take into account the way knowledge about various aspects of social life is represented in a society and shared by its members. Social representations theory provides a framework in which to study the extent to which such causal structures are socially shared and how widespread beliefs have an impact on an individual's attributions.

The social psychology which emerges is one which relates the individual psychological processes to the collective beliefs of a group or society. Although this redresses the balance between individual and social factors it does not constitute a revolutionary approach to social attribution (Farr,

1991b). The social factors simply provide the context for individual cognition rather than redefining the problematic relationship between the individual and society.

Field research

This enigma is also reflected in some of the field studies. Despite the focus on the content and transformation of social representations in natural social environments they are still open to individualistic reductionism. For example, Herzlich's (1973) highly informative study on the social representation of health and illness provides an excellent description of Parisians' understandings in relation to their urban environment. However, it has been argued that these social representations can still be conceived as ultimately individualistic, psychological phenomena (Harré, 1984, 1985). The representations were elicited in unstructured interviews with individuals and then aggregated to present a single coherent social representation. In this instance the social representation is no more than a collection of shared individual representations. Potter and Litton (1985) go on to suggest that the degree of consensus is overestimated or even created through the research procedures employed.

Contrary to this, it could also be argued that the field research is open to sociological reductionism. Herzlich attempts to explain transformations in the form and content of social representation with reference to the cultural and economic circumstances of society. Representations of health and illness are shown to differ as a function of culture and as a function of change across historical epochs within one culture. In particular, transformations in representations of health and illness are closely related to the history of medicine and changing doctor–patient relationships. Similarly, Moscovici's own study on the diffusion of psychoanalytic theory (1961) in French society provides a descriptive account of the theory's transformation in relation to Catholicism and Marxism, both in the groups' understanding of psychoanalytic concepts and the representation of the theory in the Catholic and Marxist Press. The exploration of the contents of the mass media and of other cultural objects in our environment is a distinctive feature of the field research in the French tradition. Social representations exist not only in the mind but also in the environment. It is therefore pertinent to examine social representations not only in cognition but also in the surrounding culture, in the products of human activity, including the media and the objects that constitute the environment in which we live. Unfortunately, little is said about the socio–psychological processes involved in the active construction and reproduction of social representations in either study. The origins of social representations in social interactions tend to be assumed rather than demonstrated and the role of individuals in taking up and transforming scientific concepts into social representations is all but forgotten.

To summarize, in as far as research focuses on the individual's representations of social objects, the role of representations in social interactions, or the consensual nature of social representations as shared bodies of knowledge, it remains inherently individualistic in its orientation. In as far as research focuses on the content of social representations and its relation to cultural and economic circumstances it remains sociological in orientation. This is not to suggest that either aspect is unimportant. Social representations structure people's understanding of social situations and direct individuals' actions. Shared belief systems provide a consensual universe in which individuals and groups interact and communicate. The transformation of social representations is indubitably related to the structure of society. However, it still remains open to question whether or not the research is able not only to associate, but also to integrate the individual with society in a fusion of the psychological and the cultural.

THE DYNAMICS OF SOCIAL REPRESENTATIONS: SOME PRELIMINARY STEPS TOWARDS A SYNTHESIS

In the previous discussion, concerning the distinctions between Durkheim's collective representations and Moscovici's social representations, we have seen that a prominent aspiration of the theory's proponents is to create a synthesis of the individual and society. More importantly, if we are to succeed in providing an understanding of the dynamic nature of social representations and their origins in social life it is absolutely crucial that a successful resolution is achieved. A number of modifications to those theoretical principles that deny the dynamic nature of social representations and the role of individuals in their transformation are suggested as initial steps towards such a resolution. Firstly, the prescriptive nature of social representations must be conceived in the context of a heterogeneous and changing society. Secondly, their consensual character does not imply a purely distributive understanding of social representations. Their transformation depends upon the conflicts and controversies between people living in a heterogeneous society. Thirdly, the autonomous character of social representations is rejected. Social representations cannot be autonomous from the individuals who together create and maintain them. Finally, it will be seen from the research on the dynamics of social representations that the theory must include some notion of people's identity, action or involvement in relation to social representations. These modifications go some way towards integrating the individual and society. By reinterpreting the sociological tenets of the theory we can understand the dynamics of social representations, the socio-psychological process involved in their evolution, and their perpetual recreation in social life, without losing or forsaking their supra-individual or collective qualities.

It may well be thought that the dynamic nature of social representations is contradictory to their prescriptive nature. This need not be the case. Rather than conceiving the past in terms of an immutable given, whereby social representations impose themselves upon us with irresistible force, it can be conceived as a dynamic and ongoing process, dependent upon our social interactions and communications. To put it another way, social interaction and communication are the active and dynamic processes through which social representations acquire and express their prescriptive power. Thus, social representations not only *originate* in the social interactions among individuals and groups for the purpose of understanding and communicating with others: they are also *sustained* through the same processes.

It is important to realize that social interaction refers not only to interactions between two or more people but also to interactions with the physical and symbolic products of human activity. The environment, in terms of both its physical, material characteristics and its social, symbolic characteristics are important elements of social interaction. In other words, social interaction includes interaction with other people and with the physical and social world. Similarly, communication is not restricted to 'non-verbal' and 'verbal' communications between two or more people in face-to-face interactions. Communication can occur through a wide variety of mediators: through written and pictorial materials, including books, magazines, the media, posters, films, etc.; through displays such as those found in museums and shop windows; through construction of the physical environment – for example, parks, playgrounds, sports facilities, buildings, towns, etc.; and through single but dramatic events, such as the dropping of an atomic bomb on a human population for the first time.

Given this dynamic conception of the historical aspect of social representations it can be seen that their prescriptive nature does not preclude their transformation by individuals and groups. For the purposes of clarification I shall briefly return to the distinctions between collective and social representations. For Durkheim, collective representations exist in a stable society and are embedded in the subsoil of the society's culture. In contrast, social representations exist in changing societies. Moscovici is at pains to restrict social representations to representations of our current society, to our

> political, scientific, human soil, which have not always enough time to allow the proper sedimentation to become immovable traditions. And their importance continues to increase, in direct proportion to the heterogeneity and the fluctuation of the unifying systems – official sciences, religions, ideologies.
>
> (Moscovici, 1984b: 18)

It is the heterogeneous nature of our society and the rapidly expanding forms of communication that provide the impetus for social change. Unlike people within a stable, homogeneous society, groups and individuals within a heterogeneous society do not possess the same past. There is not just one coherent system of representations but rather a multitude of systems which are diverse and controversial. These contraversions of social reality become apparent in the problems arising out of interactions and communications among individuals and groups. These require modifications in people's actions and the reconstruction of social representations. Thus, the prescriptive nature of social representations is at one with the dynamic and evolutionary nature of social representations once the possibility and significance of conflict and contradiction is realized. The confrontation between different pasts and the conflict in the expression of different representations gives rise to the transformation of social representations.

The significance of conflict in the dynamics of social representations precludes a consensual definition of social representations. The focus on 'consensus', both in research and in the critiques of the theory, is understandable, given the importance of the 'consensual universe'. However, this focus does an injustice to the aims and content of the theory as a whole and is more a reflection of methodologies which assume that the individual is the proper source of data collection. If the starting point is always the individual then the meaning of social becomes limited to those attributes which individuals share. Individual representations are then those which are not shared by a 'significant' number of people; collective representations are those shared by all members of society; and social representations are shared by members of a group within a society where some divergences exist between or within groups. However, the theory of social representations is not aimed primarily at finding out what percentage of a particular population share a given social representation, nor the level of consensus which can be considered 'significant' (Moscovici, 1963). A purely aggregative or distributive understanding of social representations does not sustain their supra-individual status, nor does it reflect their dynamic nature and their origins in social life. It is in the differences, conflicts and controversies which relate to people's pasts, their positions within society, their roles and duties and their social relations, which give social representations their distinctive dynamic character and also their supra-individual qualities. While the significance of consensus is stressed within the theory, the role of conflict, argumentation and negotiation should not be underestimated (Billig, 1987a, 1988; Billig *et al.*, 1988).

Finally, social representations are not autonomous. The need to establish the supra-individual nature of social representations must not rely on claims for their autonomy, as this denies the role of individuals in their transformation and fails to provide a psycho-sociological thesis. Markova and Wilkie (1987) have also questioned the usefulness of claiming autonomy for social representations. Any characterization which assigns agency to collective entities gives a mysterious quality to their dynamic nature. It was to such collectivist thinking that F.H. Allport so strongly objected and which, in opposition, instantiated the individualistic approach to social phenomena. Social representations are prescriptive but, in contrast to Moscovici, I would argue that they are not autonomous. They do not live a life of their own or give birth to new representations on their own – this would be a sociological thesis. Rather they are continuously modified by individuals who are involved not only in the creation of social representations but also in the maintenance of those representations. They are the products of a dialectic relationship between individuals and culture.

RESEARCH ON THE DYNAMICS OF SOCIAL REPRESENTATIONS

The role of conflict in the development of social representations is most apparent in the research on intergroup relations. For example, Di Giacomo's study on intergroup alliances and rejection showed that the student population progressively defined the protest committee as incompatible with themselves due to conflicts in beliefs, symbols and norms (Di Giacomo, 1980). The emergent social representations both anticipated and justified the students' lack of commitment to action. Unfortunately, the research does not trace the development of the incompatible social representations, their elements and their changing relationships; nor does it explore the form of communication or the processes of social interaction involved in their generation and transformation.

The psycho-sociological character of the genesis of social representations is elucidated most clearly in studies examining the development of the child in relation to its social and cultural environment. This is ironic both because Moscovici originally wished to investigate the transformation of knowledge, values and life styles in the adult world; and because these studies are often taken to demonstrate the conventional and prescriptive nature of social representations. What is important, however, is that these studies go some way towards an understanding of how the child reconstructs the social reality of the adult world and how this social reality is changed and transformed.

One of the most comprehensive field studies is that conducted by Chombart-de-Lauwe (1971, 1984) on the means by which representations of the child are socially sustained and transformed. The social transmission of cultural knowledge and values from one generation to the next during the socialization of the child involves a dynamic process of interaction between the child and the various elements of its environment; it is a 'dialectic of psycho-social phenomena'. A series of complementary studies illuminates the variation and transformation of social representations during successive historical periods and their transmission to a new generation.

The stability, evolution and transformation of social representations was explored, examining biographical and autobiographical literature, novels and films produced for both adults and children in pre-war, inter-war and contemporary periods, in relation to the structure of society. A further study examined children's essays comparing themselves to media characters. This revealed how the social transmission of representations to the next generation is related to the child's socio-biological characteristics, its social situation and its social status. Chombart-de-Lauwe goes on to explore the representation of the child in relation to the built environment. Social representations held by town planners and architects influence the construction of the environment and hence the practices, life-styles and representations of children. For example, the place of the child in an urban environment is represented as either being segregated from or integrated with the structure of the community as a whole. These representations determine the environment in which children live, the activities in which they can engage and hence the representations which they construct. From the perspectives of children these are confronted as 'social facts' which make up the environment in which they live.

This approach does more than demonstrate the prescriptive nature of social representations as it cannot be reduced to a simple indoctrination of children. Children play an active role in the internalization of social representations; in the reconstruction of the social representations presented to them in their social interactions with adults; and in the social environments created by adults. This explicitly interactional approach addresses not only the maintenance but also the origins and evolution of social representations in social life.

A similar perspective is expressed in the work of Duveen and Lloyd (1986, 1987, 1990; Lloyd and Duveen, 1990) on the development of children's social gender identities. While a description of the gender system would correspond to a sociological or anthropological analysis at the collective level, in order to understand how the prescriptive and conventional aspects of social representations become psychologically active in the regulation of social interactions, it is necessary to present a socio–psychological analysis and to examine people's participation in the active construction of social representations. The development and transmission of the social representations of gender are traced through interpersonal relations with the mother, the child's interactions with various toys and the behaviourial expression of 'maleness' or 'femaleness' in interactions with peers. Social representations exist prior to the child's entrance into the social milieu and take on an ontological significance in the child's social reality; but the child does not simply absorb or learn the prevalent social representations. Rather, through its own activity, its interactions with others and objects in the environment, the child actively reconstructs the social representations of itself, of others and of objects in its shared environment.

This research elucidates the development of an individual's identity (ontogenesis) through the course of social interactions and communications (microgenesis) in relation to the prevalent social representations. This occurs not only in childhood but also as adults participate in social life, elaborating established social representations and negotiating new or conflicting social representations. This research focuses on the process of ontogenesis by which individuals reconstruct social representations and, in so doing, acquire particular social identities. This is founded in the microgenesis of social representations in relation to social identities as they are expressed in social interactions and communications. Both the microgenesis and ontogenesis are involved in the transmission of social representations from one generation to the next and in the diffusion of social representations throughout society. Similarly, both are involved in the sociogenesis of social representations: that is, in the construction of new representations and the transformation of old ones. The inter-dependence of microgenesis, ontogenesis and sociogenesis is observed in Jodelet's brilliant study on madness and social representations (Jodelet, 1991). For a period of over seventy years the inhabitants of French villages in the region of Ainay-le-Chateau have been family hosts to numerous mental patients. Jodelet explains and vivifies the relationship between representations and action; the nature of identity and the construction of otherness; and the adaptation of customs or the evolution of understanding over successive generations.

What I wish to highlight is that the cognitive or psychological aspects of the individual and the cultural or structural aspects of society are integrated by (a) adopting a genetic or evolutionary approach; (b) recognizing the dialectics between representation and action; and (c) using identity as the expression of their interdependence. It is this perspective that will be explored and developed in Part II. However, before doing so, it is pertinent to look at the domain in which it is appropriate to apply social representations theory.

3

THE DOMAIN OF SOCIAL REPRESENTATIONS

COMMON SENSE IN MODERN SOCIETY

Moscovici conceives social psychology as an anthropology of modern culture, a science devoted to the study of thought and beliefs in the societies of our times. Astutely, he identifies science as one of the most influential cultural phenomena in modern times. The theory of social representations is explicitly designed to describe and explain the transformation of scientific knowledge as it diffuses into our common-sense understandings. He argues that, in the past, the dominant direction of influence was from common sense to science, as science merely refined and ordered common sense. However, in modern times science is now the dominant influence, transforming the very nature of common sense into social representations.

Modern society is characterized by a heterogeneity of institutions, religions, ideologies, subcultures, etc. In particular, the astounding growth of the physical sciences, including physics, chemistry, biology, astronomy as well as the human sciences such as sociology, anthropology, psychology and economics, has led to the proliferation of theories, abstract concepts, inventions and discoveries. These are disseminated throughout society by revolutionary and increasingly efficient means of communication, including the mass media, newspapers, popular discourses, books, films and television, flooding our common sense with the unfamiliar products of science and destroying our traditional modes of understanding. This gives rise to peculiarly dynamic systems of knowledge, that is, to social representations. Moscovici even suggests that common sense is now science made common. Scientific knowledge has entered into our common-sense understandings of the universe, of the human body (Jodelet, 1986), of health and illness (Herzlich, 1973) and of economic activities (Emler and Dickinson, 1985), among many others.

Perhaps the prime research example is Moscovici's original study on the diffusion of psychoanalysis in French society (Moscovici, 1961). Moscovici describes how the abstract concepts of the scientific theory including 'neurosis' and 'the Oedipus complex' come to be employed in everyday understandings and interactions.

The dissemination of scientific knowledge into common sense is not a simple process. According to Moscovici, this is because science and common sense form two distinct types of reality, each with its own form of thinking and understanding. Moscovici describes this in terms of the reified and the consensual universes. The reified universe of science is a world of objective truth and certainty that is indifferent to individuals and culture. It is founded in the objective observation of discrete objects and events and in rational thought, devoid of symbolic significance. In contrast, the consensual universe of common sense is a conventional world of symbolic and meaningful objects and events. It is founded in our belief systems, our purposes and our intentions, imbued with all that is social, cultural and historical.

The acquisition of scientific knowledge is motivated by 'a desire to consume, digest and share science', by a curiosity about how things work, the need to give meaning to one's life and to attain a competence equal to that of society. But the products of science are unfamiliar, not least because they are produced within the reified universe. From within the consensual universe the concepts and theories of the reified universe remain meaningless and unreal. As the unfamiliar products of science diffuse into society they are imbued with meaning and significance and are transformed into social objects through the processes of anchoring and objectification. This work is largely done by those who specialize in disseminating scientific knowledge, transforming the unfamiliar into the familiar, such that the lay person or amateur scientist may consume and digest the fruits of science. This detaches the concepts of science from the reified universe and transforms them into the symbolic and conventional reality of everyday life.

Thus the purpose of social representations is in direct opposition to science. Science produces the unfamiliar systems of concepts which provide the impetus for the creation and transformation of social representations. Whereas science aims to make the familiar unfamiliar, social representation re-presents the unfamiliar in terms of the familiar. This results in an ever-changing, dynamic, consensual universe as social representations are transformed and reconstituted through the anchoring and objectification of scientific information. In this way, links are forged between the purely abstract sciences and the concrete activities of daily life. The lay person, as an amateur scientist, possesses a new common sense, one which has been reconstituted and filled with images and meanings. This new common sense constitutes a mode of understanding and communicating which has transformed the scientific theories into a shared reality. They fill our minds and conversations, determining our world view and our interactions with the physical and social environment.

It would appear that the theory of social representations is concerned exclusively with the transformation of common-sense understandings initiated by the proliferation and diffusion of scientific knowledge in modern societies. However, while science may be an important determinant of the dynamics of social representations, it is unlikely to be the only determinant.

CHANGING THE BOUNDARIES

Both the wide variety of research on social representations and the theoretical principles elaborated in the theory suggest a broader domain of application. Research has not been restricted to the impact of science on everyday understanding. Furthermore, the balance between tradition and innovation, the forms of social interaction and communication and the processes of transformation are not exclusive to the diffusion of scientific knowledge.

The object of research

The early field studies conducted in France were primarily concerned with the diffusion of scientific notions from the reified universe of science into the consensual world of common sense and everyday understanding. It has already been mentioned that the first social representations study (Moscovici, 1961) examined how the scientific theory of psychoanalysis diffused into French society. Another early study explored the transmission and assimilation of scientific facts by workers in the chemical industry (Ackermann and Rialan, 1963). The focus on common-sense understanding of scientific discoveries is also evident in more recent field studies. For example, Herzlich (1973) found that illness is now understood in terms of the invasion of a naturally healthy body by external agents such as bacteria or germs. Changes in the social representation of the body are related to developments within the medical profession (Jodelet and Moscovici, 1975). To stretch a point, inhabitants' social representations of Paris are influenced by the products of cartography which might be considered a scientific representation of the city (Jodelet and Milgram, 1977). However, other French researchers have chosen objects of study which bear only a tenuous link with the products of scientific disciplines. The most compelling example in this respect is Chombart-de-Lauwe's extensive investigation of social representations of the child (1984). Transformations are not directly related to our scientific theories or to the diffusion of scientific knowledge into common-sense understandings of childhood.

Both Farr (1990) and Breakwell (1987) have commented on the problem of choosing a suitable object as the target of a representation. If social representations theory is concerned with the diffusion of scientific knowledge in society, it might be supposed that a scientific theory should be selected as the target object. However, this does not appear to be the major criterion for selecting the target object. Firstly, a knowledge of psychoanalysis had diffused fairly widely in France during the post-World War II era and it has since become a salient feature of French culture. Secondly, turning to the other major field studies mentioned above – although the transformation in their respective social representations may be related to scientific theories and discoveries – the object of study is not a scientific theory as such. There is not a scientific theory of towns and cities, or of children. Rather, researchers have selected socially significant objects which are represented in various aspects of French culture and social life. They are present in the mass media of communications, in people's social interactions, and they are often related to debates within French communities.

Other research on social representations also indicates that the theory is not exclusively applicable to the transformation of scientific knowledge into common-sense understandings. As described previously, experimental literature focuses on the representations of the self, of others, of the group and of the task within an artificial situation. These are not usually related to any scientific body of knowledge. Similarly, British work on children's social representations of economic inequalities, although they may be associated in part with economic theories, are more closely related to the children's sets of social relations, their social classes and their general social milieux (Emler and Dickinson, 1985; Emler, 1987). Again, Duveen and Lloyd's research (1987) on the socio-psychological aspects of gender is concerned not with the diffusion of a scientific theory, but with a system of ideas, values and practices that pervades the whole of society.

Thus, research on social representations has extended beyond the domain of the theory to include a wide range of socio-psychological phenomena which often focus on non-scientific, socially significant objects. It may be considered that, by breaking the boundaries set by Moscovici, the notion of social representations is in danger of becoming merely a general synonym for 'culture' or 'ideology'. Indeed, Moscovici warns against identifying social representations as a general category concerning the totality of intellectual and social products (Moscovici, 1976: 40). However, the distinctiveness of social representations theory should not rest on artificial boundaries that are not reflected either by the research or in the theory's own postulates. Rather, the theory's distinctiveness lies in the psycho-sociological origins, dynamics and evolution of collective (not consensual) beliefs; in the specific functions served by social representations; and in the specific processes by which they are transformed.

It might be argued that these distinctive characteristics of the theory provide grounds on which to distinguish between social representations of scientific knowledge and other domains of social knowledge. Firstly, the former may exhibit a peculiarly dynamic character which breaks with tradition, whereas the latter often maintain tradition. Secondly, the former are disseminated through society by means of mass media communication, whereas the latter may be more closely associated with people's first-hand experience in their social milieu. Thirdly, social representations are transformed by specific processes, which may be peculiar to the diffusion of scientific knowledge. It will be argued, however, that these do not provide adequate grounds for distinguishing scientific from non-scientific social representations. Social representations are bodies of social knowledge, oriented towards the practical and social life of a given community. As such, they not only refer to common-sense understanding of scientific theories but to a whole range of practical knowledge found in a given society.

Tradition and innovation

Some researchers may be accused of selecting 'collective' rather than 'social' representations as their object of study. Representations of gender or of childhood are phenomena which pervade the whole of society and are steeped in tradition. Furthermore, they are rarely influenced by scientific developments. It might be considered that they express the cultural traditions of collective memory, embedded in the images and meanings of language and that they do not exhibit the plasticity of social representations. However, the impetus for change and transformation does not emerge only in science. Representations of 'male' and 'female' have changed dramatically with the rise of the feminist movement. Representations of the child have undergone extensive transformations during the last twenty years. It can be seen that these non-scientific representations also possess the dynamic characteristics of social representations. Within the theory it is science that produces unfamiliar concepts which provide the impetus for transformations in social representations. However, discoveries and innovations are not peculiar to the universe of science.

From the opposite angle, tradition plays an equally important part in the understanding of scientific concepts or science-related issues. Moscovici is well aware of the role of tradition but, in some respects, he underestimates its influence. Studies of social representations have revealed the persistence and re-emergence of beliefs that are embedded in the history of our culture. The social representations of mental illness in French villages where the inhabitants are hosts to mental patients maintain traditional views associated with the nervous and contagious nature of mental illness. The need to create a feeling of otherness has restricted the diffusion of modern scientific knowledge and the mental institutions' perspective into people's common-sense understandings (Jodelet, 1991). This can also be seen in the association of AIDS with the plague (Markova and Wilkie, 1987). Similarly, social representations of Paris (Jodelet and Milgram, 1977) reflect the historical development of the city. Divisions of the urban area are constructed around the historical heart and belt of the city. The latter no longer exists in physical terms, but is still present in the collective memory and socio-spatial representations of the city. Knowledge drawn from street maps of Paris produced by cartographers is selectively emphasized and distorted to reflect these socio-psychological elements. Tradition, in terms of the historical and cultural understandings of a community, is extremely influential in the transformations of social representations associated with the products of science.

Thus, the role of tradition and innovation in the dynamics of social representations does not provide grounds for distinguishing between social representations that relate exclusively to socially significant objects and those that are related to scientific concepts and discoveries. Firstly, transformation is stimulated by innovations emerging within the consensual universe as well as by innovations from science. Secondly, the strength of tradition is seen in representations of science-related issues as well as other areas of social knowledge.

Social interaction and communication

A distinction may still be possible in terms of the forms of communication and interaction in each sphere of social knowledge. Non-scientific representations are dependent on first-hand experience and the reality of events. This is so with regard both to the transmission of representations from one generation to the next and to the creation and elaboration of representations in the consensual universe. In contrast, scientific theories are pre-existing bodies of knowledge which are disseminated through society by the mass media. However, on closer inspection, such a distinction is not upheld.

A full range of social interactions and communications are involved in the diffusion and transformation of both spheres of social knowledge. On the one hand, non-scientific representations of gender or of childhood find their expression and dissemination in the media and literature of a given society as well as in our personal relations and conversations. On the other hand, social representations of cities or of the body are constructed and maintained, not only on the basis of traditional and scientific understandings, but also on the basis of people's first-hand experience. For example, inhabitants' representations of Paris will be divergent from the representations of 'foreigners' who have not lived in and experienced the city (Milgram, 1984). Similarly, changes in the social representation of the body occur not only through the diffusion of scientific knowledge but also through knowledge acquired from people's actual experience of their bodies in social interactions with others (Jodelet, 1984a). Even in the diffusion of psychoanalysis, the theoretical concepts are taken up and assimilated into people's social representations because they answer problems of first-hand everyday experience. For example, the concept of neurosis allows otherwise unfamiliar and strange behaviours to be categorized and labelled (Moscovici, 1961). This would further suggest that some scientific theories will not readily enter into the public arena of common-sense knowledge. The diffusion of unfamiliar scientific concepts is, in part, dependent upon their efficacy in people's everyday lives.

Thus, the broader definition of social interaction and communication proffered by the theory unites, rather than separates, social representations related to scientific theories with those relating to other socially significant objects.

Processes of transformation

The dynamics of social representations is dependent upon the processes of anchoring and objectification. Once again, I would argue that these apply equally well to social knowledge that is unrelated to science. Within a system of social representations, anchoring reduces threat and unfamiliarity by imposing familiar categories and providing linguistic names. It 'excludes the idea of thought or perception which is without anchor' (Moscovici, 1984b: 36). As Billig (1987b) indicates, this is a universal socio-psychological process which applies to any unfamiliar concept, object or event, whether it originates in the sciences or in the consensual universe.

Objectification transforms abstract, unfamiliar concepts into familiar concrete experiences. This process allows the invisible to become perceptible: abstract concepts are materialized or naturalized, such that they become objects existing in the physical and social world. As Billig (1987b) suggests, objectification is a particular process but this particularity is not associated exclusively with the familiarization of abstract scientific thinking. On the one hand, just as abstract scientific concepts such as Oedipus complex are objectified in terms of a personality characteristic, so too, for example, are abstract religious concepts objectified in images of gods and religious rituals. On the other hand, there are some abstract concepts from both the reified and the consensual universes which belie objectification. Ideas of communism or socialism from the social sciences, and notions of relativity or magnetism from the physical sciences, are just as difficult to objectify as consensual notions of justice or mercy.

Despite Moscovici's initial attempt to demarcate the domain of social representations theory with reference to the diffusion of scientific knowledge into common sense, an examination of the empirical research in relation to the theoretical principles leads, necessarily, to the rejection of these boundaries. It is not possible to distinguish between social representations of scientific theories or concepts, such as psychoanalysis, and social representations of socially significant, non-scientific objects, such as childhood, either in terms of the object of study or in terms of the dynamics of social knowledge. This is with reference to the balance between tradition and innovation; to the various forms of social interaction and communication involved; and to the processes involved in their elaboration and transformation. It is, therefore, neither useful nor accurate to limit the application of the theory to social representations of scientific knowledge.

Social representations theory provides a social psychology of knowledge that extends beyond the transformation of scientific knowledge as it diffuses into common sense. I shall return to this issue in Part III not least because the distinction made between the reified universe of science and the consensual universe of common sense is highly questionable: the social constructionist view of reality presented by the theory would appear to deny the possibility of a reified universe.

NOT A CONCLUSION

In Part I, some of the internal contradictions and confusions regarding the nature, functions and process of social representations have been addressed and clarified. These developments focus on three central issues: the expression of the psychological and the cultural both in the theory itself and in its associated research; the dynamics of social representations and the balance between stability and change; and, finally, the appropriate domain for the theory's application. The proposed modifications to the theory go some way towards constructing a more coherent and consistent framework. This integrates the individual and societal aspects of social knowledge and social action; adopts an evolutionary approach that embraces the prescriptive and transformative nature of social representations; and proposes a wider domain of application which includes social representations emerging in the consensual universe of common sense as well as those related to developments in science.

However, a number of substantive issues remain outstanding. While the theory goes some way towards developing a revolutionary approach in social psychology, the theory and related research reflect the conflicts between the meta-theoretical and the methodological commitments of competing paradigms. In particular, the synthesis of the psychological and the cultural needs to be developed further if the social psychology envisioned by the theory's proponents is to be achieved. In order to construct an understanding of the dynamic nature of social representations, we must go beyond descriptions of their transformation in relation to social, historical and cultural factors and explore the nature and role of the individual in greater depth. This will involve developing a framework that expresses the interdependence of individuals, their environment and their culture in the construction of social reality. In Part II two alternative paradigms for social psychology will be discussed, and I shall suggest that, in order to achieve these aims, a paradigm shift is required.

Part II

SHIFTING PARADIGMS AND CHANGING REALITY

4

FROM THE CARTESIAN TO THE HEGELIAN PARADIGM

The re-emergence of societal psychology

Social psychology is charged with the formidable task of integrating the psychological and cultural aspects of human life, embracing individuals in their interactions with one another, their culture and their interrelations with the social structures and institutions of society. This objective is explicitly endorsed by the proponents of social representations theory. However, I argued in Chapter 2 that the juxtaposition of the individual and society has created an uneasy tension between a thesis that focuses on the individual and its antithesis that focuses on society and culture. Here, I shall broaden the scope of this debate to the discipline of social psychology as a whole. This is because the problem is not peculiar to social representations theory. It is manifest in the history of social psychology and is perpetuated in many contemporary fields of study within the discipline. I have suggested that the most constructive way to forward an integrative understanding of the relationship between the psychological and the cultural is to adopt an evolutionary approach which recognizes the social dialectics between thought and action and the pivotal role of people's identities. This involves more than extending a single theory. It involves adopting a different set of presuppositions and developing a new paradigm for social psychology, a paradigm that embraces the dynamic interdependence among individuals, their culture and their environment.

A brief outline of the historical development of social psychology illuminates how the psychological and cultural aspects of human life came to be separated in the first place and how this division has been perpetuated through diverse forms of social psychology. I argue that this divide centres on the conception of the individual and its close association with the conception of science. A positive–empiricist science demands a conception of the individual which precludes a synthesis with culture. This is rooted in Cartesian philosophy and Newtonian physics, which isolates the individual from his or her physical and social environment. In contrast, the Hegelian tradition of thought provides an alternative paradigm in which the individual is both the product and the producer of culture. Furthermore, this Hegelian tradition endorses a comparative and evolutionary approach to the study of social phenomena. Since the 'crisis' in social psychology there has been a resurgence of the Hegelian tradition of thought which is reflected in various contemporary developments such that it is possible to speak about an emerging Hegelian paradigm.

THE INDIVIDUAL AND CULTURE DIVIDED: A HISTORICAL NOTE

The division between the individual and culture was inherent in the very foundation of psychology as a scientific discipline. In 1879, Wundt established the first laboratory for the experimental exploration of the contents of individual consciousness. This was a form of psychophysics which applied the experimental methods of physiology to the psychological problems derived from philosophy. By means of introspection individuals observed the contents of their own minds. This was complementary to, but separated from, his *Voelkerpsychologie* (1900–20) which was concerned with the study of language, customs, religion, myth, magic and cognitive phenomena. The investigation of higher cognitive processes, which were a product of evolutionary and historical changes, could not be accounted for in terms of individual consciousness, since they presupposed the reciprocal interactions of a whole community or '*Volk*'. This required a comparative and historical approach to scientific investigations and drew on anthropological reports of diverse cultures (Cole, 1987). For Wundt, both were essential to a science of psychology, and the conclusions from the one should be compatible with the other (Farr, 1983).

Similarly, in social psychology, McDougall's introduction to the discipline (1908) focused on the individual's biological instincts and emotions. This was complementary to, but distinct from, his volume on *The Group Mind* (1920). The 'group mind' acquired a reality or existence which was independent of and qualitatively distinct from that of its individual members, emerging out of the interactions or relations between people. Both these perspectives are apparent in Murchison's *Handbook of Social Psychology* (1935). Many chapters in this volume adopt a historical and comparative approach in which the human mind is conceived as the product of evolutionary and historical change. But as behaviourism began to dominate psychology in general, American research and theory in social psychology became increasingly individualized. This is reflected both in the positivist's repudiation of Wundt (Danziger, 1979) and in F.H. Allport's (1924) apparently persuasive arguments that collective phenomena could be explained purely in terms of the individual. The social aspects of human life were restricted to the influence of others on an individual's behaviour. 'Social psychology is the science which studies the behaviour of the individual in so far as his behaviour stimulates other individuals or is itself a reaction to their behaviour' (Allport, 1924: 12).

With the demise of behaviourism and the rise of cognitivism both psychology and social psychology reverted from the study of behaviour to the study of mind. Despite its initial promise the dominance of the information-processing metaphor has sustained an asocial and ahistorical perspective, even within social psychology. Mind is located within the heads of individuals set over and against the objects of cognition which are located in the environment. Within this framework social cognition refers to nothing more than the individual's perception of and information-processing about social objects. The individual is conceived as a 'thinking machine' rather than a social animal embedded in a historical and cultural context (Gergen, 1982; Moscovici, 1982).

Thus, while collective forms of social psychology, focusing on culture, traditions, norms, beliefs and skills flourished in its early years, the study of social phenomena has come to be dominated by an individualistic, asocial and ahistorical approach (Pepitone, 1981; Gergen, 1985a, b; Farr, 1985, 1991c). The progressive individualization of social phenomena is evident in many fields of study within social psychology and, in particular, in theorizing and research on attitudes (Jaspars and Fraser, 1984; Graumann, 1986), on attribution (Farr, 1989), and on social groups (Steiner, 1974, Turner, 1987). Furthermore, the perpetuation of this individualistic social psychology can be seen in the series of handbooks edited by Lindzey and Aronson (1969, 1985; Farr, 1991c). This insidious focus on the individual has been institutionalized in the disciplinary and departmental boundaries which have been established between psychology and what used to be closely related disciplines such as sociology, anthropology and philosophy. Due to its close association with psychology, collective phenomena, if recognized at all, were not considered to fall within the province of social psychology. In effect, culture and history were banished from the discipline.

The conception (or social representation) of the individual as something discrete and independent from their cultural and historical context is closely associated with a positive, empiricist approach to scientific knowledge. This is incompatible with the investigation of relational and evolving phenomena because it is dependent on the primacy of independent entities. Only then can facts be identified as objective reality and only then can the known (object) be separated from the knower (subject). If culture is to re-emerge as an essential aspect of social psychology, it is necessary to conceive the cultural and the individual in relational terms and it is necessary to develop a compatible approach to scientific enquiry.

An early and highly significant influence on the development of psychology as a science was Darwin's theory of evolution. This paradoxically facilitated the emergence of both individualistic psychology through Wundt's psychophysics (Mackenzie, 1976) and sociological forms of psychology through Wundt's *Voelkerpsychologie* (Farr, 1983). On the one hand, the integration of man into the natural order provided the licence for Wundt to apply the methods of physiology to the phenomenon of the human mind. Scientific enquiry could be geared to the problems and theories of mind and psychology could be included in the natural sciences. On the other hand, Darwin's evolutionary science had been content or problem oriented, and had broadened the available conception of scientific method. He had conducted a major study which was wholly naturalistic: it used historical and comparative methods, drawing on an eclectic data base. Moreover, his theory of evolution employed a variety of explanatory and descriptive terms which were not restricted to physiology, chemistry or physics. In order to study the varieties of culture and its relationship to the individual, Wundt's Voelkerpsychologie adopted this comparative and evolutionary perspective.

With the establishment of psychology in America, the former model of science was given priority over the latter and, by association, the significance of language and culture was virtually ignored. Behaviourists were guided by their commitment to their model of natural science rather than to any substantive theoretical perspective or any understanding of human nature (Mackenzie, 1977). In order to be scientific, psychology had to employ empirical methods of objective observation and experimentation and its theories had to conform to the restrictions of behaviourism, operationalism, and causal mechanisms.

The social representation of science adopted by behaviourists was based on classical theoretical physics, as exemplified by Newton's *Philosophiae Naturalis Principia Mathematica* (1687). It involved a mechanistic conception of nature in which elementary and independent particles of matter operated according to discoverable laws. Laboratory experimentation was an ideal method for controlling and isolating independent and dependent variables. For psychology, a new particle entered into the equation of simple cause and effect relationships – the individual. In order to be consistent with the social representation of science, the individual had to be conceived as an isolated object, in a linear causal mechanism of stimuli and responses. Furthermore, statements were only meaningful in terms of their operationalization and in terms of their verifiable observations. By adopting the methodology of physics and its style of constructing the world, behaviourists attempted to gain the prestige of the physical sciences but, in so doing, they restricted any critical assessment of its appropriateness as a model of science for the study of human phenomena.

With the rise of cognitivism, some of these restrictions were removed (most notably behaviourism and operationalism) but the doctrines of empiricism, reductionism, individualism and mechanism proved to be an all-pervasive influence on theory and research. Information from the environment is processed in a mechanical, linear fashion such that the stimulus–organism–response sequence is sustained in much cognitive theorizing. Thus, despite their explicit concern for social phenomena, social psychological theorizing and research remained a largely individualistic and positivistic enterprise.

DESCARTES AND THE PHILOSOPHICAL ROOTS OF INDIVIDUALISTIC (SOCIAL) PSYCHOLOGY

In its emergence as a science, psychologists created a divide between psychology and its parent discipline of philosophy. However, social psychology and psychology are not independent from philosophy. In failing to recognize their philosophical roots they have failed to realize the assumptions which they had inherited and the philosophies which would have supported alternative psychologies. Embedded in the individualistic and positivistic form of social psychology are various philosophical presumptions which are rarely made explicit. In her insightful book on *Paradigms, Thought and Language*, Markova (1982) elucidates the Cartesian tradition of thought which has structured both behaviouristic psychology (empiricism) and cognitive psychology (rationalism). Both have inherited the Cartesian dualism between the individual and culture. Descartes' scepticism led him to doubt everything but the fact that he was doubting. This gave primacy to the individual mind which had a number of implications for social psychology. Most significant is that the dualism between mind and body also creates a dualism between individuals and their environment and between self and other.

Firstly, mind is separated from reality: while one's body interacts with the environment these are of a different substance and nature to mind. Consequently, mind is independent of the body and of the environment. An individual's subjective knowledge is in some way divorced from the objective reality of the physical environment. The 'world of consciousness' is separate from the 'world-in-itself', the subject from the object, or the knower from the known. Secondly, knowledge and certainty are located in the minds of isolated individuals. An individual's mind is static and passive in the acquisition of knowledge through the recognition of universal ideas. Consciousness and subjective reflection are considered to be innate attributes of the human mind. They are givens in nature which require no further explanations. Thirdly, consciousness is given priority over actions in the world and communications with others about the world. Action and communication do not play a significant role in the acquisition of knowledge. Rather, knowledge is somehow acquired through reflection and is assessed by stable external standards such as mathematical and logical systems and the laws of nature.

Fourthly, the Cartesian paradigm provides a mechanistic conception of the world that consists of discrete, independent and stable entities. This has a number of implications for social psychology. Phenomena can be reduced to their simplest form or divided into separate parts as each entity maintains its independence. These entities still remain the same despite any changes in their surrounding context. They are givens in nature that can move freely from one context to another without being changed themselves. As a consequence, scientific generalizations about human behaviour or cognition can be accepted as universal, unrestricted and stable. This means that we do not need to consider the cultural or historical context of the phenomena that we study.

Cartesian philosophy was not the only viable paradigm on which to build a new psychology (Markova, 1982; Hearnshaw, 1986), but it provided the foundation both for the philosophy of mind and for experimental physiology from which psychology was born. As psychology gained its independence from philosophy and was rapidly transformed from a science of mind to a science of behaviour, it appeared that psychology no longer bore any relationship to Cartesian philosophy. Introspectionism had adhered to Descartes' conception of mind but behaviourism, with its faith in empirical objectivism, had banished all reference to mental phenomena. However this, in itself, did not constitute a paradigmatic revolution: many of the Cartesian principles were embedded within the behaviouristic framework. Most significantly, mind was still separated from behaviour. Behaviourism focused on the body and the behaviour of 'the other one'. By the time cognitivism emerged as the dominant tradition, psychology already had its own history and apparently did not need to reflect on its philosophical past. However, cognitivism simply shifted the perspective back to the mind of the individual while remaining within the Cartesian paradigm. The knower was still separated from the known, from the world which is given in an external reality. Priority is given to the human mind which, while active in the acquisition of knowledge, is still isolated from other minds. The Cartesian philosophy was also compatible with a social representation of science based on Newtonian physics. Psychology's aspiration to the natural sciences only further entrenched the discipline in the dualism between mind and body, between self and other and between the individual and society.

AN ALTERNATIVE PARADIGM FOR SOCIAL PSYCHOLOGY

The influence of Cartesian assumptions in contemporary social psychology becomes apparent when we examine the contrasting pre-suppositions and implications of an alternative framework. Such an alternative is offered by the Hegelian traditions of thought (Markova, 1982; Singer, 1983; Hegel, 1990) which transcends the dualism between mind and body and constructs a synthesis of the individual and culture. The psychological activity of individuals is conceived as a cultural product and culture is conceived as a human product. Essentially, this is an expression of Hegelian dialectics. It refers to the unification of opposites, in this case the synthesis of the psychological and the cultural, of individual thought-processes and social reality, through their dynamic interrelations. In other words, individual thought-processes and social reality are mutually interdependent. Cultural products such as language, myth and customs have an objective existence which is dialectically related to the mental functioning of individuals. For example, language is an inherently social phenomenon which is related closely to self-reflexive awareness. It constitutes a system of gestures and symbols of communication which link the psychological processes of associated individuals. The mind of an individual is thus part of a trans-individual psychological system, and language can express the mentality of a nation. With this as the basis, the Hegelian tradition of thought contrasts drama-tically with the Cartesian paradigm, as outlined in Table 1.

Table 1 A comparison of the Cartesian and Hegelian paradigms

Cartesian paradigm	*Hegelian paradigm*
DUALISM:	MUTUALISM OR RELATIONISM:
between mind and body	among mind
between individual and	body
environment	environment
between self and other	culture
Consciousness and subjective	Reflexive self-consciousness
reflection are innate	develops through mutual interaction
Mind and consciousness are	Mind and consciousness
given priority over action and	depend upon action and
communication	communication
MECHANISTIC:	ORGANIC OR RELATIONAL:
Individual is independent and	Individual is dependent and
stable entity	dynamic
Reductionism	Holism
Change is quantitative	Change is qualitative
Scientific laws are universal	Scientific laws are indeterminate
How the world works	How the world is constructed

Firstly, the dualism between mind and body, between the individual and the environment, is transcended by re-conceptualizing the relationship between the knower and the known. For Hegel, knowledge is acquired through a circle returning within itself; through interacting with the environment. It is as if a person's mind and body join forces with the environment to express an idea. Secondly, self-consciousness and subjective awareness are not things that are given in nature. Rather they develop out of the mutual encounter of one person with another. During interactions people take other people's perspective towards themselves and, in so doing, they attain a reflexive self-consciousness. Our awareness of ourselves and our ability to think both depend upon our interactions with other people. In this way, the individualistic conception of mind, reflection and consciousness are transformed into dynamic and social conceptions, transcending the dualism between individuals and culture. Thirdly, it can be seen that mind and consciousness are dependent upon our interactions with the environment and our communications with other people. Mind is not given priority over action, rather it is through practical activity that the individual develops a mind of his or her own. Thus, mind involves both self-reflection and action and knowledge is dialectically related to activity in particular environmental and social contexts.

Here we must go a step further and break with the constraints imposed by a direct comparison with the Cartesian paradigm. The Hegelian paradigm adopts an evolutionary perspective involving the historical dimension of change through time. It is not only that humans are active in the acquisition of knowledge, it is also that there is a circle of interaction by which both the person who knows something and the object that is known are transformed. All aspects can be transformed in the expression of an idea through the interaction between a person and his or her environment. It is through the interdependent development of individuals and culture that social reality is gradually reconstructed and recreated.

This leads us to the fourth point of comparison. In contrast to the mechanistic conception of the world inherent in the Cartesian paradigm the Hegelian tradition of thought provides an organic or relational conception of the world that consists of interdependent and changeable entities. It is a world of vibrant activity that is continually being re-created and transformed. The individual is conceived as an active and dynamic entity that cannot be divorced from their physical and social environment. It is not so much that one individual responds to some discrete object or individual but, rather, that the individual and the object or person come together to act in unison and, in so doing, they create and reconstruct reality. As a consequence of this relational perspective, phenomena must be investigated in all their complexity in order to maintain the integrity of the system as a whole. A single entity must always be considered in association with related entities. If aspects of the system are reduced or divided up then the elements no longer remain the same. It is like the difference between a line drawing and a post-impressionist painting. In the line drawing, different objects in the picture can still be easily identified even when they are moved around. In the painting, the identity of objects depends upon their relation with other objects as there are no clear boundaries dividing one from the other. Finally, a change in context always involves a change in the entity itself. Any scientific generalization is therefore always indeterminate, unstable and relative. It is dependent upon the social and historical context which must be embraced in our understanding of social-psychological phenomena.

While the Cartesian paradigm may still provide a useful framework, just as Newtonian physics is still useful despite being superseded by Einstein's theory of relativity, the Hegelian tradition of thought provides a more appropriate framework for the study of social phenomena. This is because individuals are conceived as social beings in relation to their physical and cultural environment and because reality is conceived as a dynamic and open system. The inherent dualism of the Cartesian paradigm can only offer social psychology an individualistic conception of reality. The mechanistic conception of phenomena also precludes any understanding of real change. We would be concerned only with how the world works, as it is. This restricts our research and theorizing to a description and explanation of those social factors that influence the individual.

The fundamental mutualism of the Hegelian paradigm gives us a relational or social conception of reality. This provides an alternative framework in which the individual's psychological processes are dialectically related with culture. Culture is the product of individuals who are themselves the product of culture. They are essentially different aspects of the same process. This allows us, as social psychologists, to explore the active and creative relationship between individuals and their culture and to theorize about and examine the dynamics of stability and change. Social psychologists then would be concerned primarily with the social construction of reality: that is, how the world came to be as it is.

THE INTEGRATION OF THE INDIVIDUAL AND CULTURE

The Hegelian tradition of thought flourished in the human sciences until the mid-1930s since when it has been poorly represented, especially in social psychology, which has been dominated largely by the theoretical and methodological commitments of the Cartesian paradigm. However, since the crisis in the 1970s there has been a gradual paradigm shift in which increasing numbers of social scientists have adopted Hegelian presuppositions and elaborated their implications for particular areas of study.

During the 1970s a number of penetrating critiques against mechanistic and reductionistic approaches initiated and sustained a crisis in social psychology. At the heart of the crisis was a loss of faith in objectivity. The work of Orne (1962) and Rosenthal (1966) indicated the highly reactive nature of laboratory experimentation and led to doubts concerning the validity and certainty of such scientific investigations. Kelman (1968), among others, questioned the notion of value-free science and issues regarding the ethics of research in the social sciences further destabilized the establishment. This gave rise to meta-theoretical analysis and debate which challenged the traditional assumptions rooted in Cartesian philosophy and positivistic empirical science.

The debate was closely related to heated disagreements between psychologists who considered their discipline to be a branch of the natural sciences and others who argued that psychology was a social science. Psychology, as an experimental science, tended to isolate phenomena in the laboratory in order to establish universal laws or truths. The scientist attempts to create a cultural and temporal vacuum within the laboratory such that the relationships found in the experimental manipulation may be said to apply to all people at all times. Psychology, as a social science, includes the dimensions of time and space, recognizing the influence of history and culture. Any one culture will exhibit changes over time and at any one time there exists a variety of cultures and subcultures. As cultures differ and change the very subject-matter of social psychology changes and this must be reflected in our social-psychological theories.

This debate was resumed in a slightly different form with the publication of Gergen's article on social psychology as history (1973). Gergen argues that the diffusion of scientific knowledge into common sense changes the very subject-matter which psychology attempts to study. It changes people's understanding of themselves and others, their communications and their social interactions. Moscovici's own study on the diffusion of psychoanalysis within French culture is a case in point. Other examples include the work of Festinger on cognitive dissonance (1957), of Asch on group conformity (1956) and of Milgram on obedience to authority (1974).

Over the past twenty years new approaches to psychology and social psychology have emerged. In particular, there has been a resurgence of interest in cultural or societal forms of social psychology and the emergence of a contextualist or constructionist approach to social psychological phenomena. Despite their differences they display a number of common themes, emphasizing the active role of individuals in the construction of social knowledge, the significance of meaning and symbolism, the dynamic and changing nature of reality; the role of culture and social structure; and the wider socio-historical context of human life (e.g. Harré and Secord, 1972; Israel and Tajfel, 1972; Mixon, 1972; Armistead, 1974; Shotter, 1975; Strickland et al., 1976a; Gauld and Shotter, 1977; Meehl, 1978; Tajfel, 1978a, 1984b; Gilmour and Duck, 1980; Billig, 1982; Cranach and Harré, 1982; Gergen, 1982, 1985a, b;

Markova, 1982, 1987; McGuire, 1983; Farr and Moscovici, 1984a; Henriques *et al.*, 1984: Graumann, 1986; Margolis *et al.*, 1986; Cole, 1987; Jaeger and Rosnow, 1988; Rijsman and Stroebe, 1989; Himmelveit and Gaskell, 1990; Himmelveit, 1990; Farr, 1991a). Apparently diverse alternatives in contemporary social psychology, including the historical–social psychology, ethnogenics, dialectics, hermeneutic analysis, discourse analysis and ethno-methodology, as well as a more critical analysis of the philosophical and meta-theoretical history of social psychology, fall within the Hegelian paradigm (Gergen and Morawski, 1980). Moreover, its manifestations are not limited to social psychology; its principles have also been explored in cognitive psychology, life-span development, personality, communications and environmental psychology. Although the Hegelian paradigm is by no means fully articulated in these fields of study, together they indicate a decline in the power of the Cartesian paradigm to structure our theorizing and research and the gradual emergence of an alternative paradigm which embraces Hegelian presuppositions and a dialectic perspective.

SCIENCE AND SOCIAL PSYCHOLOGY

The paradigm shift from Cartesian to Hegelian presuppositions has significant implications for our understanding of science and for the conduct of research. We have already seen that a Cartesian conception of the individual as a discrete and independent entity is associated with a positive–empiricist conception of science. A Hegelian conception of individuals in relation with others, or as members of a collective with its own language and culture, requires a different conception of science. This should reflect the constructionist epistemology inherent in the Hegelian paradigm. Knowledge, including scientific knowledge, is conceived as an active, practical and constructive affair. As such, it is relative to specific socio-historical and cultural contexts which evolve and transform. Knowledge is thus relative to time and space and cannot be divorced from either the knower or their context within a particular culture (Gergen and Davis, 1985; Gergen, 1978, 1982, 1985a, b; Hollway, 1989).

The development of a Hegelian approach to scientific enquiry should be guided by the principle of self-reflexiveness. It is difficult, if not impossible, to conceive of a human science which is independent of its subject-matter, or how the community of scientists and the community which it studies live and function within different forms of reality. Being a human science, the assumptions applied to people as the object of study must also be applied to scientists as the agent of study. In conjunction with this we cannot apply one epistemology to common-sense knowledge and a different epistemology to scientific knowledge.

Behaviourism, by limiting itself to the observation of other people's behaviour, excluded from its analysis the role of the scientist both as a participant in research and in the construction of the research situation. This conformed to the social representation of science which behaviourists adopted from the natural sciences. The reactive nature of psychological research could not be formulated within such a framework and consequently did not appear to be a problem. With the emergence of cognitive psychology it was realized that the human subject does not passively respond to a given situation; rather, he or she actively construes the situation in accordance with his or her beliefs, values and desires. This is as true for everyday life as it is for the research situation. However, this constructive epistemology was restricted to the object of study: an empiricist epistemology was maintained with regard to the scientists.

Within a self-reflexive approach to social psychology these contradictions must be avoided. We must apply the same principles both to the object of study and to our understanding of science itself. Social psychology within the Hegelian paradigm must conceive both the subject and the scientist as social beings and both the reality of people and the products of science as social constructions. Scientists are social individuals who are actively engaged in the social construction of scientific knowledge. They are participants in the construction and transformation of theory and research. Furthermore, science is a human activity which is culturally and historically situated. Scientists' observations are dependent on their theories and theories are relative to the social and cultural milieu of which they are a part. Scientific knowledge is thus not objective, individualistic and ahistorical; it is perpetually open to revision and transformation and can lay no claim to certainty.

By now it should be apparent that the Cartesian and Hegelian paradigms have divergent implications with regard to the formulation of research problems, the appropriate methods of research and the construction of acceptable solutions. In particular, while the Cartesian paradigm favours experimental methods, data collections, short time spans and quantification, the Hegelian paradigm favours comparative methods, theory construction, extended time spans and qualifications. Furthermore, the latter encourages the use of multiple and complementary methods within a programme of research.

With the dominance of the Cartesian paradigm experimental methodology has enjoyed an unrivalled hegemony in social psychology since its early adoption as the primary method of investigation in the 1930s. Despite various critiques which have challenged this approach it has remained the dominant mode of investigation. Chapters and books on methodology continue to focus on experimentation (e.g. Greenberg and Folgar, 1988; Manstead and Semin, 1988) and experimental reports dominate the most prestigious journals. Rather than adopting alternative methods of research which are now available, many social psychologists have concentrated on developing new and more complex experimental designs in order to overcome problems associated with experimenter effects, demand characteristics, ecological validity and social or cultural context effects (e.g. Campbell and Stanley, 1963; Webb *et al.*, 1966, 1981; Campbell, 1967; Doise, 1986).

The methodological commitments of the Cartesian paradigm favour the experimental method of research. The manipulation of independent and dependent variables in a controlled environment depends on the conception of phenomena as discrete and independent entities. For example, attitudes are studied independently of perceptions, cognitions, beliefs or emotions, and message content is studied independently of other environmental variables. Of even greater significance is the duality which this methodology establishes between the individual and the environment. The individual is envisioned as a stable, inert entity influenced by environmental stimulation. Thus, the experimenter manipulates the environment and observes the response (S–R psychology). Furthermore, the independence of entities justifies a reductionist approach whereby the relations between phenomena can be reduced to their simplest form. In this way, the experimenter 'discovers' basic cause–effect relationships between the variables (determinism) and can postulate various intervening mechanisms (S–O–R psychology).

These methodological commitments cannot be accommodated within the Hegelian paradigm. Entities are not independent but are interdependent or dialectic, such that a single entity can only be considered in association with related entities. As these relationships change the essence of the entities involved also change. Thus, a person's attitudes are dependent upon their perceptions, cognitions, beliefs and emotions. Furthermore, there is a unity between the individual and the environment. The individual can only be understood as a purposefully functioning unity which embraces the environment. This unity is achieved through the individual's activity and participation within the environment. This requires a reconceptualization of the methodological commitments such that reductionist and mechanistic explanations are avoided. In general terms, there must be a commitment to structural and comparative analyses of phenomena that incorporate the historical and cultural milieux.

The Cartesian paradigm also favours data collection over theory construction. This is endorsed by the positive-empiricist epistemology whereby the scientist is considered to be an objective observer of nature. This perspective on the process of science is rejected by the Hegelian paradigm. Science is a social activity in which scientists actively construct knowledge and, in so doing, transform both themselves and the world in which they live. Observation is an activity that depends upon theory and is effective within the system being studied. That is, both scientific knowledge and the phenomena being studied are essentially interactive – they are both active and reactive. This perspective takes into account the theory-dependent nature of observation, indeterminacy and reactivity to be discussed in Chapter 7. Theory construction thus plays a central role within the Hegelian paradigm.

Furthermore, the historical and evolutionary character of the Hegelian paradigm means that a new dimension must be taken into account in research – the dimension of time. This is not an important dimension within the Cartesian paradigm; as entities are stable and enduring, change is limited to quantitative redistribution. It is not surprising then that the methods of research adopted within the Cartesian paradigm are unsuitable for studying the transformation of phenomena over time. For example, experimentation only provides knowledge of temporally truncated sequences of events. The length of experiments is reduced to a minimum in order to eliminate contaminating variables. An equally pervasive influence has been the preference for quantitative, as opposed to qualitative, research. It is almost as though scientific research is synonymous with quantitative research (see Lindzey and Aronson, 1985). If we wish to study the creation and development of new things and new ideas then we need to develop alternative methods of research.

Finally, within the Cartesian paradigm the aim of science is to discover universal principles that exist in nature. This relies upon the quantitative analysis of stable relations between independent entities. As a consequence, there are methodological commitments to prediction, hypothesis-testing, validity, replication and control. Within the Hegelian paradigm the aim of science is to construct understandings of a dynamic and open-ended system. This relies on the qualitative analysis of changing interrelationships between interdependent entities. The meaning of concepts of the essence of things cannot be described in mathematical terms. As a consequence, the conventional criteria for trustworthiness are inappropriate within the Hegelian paradigm. Alternative criteria for the evaluation of research must be constructed. Lincoln and Guba (1985) suggest that credibility, transferability, dependability and confirmability are more appropriate criteria. Alternatively, Gergen (1984) emphasizes the role of empirical research in the construction and development of theories. Research should clarify, demonstrate, illustrate and vivify theoretical statements.

The dominance of the Cartesian paradigm has resulted in a social psychology that is both individualistic and static. This applies to research as well as to theory. By relying on experimentation as the primary method of investigation, social psychologists have produced a discipline that is both acultural and ahistorical. We know a great deal about individuals behaving on their own in strange situations but very little about ongoing social activity within its natural context. In order to establish a social psychology based on the meta-theoretical principles of the Hegelian paradigm we need to develop methods of research that take account of the relational, constructive and evolutionary character of social phenomena. Traditional methods of research need to be adapted and new ones developed, especially with respect to the historical dimension (Gergen and Gergen, 1984; Semin and Gergen, 1990). These would include the scientist as an active participant in research. They would incorporate the historical, cultural and social context; deal with the qualitative or meaningful nature of phenomena; and examine the transformation or evolution of phenomena over time.

This does not dictate the rejection of traditional research methods such as experimentation, as has been suggested by some social psychologists working within the constructionist tradition (e.g. Harré, 1979). Experimental research can be adapted to and interpreted within the Hegelian paradigm, taking account of the role of language in the research context, the role of the researcher in construing experimental situations and in the interpretation of events; and the importation of culture and history into the laboratory (see Chapter 2; Mackenzie, 1977; Doise, 1978; Markova, 1982). This would go hand-in-hand with a recognition of their limitations. In particular, the Hegelian paradigm is committed to the 'definitional sanctity of the whole'. Individual objects or events derive their social meaning from their position within the whole over extended periods of time (Gergen, 1984). Isolated fragments are significant only in relation to their extended context. Thus, it is necessary to have experimental investigations on ideas that have emerged from research which addresses the social, cultural and historical aspects of socio-psychological phenomena. Experimentation would no longer be used to generate foundational elements of a theory, rather it would be used to clarify, demonstrate, illustrate or vivify theoretical understandings which had been gained from studying social phenomena in all their complexity.

This can only be achieved by employing diverse but complementary research methods within integrative programmes. Within the Cartesian paradigm the adoption of a multi–method approach might be justified in terms of the accumulation of knowledge from multiple data sources. A more sophisticated justification could be given in terms of triangulation, whereby the use of multiple data sources and various research methods offers the opportunity to validate findings by systematically comparing the research results (Fielding and Fielding, 1986). However, these justifications fail to take into account the process of research as defined by the Hegelian paradigm. Here, different methods of research provide the investigator with an array of tools that are particular to specific research problems.

Within a research programme complementary methods would be employed to examine different aspects of the research object and to overcome the problems and limitations associated with any one particular method or data source. For example, it is not so much that an experimental study can be used to validate the results of a content analysis but, rather, that the results of one investigation are used to formulate research problems and to inform the design and interpretation of a complementary investigation. Furthermore, it is not possible to predetermine the structure and content of a research programme, for the very reason that it is not possible to predict the outcome of research. There is little point in carrying out research when we already know the answer. Rather, research focuses precisely on the unconfirmed, where there are contradictions and conflicts to be resolved. This is achieved through the meaningful and ongoing interaction between the researcher and the object of research. The research programme thus emerges and evolves during the process of research. It involves a set of complex and dynamic relations among theory construction and transformation, formulation of research problems, the design of research, the various sources of data and methods employed, the objects of investigation, the active participation in research, the negotiation of meanings and the interpretation of research findings, etc.

A NOTE ON SOCIAL REPRESENTATIONS THEORY

While the scope of this chapter has been broad, giving an exposition of the contrasting paradigms and their expression in the distant and recent history of social psychology, it is worth refocusing on social representations, if only briefly. The theory of social representations does not stand in isolation from the evolution of social psychology as a discipline and the emergence of alternative orientations in the human sciences. It is, at one and the same time, an initiating force and an expression of this reorientation. This is reflected in both its theoretical perspective and its methodological approach. However, even though social representation theorists propound a cultural social psychology, they have not entirely broken with its Cartesian predecessors.

One of the distinguishing characteristics of research on social representations is the diversity of methods which have been employed, including experimentation, questionnaires, multi-dimensional scaling, observational studies, participant observation and content analysis of interview transcripts and media. This has given rise to considerable debate within the research community (Breakwell and Canter, 1993). In particular, if social representations theory is to be successful in developing a social psychology which goes beyond the individualistic traditions of the discipline then it is also necessary to operationalize the social principles of the theory in research practice. Parker (1987) argues that the social-constructivist orientation of the theory has been betrayed by the choice of individualistic methods. Farr (1993) similarly suggests that many of the methodological debates have arisen because British social psychologists have applied positivistic (Cartesian) principles of research. I have also argued in Chapter 2 that much of the research on social representations fails to reflect the relational and interdependent quality of the psychological and the cultural.

Moscovici's answer is to revert to methods of observation for the purpose of describing the content, structure and evolution of social representations and that progress will be made through the comparative study of such descriptions (Moscovici, 1985b, 1988). But observation, in itself, is inadequate. Within the Hegelian paradigm the conduct of research and the development of theory go hand in hand: both description and explanation are essential components of understanding. All too frequently researchers have employed social representations theory as a framework in which to describe a particular phenomenon but have failed to explicate the implications of their research for the theory or to develop any of its theoretical principles. In order to understand the transformation of social representations it is necessary to construct both descriptions of the phenomenon of social representations and explanations in terms of the socio-psychological processes of social representations. This can only be achieved by developing research programmes which adopt a multi-method approach. Only by combining the strengths of diverse research methods are we able to provide descriptions of the content and form of social representations, examine their behavioural aspects, explore their association with groups, inspect their role in socialization and understand their dynamics and the processes by which they are transformed (Moscovici, 1961; Jodelet and Moscovici, 1975; Chombart-de-Lauwe, 1984; Jodelet, 1991; Purkhardt and Stockdale, 1993).

Many of the conflicts and ambiguities evident in various writings on social representations arise from the fundamental differences between the Hegelian and the Cartesian paradigms. In Part I we discussed the contradiction between the individual and society and made some progress towards a synthesis. This is elaborated in the next chapter, where I develop the theory of social representations within the Hegelian paradigm, focusing on the nature of the individual in relation to the social construction of reality. Unfortunately, this does not resolve all our problems. While the theory constitutes a powerful and valid critique of individualism in conventional social psychology, Moscovici subscribes to a positivistic view of science and this leads him to make a false distinction between the world of science and the world of common sense. In opposition to Moscovici, I shall argue in Part III that the theory must adopt a constructivist approach to both realms of knowledge. Furthermore, far from being exclusive to common sense, the theory of social representations is also applicable to the dynamics of scientific knowledge.

5

THE SOCIAL INDIVIDUAL AND THE NATURE OF REALITY

The shift from a Cartesian to a Hegelian paradigm outlined in the previous chapter involves a transformation in our social representations, both of the individual and of science. The relationship between science and social representations is discussed in depth in Part III. In this chapter I shall concentrate on the social representation of the individual, a crucial component in the synthesis of the psychological and cultural. Inevitably, this is linked with our understanding of reality. By elaborating a social representation of the individual as a social being and explicating what is entailed in the social construction of reality, I hope to transcend the contradictions within the theory and construct a coherent and unified account regarding the dynamics and transformation of social representations. These developments, within the Hegelian paradigm, allow us to reassess the role of individuals in the construction of social reality.

The notion that the 'individual' and the 'social' are indeed social representations is indicated by the diversity of their representations in different cultures (Kon, 1984) and their transformation in different historical eras (Foucault, 1974). The significance and insidious influence of these social representations within social psychology was discussed in the previous chapter and is evident from the numerous discussions concerning the image of man and its place in psychology (e.g. Shotter, 1975; Semin, 1986). It is also raised within the field of social representations itself. For example, Duveen and Lloyd (1986) argue that theoretical confusion arises when the constructed and constructive natures of the categories 'individual' and 'social' are ignored. Farr (1987a) develops a similar argument, drawing on the work of Ichheiser, in his study of the collective representation of individualism and its profound effect not only in our social, economic and legal practices but also in shaping modern psychology.

Some theorists have re-socialized our social representations of the individual by emphasizing the importance of language. The individual human mind is pervaded by the cultural tradition of society through the medium of language. Language is clearly of prime importance (Farr, 1984; Jodelet, 1984b; Moscovici, 1984b; Rommetveit, 1984). It provides the means by which we think, by which we structure our understandings and by which we communicate and create our social representations. It relates the observations of something (the iconic) to an abstract category (the symbolic). Just as an individual is always a particular person and also a member of a social category (Jaspars and Hewstone, 1990) so, too, an object is always a particular thing and also a thing belonging to one or more categories. These categories which structure and express the representation of an object are drawn from our common culture and are embedded in our language. Thus, even where the focus is on the individual's system of representations, as in the case of the experimental studies, this cultural element is always present.

Despite the significance of language a much stronger argument for the re-socialization of the individual can be constructed. It is not only that an individual's mind is imbued with the social but also that it is social in origin. Moreover, mind exists not only in an individual's head but also in people's social interactions and in their cultural environment. This argument is developed by drawing on the writings of Dewey, Mead and Vygotsky in order to elaborate an evolutionary perspective on the mutual relations between the organism, their environment and their culture. In this way individuals are conceived as inherently social beings embedded in a physical, cultural and historical context. Furthermore, reality is conceived neither as an external given nor as a collective illusion but as a product of people's social activity within an ongoing physical and cultural environment. This provides a framework within which to reconsider the role of the individual in the dynamics and transformation of social representations.

THE SOCIALIZATION OF THE INDIVIDUAL AND THE DE-INDIVIDUALIZATION OF THE SOCIAL

I have argued that, in order to understand the origins and transformation of social representations, it is necessary to integrate the psychological and the cultural. This can be achieved by conceptualizing the human mind and 'individual' thought as a thoroughly social affair. The human mind is not only pervaded by the social, by the language and traditions of a society, but it is also social in its genesis. The individual's psychological processes and the contents of their representations are the products (as well as the producers) of social processes and cultural phenomena. This denies the existence of purely individual representations. In effect, it entails the reverse of Graumann's exposition on the individualistic psychology of groups and crowds in which he states 'the individual-ization of the social is identical with a desocialization of the individual' (Graumann, 1986: 100–1). For social representations theory to overcome individualistic reductionism it requires the socialization of the individual which is identical with a de-individualization of the social.

The idea that the relationship between the individual and society can be understood by propounding the social nature of the individual is not new. Much of the discussion below draws on the seminal work of G.H. Mead (1934, 1956) from Chicago, USA, and of Vygotsky (1929, 1962, 1978; Luria, 1976; Wertsch, 1985) from Russia. With the re-emergence of culture in social psychology, and social constructionism in psychology more gener-ally there has been a resurgence of interest in their work. Mead and Vygotsky both adopted and elaborated the Hegelian paradigm (independently of each other) in an explicit attempt to reconcile Wundt's two psychologies. The integration of Wundt's individual and folk psychology required that consciousness be reconceptualized as a social phenomenen: thought and self-awareness arise out of culture and are inherently social in nature. Although the writings of Mead and Vygotsky contain some significant differences, their fundamental characteristics are surprisingly similar. Both were committed to an evolutionary and historical approach in which psychology cannot be divorced from the study of culture. Both sought the origins of mind in the communicative act. Both emphasized the dialectic relationship between language and thought. Furthermore, both focused on symbolic meaning and the means of communication.

Before considering the social nature of the individual in any depth I shall draw on Dewey's classic article against the use of the reflex arc concept in psychology in order to establish an 'organic' as opposed to a 'mechanistic' conception of the relationship between the organism and the environment (Dewey, 1896). Mechanistic conceptions construe organisms and their environments as separate parts in isolation and existing independently of one another, such that the characteristics and functions of each can be considered irrespectively of their context. In psychology, this mechanist approach is epitomized by behaviourism in which causes are located in the environment and responses in the behaviour of the organism. As a result, the analysis of behaviour has been constructed in terms of a sequence of an organism's responses to environ-mental stimuli (S–R). In contrast, an organic conception construes the organism and the environment as a system of mutual influences by which the 'parts' all determine one another's characteristics and functions.

Furthermore, the organic system transforms itself qualitatively in a continual process of exchange and growth. The organism is not set in opposition to the environment; rather, they are interdependent aspects of an organic system which function together and define each other at every step.

Dewey illustrates the organic conception using the example of light. Light is construed not as a stimulus in the environment, but as an act of seeing. Similarly, sound is construed as an act of hearing. Seeing and hearing involve both the organism and the environment simultaneously and interdependently. Furthermore, the meaning and value of seeing or hearing are transformed through the action of the organism–environment system over time. This organic conception is difficult to express in ordinary language in which the separation of the organism and environment is both implicit and insidious. For example, the statement 'the child sees the candle' immediately locates the seeing in the organism and the candle in the environment. Similarly, the action is located frequently either in the organism or the environment; the child reaches for the candle and the candle burns the child. But the meaning and value of both 'reaching' and 'burning' are dependent upon the organism–environment system. Furthermore, it is through such action that meanings and values are transformed. Rather than assuming that the stimulus and response are givens which exist in nature it is necessary to examine the genesis and development of the organic system over time.

So far, we have an understanding of the organism in the environment. However, when we come to consider the human organism–environment system a third term enters into the analysis – that of culture, with all its social and historical concomitants. This does not enter as a variable to be included in a mechanistic analysis. Rather, the organism–environment–culture system entails a qualitative shift in the explanatory principles of psychology. Both Mead and Vygotsky propounded an organic conception of the organism–environment system which emphasized its evolution or genesis in socio-cultural processes. The individual and the environment mutually determine each other through the activity of the individual in the environment. Objects in the environment change as the patterns of activity or responses to those objects change. What is distinctive about humankind's evolution is that it has been directed through intelligent action, made possible by symbolization. In human societies, the environment is partly constituted by significant symbols, signs and tools of mediation, which are themselves constructed in human interaction. Mead emphasizes the role of language as a system of symbolic gestures by which individuals communicate and develop shared understandings of the world in which they live. Vygotsky emphasizes the creation of systems of communication or cultural elaborations in the environment, such as notched sticks, signs and written language. Both emphasize that the locus of the mind is not in the individual but rather in the significant gestures and cultural artifacts which have a shared symbolic meaning for members of a given society.

Drawing on the writings of Mead, the individual is conceived as an essentially social being. Through the process of the self, which has its origins in social interaction, the individual is able to take the attitude of the other in a process of symbolic interaction. Individuals adjust to the indications or gestures of other individuals in the social process of behaviour: and gestures become significant symbols when they have the same effect on the individual making it as they have on the individual who responds to it. Individuals acquire a communality of perspective with others by learning the symbols by which they designate aspects of their world. Moreover, the shared meaning of a gesture, or significant symbol, is determined by the response to which it gives rise within the social interaction. Thus, meaning is defined in terms of action and involves subject, object and third person or generalized other. In other words, meaning is dependent upon the actions of the individual, the environment and other individuals. For Mead, as for Vygotsky, in order to provide an understanding of human thinking and communication among individuals it is necessary to understand the origins of mind in the process of human interaction or what he terms a 'conversation of gestures'. 'Mind arises through communication by a conversation of gestures in a social process of context of experience' (Mead, 1934: 50). Thinking is the internalization of external conversations or gestures (social interaction) and, once internalized as significant symbols, they have the same meanings for individual members of a society or social group. Thus the existence of mind or thinking is only made possible through social interaction.

The implications for our understanding of mind and of the individual are quite profound. Mind finds its genesis and its expression in the social interaction between people in a given environmental context. Furthermore, as Vygotsky argues, human society is distinguished by the creation of cultural artifacts which exist in the environment and which are imbued with symbolic significance. In this way, the social development of mind is dialectically dependent upon the socially constructed environment. This implies that 'mind' does not exist purely in the heads of individuals, but exists in the social interactions and cultural elaborations of society. In this way, priority is given to the social. The individual does not exist independently from his or her surrounding culture, as something over and against society. Furthermore, the individual is not assumed to be a given in nature, prior to any kind of analysis. By adapting an evolutionary or historical approach, it can be seen that the individual cannot be understood outside the social relations and culture of which he or she is a part. The individual is social through and through. At the same time, society is not set apart from individuals. It is individuals who together sustain and create the social and cultural environment in which they live.

Once the origin, function and expression of mind is understood in this way the interaction among minds, the communication between people and the consensus of meaning on which they depend, cease to be problematic. Moreover, it transcends the dualism between mind and body, between organism and environment and, most importantly in the present context, between the individual and culture. The individual and culture are inextricably interwoven in a dialetic relationship, embedded in a socio-cultural historical context. The representation of the relationship between the individual and the social in terms of an evolving organism–environment–culture system provides a framework in which to avoid both individualistic and sociological reductionism.

If the above argument is accepted then it may well be assumed that everything is social and, as a consequence, there is no need to have a theory of *social* representations. If the individual's mind is a social phenomenon, then cognitive psychologists and individualistic theorists are necessarily studying the social processes and social contents of mind. The problem is not that these psychologists have studied something which does not exist but rather that they have failed to realize the evolutionary and social nature of their object of study. The framework presented above suggests that we look in different directions for solutions to the problems of social psychology. It is necessary to examine not only the individual but the individual with other individuals in their environmental context; to examine not only individual cognitive processes, but social cognitive processes and the significant context of social interactions in the environment; to examine not only behaviour (in the broadest sense of the term) at a given time but the evolution and transformation of actions in its historical and socio-cultural context. It may well come to pass that lengthy expositions of the social nature of mind will prove unnecessary. The history of social psychology tells a different story. The dominance of individualistic approaches to social phenomena demands that the 'social' is propounded and explicated every step of the way. It must be remembered that this book is written in the context of modern social psychology. This refers both to its argument against the individualization of the social and to the re-emergence of culture in social psychology.

THE DEFINITION OF SOCIAL REALITY

Social representations are the constituents of our social reality. It might be assumed, then, that a definition of social representations would simultaneously offer a definition of social reality. We know that the symbolic and meaningful nature of reality is constructed through the social processes of interactions and communication. This view of reality is a legitimate reaction against a positive–empiricist definition in which the individual does no more than passively perceive the external objective world and meaning is either ignored or located in the objects themselves. However, the opposition to an empiricist notion of reality does not, in itself, provide a definitive idea of how we should conceive social reality. It is also necessary to deny the extreme social constructionist thesis which suggests that reality is no more than what we believe it to be.

Reality is not located in the heads of individuals: it is not purely the subjective reconstruction of an individual or, for that matter, the inter-subjective reconstruction of several individuals. If this thesis were pro-pounded, objects would be social creations which only exist in human experience: they would be no more than their socially created meaning. This position is completely untenable. If reality were purely a social construction, the absence of the physical world would not impinge upon normal life at all. The world would be nothing but an illusion. Clearly, even if we accept the symbolic and meaningful nature of reality its social construction cannot be given primacy over the physical world. Wells (1987) presents a similar argument, drawing on the philosophical writings of Quine (1976). Culture and its assimilation are dependent upon (but not determined by) the physical senses of our bodies – that is, to light, sound, touch, etc. Social reality may be imbued with meaning and social significance but it is also imbued with physical force.

The theory of social representations requires a definition of social reality which assimilates the physical with the social and does not dissociate human beings from their environment. This can be achieved by a conception of social reality in terms of a 'historical intersubjective objectivity'. This is a dreadfully cumbersome term, but it indicates the importance of adopting an evolutionary perspective; it emphasizes the significance of interrelations among people, and it obviates the distinc-tion between subjective and objective through their juxtaposition.

This can be illustrated by examining Mead's understanding of objects and its association with the notion of perspective. An object has definite qualities that are dependent on both the physical structure of the biological organism and the physical qualities of the environment (see Dewey, above). The significance or meaning of an object, event or symbol is dependent on the experience of the object or gesture. This meaning will be the same when individuals share a common perspective and this common perspective is dependent on both the language of significant symbols and the physical structure of organisms and their environments. It is not a given in nature but rather it is socially constructed through ongoing interactions between people in their environment. The Meadian notion of social reality is the most appropriate for the theory of social representations. It goes beyond the active observation of the environment inherent in much cognitive psychology to the active construction of reality within an organism–environment–culture system. As such, it transcends the dualisms between mind and body, between the individual and the environment and between the cultural and physical.

Reality is not located in one particular element but within relations of a continuously changing system. The human individual is not an independent entity but a social being that is part of a physical and cultural context. It should not be forgotten that a person is both essentially social and essentially physical. At the same time it should not be forgotten that the environment of objects and events is imbued with meaning and with social significance. It is not a collection of independent, stable and static objects but is rather part of a dynamic and evolving system. The environment is made up of physical objects with a physical force and is perceived through physical media, but these exist in a social, cultural and historical context from which they cannot be divorced. For example, Paris has a physical existence which cannot be denied but nor can it be known outside its social and historical context (Milgram, 1984). Finally, we can see that culture exists in the emerging relationship between people and their environment. It can neither be located purely in the heads of individuals nor simply in the cultural objects of the environment. The former conception individualizes culture while the latter reifies culture. Rather, culture, as an aspect of the organism–environment–cultural system, denotes an objective social reality. Reality is no less real for being social. Rather, it includes people and culture in our ontology, an ontology that is essential to any social science.

It is important to realize that this conception of social reality provides the basis for our broader definition of social interaction and communication. 'Social interaction' not only refers to interactions between two or more people, but also to interactions with the physical and symbolic products of human activity. The environment, with its material, physical characteristics forming the foundation for its social symbolic characteristics, is an important constituent element of any social interaction. Similarly, communication not only refers to 'non-verbal' or 'verbal' communication between two or more people; it also refers to communication through written and pictorial materials including magazines, papers, posters, films, television, etc., through displays in museums, shops, exhibitions, etc.; and through the structure of the 'physical' environment, including parks, offices, homes, etc. (Chombart-de-Lauwe, 1984). While this broader definition is implied by the diversity of research on social representations, from studying people's actions and conversations to examining the media and the structure of physical objects, the definition of social reality presented here provides a theoretical basis for their integration.

A final point needs to be made about the dynamic nature of social reality. Not only do relations and meanings evolve in the course of interactions but new objects or events are created. For example, the sciences not only create new concepts or ideas, as was the case for psychoanalysis (Moscovici, 1961), they also create new objects which enter into our daily lives. The invention of toothpaste was of great physical and social significance; the computer has and will continue to revolutionize our social realities; the existence of atomic bombs and the prospect of nuclear warfare has irrevocably changed reality. In more general terms, human activity is continuously transforming the environment in which we live. We build houses, roads, offices, towns; we plough fields, plant forests, build dams; we construct and destroy such that not only do the meanings change but the physical environment upon which the social environment is constructed also changes. All aspects of the organism–environment–culture system are involved in social change. Thus, there is not a single underlying absolute reality. Reality is never independent of its socio-historical context: it will be different depending on one's perspective or one's position in space–time, and it will be different depending on the environmental and social products of human activity.

To return to where we started this section, social representations can be said to constitute our social reality if, and only if, they encompass our thoughts and beliefs, our behaviours and social interaction, and the environment in which we live. It is not simply that the social representations in our minds determine our perceptions of the environment and direct our behaviour. Rather, social representations originate, evolve and exist within the dynamics of an evolving organism–environment–culture system.

THE INDIVIDUAL'S ROLE IN THE DYNAMICS OF SOCIAL REPRESENTATIONS

The organism–environment–culture system creates an understanding of individuals and of reality that is social, relational and dynamic. This provides a framework in which to re-examine the role of individuals in the maintenance and transformation of social representations. Social representations only exist in relation to people and people's relations in a physical, social and cultural environment. They constitute a social reality constructed and sustained by people's communications and interactions that are themselves interdependent with people's physical, cultural and historical contexts. This interdependence between social reality and social individuals can be re-presented, in theoretical terms, as the interdependence between social representations and identity. In order to understand the dynamics of social representations we must also consider the role of people's identities in the social construction of reality (Breakwell, 1992).

Let us consider, firstly, the role of individuals in the perpetuation of social representations. This relates to our previous discussion on the conventional and prescriptive nature of social representations (Chapter 2) which must be conceived as a dynamic and ongoing process dependent upon people's communications and interactions. As people assimilate and express the social representations of a group or community, they are simultaneously locating themselves in society, defining their identities in relation to other people and other groups (Moscovici and Hewstone, 1983). In this respect, an individual's identity can be seen as an effective representation of his or her community, created in collaboration with others (Moscovici, 1990). However, the subsequent maintenance of their identities goes hand-in-hand with sustaining the relevant social representations, in all their aspects. Social representations not only direct the formation of identities by constructing the consensual universe of common meanings in which we communicate and interact, they are also maintained through the expression of our identities. In this way, social reality is collectively maintained through the activities of social individuals within the organism–environment–culture system. Furthermore, the mutual dependence of social representations and identity underlies the process of objectification. Social constructions become 'reality apparent' when their origin and association with particular individuals or groups are forgotten, when the subjective beliefs of an individual are transformed into the objective concerns of a group; and when they are established in the language, institutions and practices of a group or society. These realities, however, are inseparable from the people or groups that have created and objectified them through the communications and interactions that maintain their social representations and their identities.

Surprisingly, within the theory of social representations, we are told little about the individual's role in *changing* social reality. The theory must deal explicitly not only with the socialization of individuals but also with the creativity of individuals; not only with the influence of society on the individual but also with the influence of the individual on society; in sum, it must deal explicitly with the dialectics of the individual with his or her culture. In some respects the theory is a social psychology of knowledge (where knowledge is used in its broadest sense) and, as such, it must explore not only the content and diffusion of social representations but also the origins of those social representations and the individual's role as a source of innovation and change. This will depend on their identities, on their location within society and the objectives of their groups in relation to their social representations. Just as conflict within or between social representations stimulates change so, too, conflict within or between people's identities directs the transformation of social representations (Mugny and Carugati, 1989; Breakwell, 1993).

Elsewhere in the writings of Moscovici there is greater emphasis on the processes of innovation and change which give clearer indications of the individual's role in the dynamics of social representations (Moscovici, 1985a, c). Since the mid-1960s there has been a growing tradition of literature and research that has examined the effect of minorities on majorities. As yet, this work has not been integrated within the literature on social representations. It would normally be considered to fall under the rubric of group psychology and can be seen as a reaction against the 'conformity bias' in North American social psychology. But it is highly germane to issues concerning the dynamics and transformation of social representations (Farr, 1987b).

The early experimental research (e.g. Faucheux and Moscovici, 1967; Moscovici *et al.*, 1969) demonstrated the influence of a minority in a group on the perceptual judgments of the majority. More recent research has examined the behavioural styles of minorities (Moscovici, 1976; Mugny, 1982; Moscovici *et al.*, 1985) and the social and cognitive processes of minorities in society (Tajfel, 1978a). Majorities tend to maintain the status quo by perpetuating systems of social representations, including the social beliefs, the social relations and the environmental structures which sustain their relative positions in society. In contrast, minorities try to change existing social representations by inducing social conflict and instability, by emphasizing different aspects of the situation and by proposing novel solutions or alternative perspectives. The minority creates a new social reality by posing new problems and constructing conflict with the social representations of the majority. A minority's success in transforming the social reality of the majority depends upon their behavioural consistency and their ability to negotiate that reality. They must be firm, coherent and personally involved consistently over time but they must not appear to be dogmatic or inflexible (Mugny, 1982). With the diffusion and transformation of social representations a minority can change significantly the social reality of a society. For example, feminism and, more recently, the Green Movement, have transformed radically our social relations, the environment in which we live and our perceptions and beliefs.

However, much of the research on minority influence has focused on the behaviours of minorities which are more or less successful in influencing the majority. Little attention has been paid to how minorities themselves establish alternative perspectives or the processes by which radical social representations emerge. Similarly, the processes by which the majority assimilates these novel social representations has not been examined in any depth. The integration of the literature on minority influence and the literature on social representations present social psychologists with a field that is ripe for development.

We must not forget that minorities and majorities are made up of people. As Farr (1984) points out, an individual is, in effect, a minority of one. In Moscovici's work in the sociology of knowledge the individual is seen as a source of innovation and change in society. In *The Age of the Crowd*, Moscovici (1985a) describes how new bodies of scientific knowledge came into existence. He explores the influence of Le Bon's mass psychology on Freud's collective psychology and their impact on the social history of Europe. The creative role of individuals in the transformation of social representations is most apparent in science. Copernicus, Darwin, Einstein and Freud were all individuals who constructed new social representations of the world and the place of humans in that world. These eventually transformed the social reality of whole societies.

While it is relatively easy to identify scientists or political leaders who have had a huge impact on social reality it is not so easy to recognize the creative activity of the person-in-the-street. However, every individual is, to some extent, active and creative in breaking with the prescriptions and conventional forces of social representations and in constructing new identities (Markova, 1987). When individuals face a problem, a contradiction or dilemma, they will develop or construct their own perspectives against the conventional ways of thinking and communicate their perspectives to other people through their conversations and behaviour. This is not to suggest that either problems or their solutions are purely individual phenomena. Problems belong to the history of a human community and their solutions are constructed in reflective thought and interaction within the organism–environment–culture sytem. The individuals' perceptions and understandings of the world are structured by the social representations extant in their society. These constrain their identities, thoughts and activities. But the organism–environment–culture system is not perfect. It presents inconsistency, contradiction, antagonism and conflict (Billig, 1982) within or between social representations and their related identities. Discrepancies within an individual's own social representations or identities will give rise to mutually antagonistic reactions. Alternatively, differences between individuals or groups may create conflict. The contradiction or dilemma will give rise to creative thought, novel actions, and the reconstruction of an object's or person's symbolic significance. Once again, through communication and interaction, a new social reality is established, transforming people's social representations and reconstructing their identities.

SUMMARY

In this chapter I have addressed some central issues in social representations theory and constructed theoretical clarifications and developments within the Hegelian paradigm. The social representations of the individual as a social being is taken to be a key component in understanding how the individual is both the product and producer of culture and vice versa. This overcomes the inherent dualism of the Cartesian paradigm and the contradictions between the individual and society. It escapes the individualistic thesis that reduces everything to individual cognition and, simultaneously, obviates the sociological antithesis that claims the autonomy of social representations. In other words, it presents a socio-psychological synthesis that recognizes the role of the individual in maintaining and transforming social representations without denying the conventional, prescriptive and collective nature of social representations.

The understanding of the individual as a social being goes hand-in-hand with a definition of reality as a dynamic and evolving social construction which exists in the interdependence between mind and the environment. This is expressed in terms of an organism–environment–

culture system, a dialectic system which embodies both mind and reality. Thus, social representations are not to be found 'in the air': they are located in the heads of individuals; in people's symbolic physical actions and interactions with the world; and in the symbolic and cultural artifacts in the environment. Furthermore, wherever there are social representations so, also, there is mind. An individual's mind cannot be divorced from the physical and cultural milieu in which it developed and in which it is immersed. Mind is not simply located in the heads of individuals. It is also expressed in our social interactions and in the cultural products of society.

Finally, I reassessed the individual's role in perpetuating and changing social representations within this framework, arguing that we must consider both people's social representations and their identities in the social construction of reality. Despite some major differences, the theoretical principles propounded here are in keeping with Moscovici's general perspective. They present a societal psychology which emphasizes the social, cultural and historical nature of human life within an evolutionary framework.

Part III

SCIENCE AND COMMON SENSE

6

THE REIFIED AND THE CONSENSUAL UNIVERSES – REALITY OR MYTH?

Moscovici is one of the foremost proponents of *social* social psychology: a social psychology that (a) goes beyond the individual to embrace culture and meaning; (b) goes beyond the status quo to examine the social construction of reality; and (c) rejects an objectivist ontology in the study of social phenomena. I am indebted to Moscovici, among others, for introducing me to this perspective in which I am, by now, thoroughly immersed. But, while acknowledging this debt, I also take issue with Moscovici's views concerning the relationship between social representations and science. Moscovici does not push his social thesis of knowledge to its logical conclusion, that *all* knowledge is socially constructed. In failing to do so, he not only creates a number of substantial theoretical and methodological problems, but also excludes social representations from the realm of science.

My purpose in this part of the book is to argue that, far from being exclusive to common sense, social representations theory can be usefully applied to the transformation and evolution of science itself. In the following chapters I shall draw upon developments both in the philosophy of science and in the sociology of knowledge to justify this claim. However, before elaborating this perspective, it is necessary to examine the characterization of, and the distinction between, the reified universe of science and the consensual universe of social representations, as they are presented within the theory. Following a review of these two universes, I shall examine briefly their historical roots and the reasons for creating such a distinction. I shall then turn to a discussion of the problems that arise from this distinction. These lie both in the interaction between science and common sense and in the conception of the reified universe itself. However, the present critique goes much further than this. I shall argue that the reified universe is itself a social representation of science that is antithetical to the Hegelian paradigm. Moscovici broke with traditional social psychology by insisting that the study of social phenomena requires a social constructionist approach. It is argued here, however, that the constructionist approach should be applied to both common sense and science.

THE REIFIED AND CONSENSUAL UNIVERSES – A USEFUL DISTINCTION

On numerous occasions (e.g. Moscovici and Hewstone, 1983; Moscovici, 1984b, 1987, 1988), Moscovici distinguishes between the reified universe of science and the consensual universe of social representations. Firstly, the reified universe is a world of discrete objects of solid, basic, unvarying entities that are indifferent to and autonomous from human collective life. It is a system of independent entities devoid of human meaning. Mind is nothing more than a reaction to reality, our thoughts being shaped by the objects of the world. In contrast, humans are an integral part of the consensual universe in which society is a 'visible, continuous creation, permeated with meaning and purpose' (Moscovici, 1984b: 20). It is a world of social objects in which reciprocal, symbolic understanding emerges through communication and interaction. Here, mind shapes reality and acts upon it.

Secondly, in the reified universe ambiguities are overcome by the precise and objective collection of data and the negation or confirmation of conclusions derived by rational and reflective reasoning. The world of science is dominated by the use of concepts and signs. Its validity lies in empirical observation of discrete entities which function under a set of laws, independent of society and individuals. The 'legalistic' truth of science continually asks for proof and replication, having more confidence in rules than in people. This results in a precise and totally unambiguous universe of facts, which are valid for all people, in all places and at all times. The reified universe is thus one of rigour, predictability and control in which values are concealed and the creation of reality is ignored. However, in the consensual universe the world is ambiguous and remains so, being both spontaneous and creative. Through the social processes of interaction and communication, conventions and mutual acceptance are established. These are first and foremost influenced by prior beliefs or theories and the interests and purposes of the group. The world of social representations is thus a conventional system of symbolic and meaningful objects and events. Its validity lies in consensus and in 'fiduciary' truth that is manifest in both content and judgment. It provides a consensual universe in which we can converse, interact, understand and explain. Thirdly, the reified universe exists in the professional and disciplined spheres in which pre-established organizations are generally accepted, along with its rules and regulations, and individuals are constrained by their prescriptive rights and duties. The consensual universe is associated with everyday life and individuals are equal and free to acquire any competence required by their circumstances.

These two universes, the reified and the consensual, the world of science and the world of common sense, form two distinct types of reality, each with its own logic, limits and attributes (Moscovici and Hewstone, 1983). They have different forms of thinking and a different knowledge of the world which require different modes of examination. In particular, they are characterized by different forms of causality and explanation. For 'scientific causality' in the reified universe the effect is explained retrospectively by attributing a cause. The direction of causality is determined by the sequence of events: that is, the cause always precedes the effect. In order to establish causality certain rules must be followed. These include non-involvement by observers, repetition of correlations and independence from authority and tradition. By keeping to these rules the data may be collected and processed impartially so that specific effects can be associated with specific causes. Scientific causality is, in this way, divested of the intentionality and responsibility associated with conversation, social interactions and other phenomena of the social world. It provides an objective causal analysis of events in the world, independent of social, cultural and historical phenomena.

In contrast, the 'social causality' of the consensual universe is dependent upon our social representations. We perceive the events and designate effects and causes in accordance with our social representations. Any explanation depends primarily on the ideas we have of reality not only by determining when an explanation is required but also the form and the content of that explanation. Effects can be explained retrospectively by attributing a cause on the basis of our education, language and world view. Alternatively, a sequence of events can be explained prospectively or teleologically by inferring the intentions or purposes of others. In either case, whether we attribute or infer causes, our explanations are dependent on the social, cultural and historical context in which they are constructed.

It is clear that, for Moscovici, the reified universe of science and the consensual universe of social representations constitute two contrasting forms of reality. The former is a world of objective truth and certainty that is indifferent to context and culture. The latter is a created world of symbolism and meaning dependent on its historical and cultural context. In the former, thought is rational and based on observation. In the latter, thought is social and rooted in interaction and communication. (This is not to suggest that social thought is irrational, only that it is different from so-called absolute rationality.) It is clear that Moscovici wishes to differentiate science from social representations and common sense: but the contrast between these two realms is presented in a cavalier fashion, with no justification for its acceptance or any considerations of alternative perspectives. This distinction continues to be employed by researchers and theorists in the field (e.g. Farr and Moscovici, 1984b; Billig, 1988; Carugati, 1990), although some critics have briefly questioned the plausibility of the reified universe (Jahoda, 1988; Palmonari, 1988). In this chapter, it will be shown that there are a multitude of reasons why Moscovici's notion of the reified universe should be rejected. But, before presenting these arguments, it is worth examining the historical antecedents of this distinction and the role it plays within social representations theory.

The obvious place to look for the historical antecedents of Moscovici's distinction between these two universes is in Durkheim's sociological writings. Durkheim (1915) postulated a dichotomy between the profane and the sacred which constituted completely different ways of knowing about the world and, in many respects, contradicted each other. The profane consisted of objective knowledge which was independent of context or culture. It characterized industrialized societies and was epitomized by scientific truth which expressed the world as it is and, as such, could falsify magical and mythological beliefs. The sacred was socially constructed knowledge which was context and culture dependent. This also applied to industrial societies but was epitomized by primitive and religious societies (Lukes, 1973). Douglas (1975) suggests that Durkheim maintained this distinction for two reasons. As in the cultural anthropology of that time, he believed that primitive and civilized societies were utterly different; they were literally worlds apart. He also believed in objective scientific truth which could not be challenged by his sociological thesis on the social determinants of knowledge.

Moscovici, in a peculiar way, both challenges and maintains these assumptions. In effect, he shifts the boundaries but does not obviate the distinction. He challenges Durkheim's thesis by proclaiming the theory of social representations to be an anthropology of modern culture, focusing on the consensual universe and its place in modern 'civilized' societies. Furthermore, as a social psychology, it denies the legitimacy of objective scientific truth in the study of social phenomena. On the other hand, by including the reified universe within the theoretical framework, Moscovici maintains both a belief in 'the world as it is' and a clear demarcation between science and common sense. Moscovici is by no means alone in proposing the existence of distinct forms of knowledge. Berger and Luckmann (1966) distinguish between non-social and social reality; Vygotsky (1962, 1978) contrasts scientific and spontaneous concepts; and Mead (1934) discusses the differences between knowledge and information. All these theorists propound a constructionist perspective for the study of social phenomena and consider science to be a special realm of interest. But Moscovici goes a step further by suggesting that science and common sense constitute two different realities.

Why should Moscovici preserve a model of science which is not only antagonistic to his own constructionist approach but is also largely discredited? The only reason I am able to suggest is that the distinction between the reified and consensual universes provided the context in which social representations were first defined. It identifies simultaneously the phenomenon of social representations as an object of study and defines the boundaries of the theory's application. The theory of social representations focuses on the transformation of the concepts and signs produced in the reified universe as they diffuse into the consensual universe. Social representations are science made common.

FROM SCIENCE TO COMMON SENSE – A TWO-WAY INTERACTION

According to Moscovici (1984b), World War II marks a watershed in the changing relationship between the reified and consensual universes. Prior to World War II, the direction of influence was from common sense to science. Knowledge which had emerged in the consensual universe was clarified and modified by the sciences in the course of research and debate. Since World War II, the direction of influence has been reversed. Science now modifies common sense. The sciences have become more refined and more removed from common sense and their products have to be assimilated into the consensual universe as they impinge upon daily life. Some of the most dramatic examples include the products of nuclear science, biophysics and biochemistry.

This characterization of the relationship between science and common sense has also identified the common-sense understanding of science as a new object of study for social psychology. More significantly, perhaps, it has encouraged a reappraisal of the nature of common-sense understanding. It is no longer static and all-encompassing, or unquestioning and irrational. It is a dynamic system of representations which is modified according to the purposes of different groups and adapted to a changing world.

However, the relationship between science and common sense is not as simple as Moscovici suggests. The dominant direction of influence has not simply been reversed. Rather, there has been a persistent two-way interaction between the reified and consensual universes. Firstly, the sciences most certainly transformed the consensual universe before World War II. Secondly, common sense is by no means impotent in the reified universe today.

The influence of science on common sense was established well before World War II. Many of the social representations which are now taken for granted originated in the sciences before the turn of the century. The most dramatic of these have involved the reconception of mankind's place in the universe. The earth is no longer thought to be flat or to lie at the centre of the universe. With the discoveries of astronomy and the Copernican revolution these conceptions were transformed; for centuries it has been known that the earth is round and but one sphere that revolves around the sun. Similarly, man was once set apart from the rest of nature, closer to God than to the natural world. But, with the Darwinian revolution, man was seen to be but a small part of the natural order. Again, with regard to Moscovici's study of psychoanalysis, Freud's major impact on common-sense understandings of consciousness occurred prior to World War II, during his own lifetime. No doubt there are many other instances in which the sciences transformed the consensual universe prior to World War II, but these will suffice.

In the opposite direction, the reified universe is by no means separated completely from common sense in contemporary society. Social representations which are prevalent in society are embedded in the content and progress of science. The following examples tend to be drawn from periods which extend into the early and middle twentieth century, largely because contemporary studies of this nature are hard to find. It is easier to identify the social representations in science when they diverge from one's own social representations. But there is no reason to believe that today's science is any more 'pure'.

In psychology, social representations of science and of the individual which were prevalent in society have had a dramatic impact on the structure and content of research and theory. These implicit social representations of the individual and society in psychology and social psychology tend to go unnoticed because they reflect the social representations prevalent in society. For example, the social representation of science as an objective empirical endeavour in search of truth has persisted in psychology, despite the fact that it had long been abandoned by physicists, not least because it has been the dominant representation of science in the consensual universe. Also, the contrast between Russian and American psychology reflects the divergent social representations in their respective cultures. In Russia, the individual is determined by his or her social activity within a social system. This is reflected in Russian psychology, in which cognition is studied within its social context (Strickland, 1984). Similarly, Luria's (1973) contribution in *A History of Psychology in Autobiography* focuses more on his laboratory than on himself. In contrast, the strong individualism of American society has led to the psychological study of the individual set apart from his or her social relations and environment. The insidious power of these social representations is highlighted by the transformation of originally socially oriented theories as they reached America from Europe (Farr, 1991a).

Social representations in the consensual universe not only enter into the construction of psychological theory; they also structure our methods of measurement and the interpretation of results. In *The Mismeasure of Man* (1981), Stephen Gould gives a brilliant exposition of the influence of social representations and social values in the measurement and definition of intelligence. Since the acceptance of Darwin's evolutionary theory the social representations which supported racial and sexual distinctiveness as part of the natural social order were maintained through scientific, as opposed to religious, argument. So-called objective measurement techniques, statistics and ranking procedures were designed and employed, not so much to generate new theories, but more to confirm *a priori* representations and prejudices.

The possibility that statistics reflect the social representations of society is explored similarly by MacKenzie (1981). In his study of British statistics and its development from 1865 to 1930, MacKenzie reveals its intimate connection with the eugenics movement and the social interests of the professional middle classes. He elucidates how Pearson and Bateson constructed different statistics and different biologies to defend opposing representations of the social order. Furthermore, it appears that not even mathematics can escape the consensual universe. Dickson (1979) argues that the formal characteristics of calculus correspond to representations of the material world and the labour process in a capitalistic society.

Thus, social representations of the consensual universe provide assumptions about individuals, society and the environment which are incorporated into science; they influence the questions asked, the evidence sought and the interpretation or conclusions which are accepted. I would suggest also that contemporary society, with its ever-increasing rate of change, frequently initiates developments in the sciences. Social movements such as feminism, anti-racism and environmentalism set new agendas for scientific investigation, both in terms of what is studied and what are acceptable solutions.

In sum, the relationship between science and common sense involves a two-way interaction. Not only do the products of science enter into the consensual universe but social representations also enter into the reified universe. This creates the difficulty of explaining how two distinct universes of reality interact and influence each other. How do the unfamiliar products of science enter into the consensual universe? The difficulties associated with Moscovici's conception of the unfamiliar will be discussed more fully in Chapter 8. For the current argument it is enough to realize that, as social representations are the constituents of our social reality, it is problematic to conceive the unfamiliar as something outside this reality.

The reverse process is also problematic. How can social representations of the consensual universe enter into the reified universe of science? Not denying the initial appeal of Moscovici's distinction between the reified and consensual universe, it creates unnecessary theoretical complexities. The transformation of social representations is not dependent upon the reified universe. As we discussed in Chapter 3, the theory applies equally well to the transformation of social representations which are not associated with the products of science. This being the case, it is detrimental to hive off the unfamiliar into a different realm of reality. The social construction of the unfamiliar must be included in a theory which purports to explain the dynamics of social representations.

REJECTING THE REIFIED UNIVERSE

It is not only the interaction between the reified universe of science and the consensual universe of common sense that is problematic. The range and diversity of scientific disciplines makes any clear demarcation between the reified and consensual universes extremely difficult. At first sight, it appears perfectly clear that all sciences fall within the reified universe. But science itself is not so clearly defined. There seems to be general agreement that physics, chemistry and biology are sciences, but what about economics, sociology, anthropology or geography? To take a case in point, it is uncertain whether or not the discipline of psychology should be considered a member of the reified universe.

When discussing the influence of science on the nature and content of common sense in modern societies, Moscovici refers to a broad selection of disciplines ranging from physics and chemistry to anthropology and sociology and even including psychoanalysis and Marxism. All these disciplines are considered to fall within the reified universe of science, producing theories and concepts which are alien to the consensual universe. It would appear then that psychology is conducted within the reified universe. However, Moscovici argues that the principles of the reified universe cannot be applied to the study of social life and human meaning. If psychologists are to study the consensual universe of social representations they must employ a different framework and different methods from those adopted in the natural sciences. He claims that it is a mistaken endeavour to use the methods and assumptions of science in the study of social phenomena. The theory of social representations and the conception of social reality which it enshrines is 'incompatible with a positivist conception of science and a behaviourist approach to reality' (Moscovici, 1982: 115). In this case, it would appear that the discipline of social psychology would not conform to the principles of the reified universe.

This contradictory position is further confused by the views propounded by Moscovici on research and theory development. Rather than starting with precise definitions and narrow hypotheses which identify specific causes and effects, the development of a theory should be based on observational and comparative studies which reflect the complexities of social and cultural phenomena. On the one hand, this appears to reject the principles of the reified universe. On the other hand, he suggests that descriptions of the content, structure and evolution of social representations constitute the proper foundations for theory development (1985b, 1988). In other words, we can first collect the facts and then build the theory (Gergen, 1989). This adheres to the principles of the reified universe. It ignores the problems associated with the theory dependence of observation and the role of the researcher and the research methods in constructing such descriptions. Thus, we are left in some confusion as to the proper location of the social psychology envisioned.

This confusion is exacerbated by Moscovici's choice of appropriate objects of study for the theory of social representations. Those sciences which he has studied have been explicitly rejected by some scientific communities. The Vienna Circle, for example, did not accept either psychoanalysis or Marxism into the realm of science. Furthermore, I suspect that the majority of scientists today would argue that they are not true sciences, as they do not conform to the generally accepted standards and criteria of science. I have already suggested that the selection of psychoanalysis and Marxism was based on practical rather than theoretical grounds. In order to conduct an empirical investigation of social representations, Moscovici had to select those theories or sciences which were widely diffused within French culture.

91

Other disciplines, such as geography and history, must also be taken into consideration. Like the natural sciences, they have produced ideas which have diffused into common sense. If the influence of these disciplines is to be excluded from the realm of social representations it would be necessary to establish the criteria that differentiate them from other disciplines which fall within the reified universe.

A further problem arises in the demarcation of the reified universe when we consider the distinction between scientists and lay people. In order to make the distinction between the reified and the consensual universes feasible it would be necessary to establish how the lay person is denied access to the reified universe: why is it that the lay person is dependent upon and embedded in a consensual universe while the scientist is not? Similarly, how does the scientist deal with two distinct realities: the reified universe at work and the consensual universe in everyday life?

Taken together, these difficulties make the continued usefulness of Moscovici's distinction between the reified and consensual universes highly questionable. Rather than providing a coherent framework for social representations theory, it engenders confusion and creates problems for the dynamic, social constructionist thesis of the theory. In conclusion, I would argue that the notion of the 'reified universe' is neither an essential nor a useful component of the theory.

Here, I shall take the line of argument further. The reified and consensual universes do not constitute two distinct realities. Rather, they embody two alternative and contradictory epistemologies. On the one hand, individuals acquire knowledge independently through the passive and objective observation of events occurring in an external reality which is itself made up of independent causes and effects. In previous chapters I have described this approach to knowledge in terms of positive empiricism and I have argued that it is founded in the assumptions of Cartesian philosophy. On the other hand, individuals actively construct knowledge through social interaction and communication in a cultural and historical context. I have previously described this alternative approach to knowledge in terms of social constructionism, founded in Hegelian philosophy. As we discussed in the previous chapter, knowledge is constructed in a dynamic and interdependent evolving system that encompasses the environment, the social individual and culture. Moscovici uses the latter epistemology to characterize the consensual universe of the lay person. However, for reasons discussed above, he characterizes the 'reified universe' of the scientist in terms of the former epistemology. This is a mistake.

Moscovici goes some way towards revolutionizing social psychology by insisting that the study of social phenomena requires a social constructionist approach. Social representations theory constitutes an exciting alternative to traditional social psychology theories which have been profoundly influenced by a positive-empiricist epistemology. It explicitly elaborates a social constructionist epistemology for the study of common-sense understanding and everyday social life. However, while championing social constructionism, Moscovici fails to apply the same epistemology to science itself. The conception of the 'reified universe' perpetuates a positive-empiricist epistemology which is contradictory and antagonistic to the theory's main thesis. Not only does this create the difficulties outlined above but it also stands at odds with recent developments in the philosophy of science and the sociology of knowledge. Science is a human endeavour and, like common sense, is better conceived in terms of dynamic social representations than in the asocial and static terms of the 'reified universe'.

7

PHILOSOPHIES OF SCIENCE AND THE SOCIOLOGY OF SCIENTIFIC KNOWLEDGE

Developments in the philosophy of science and in the sociology of scientific knowledge suggest that social representations theory *is* applicable to science. This does not refer to the theory's depiction of the reified universe. Rather, the communality between the two subdisciplines explored in this chapter and social representations theory lies in the latter's depiction of the consensual universe. It is the consensual universe of social representations that provides the more appropriate framework for the study of science.

In the first section, I shall provide a brief overview of developments in the philosophy of science from the received tradition of positive empiricism to the social constructionist perspective which focuses on the process of science and the transformation of scientific knowledge. It will be seen that it is the traditional view of science which Moscovici adopts in his description of the 'reified universe'. However, this view was challenged by significant advances in physics – namely, the general theory of relativity and quantum mechanics. This encouraged the development of alternative philosophies, most notably by Popper, Kuhn, Lakatos and Feyerabend. The present discussion focuses on the writings of T.S. Kuhn (1962, 1970) who propounds a historical, cultural and social-psychological approach to the understanding of scientific knowledge and its transformation. It will be seen that this approach bears many similarities to social representations theory. World views are comparable to social representations; paradigms are comparable to social realities; and the growth of scientific knowledge is comparable to the transformation of social representations.

In the second section, we shall turn our attention to the sociology of scientific knowledge. In general terms, this field is concerned with 'the relationship between human thought and the social context within which it arises' (Berger and Luckmann, 1984: 16 (1st edition, 1966)). It addresses the variety of knowledge in different societies and the processes by which knowledge is socially established as real. This section is not intended to provide an overview of the diverse approaches that have been adopted or to debate the various perspectives on the social construction of science. However, reading the theoretical and research papers in the sociology of knowledge convinced me that science could be legitimately characterized in terms of social representations. I also believe that the theory of social representations would provide a useful framework for the integration of at least some of this material.

PHILOSOPHIES OF SCIENCE AND THEIR IMPLICATIONS

Challenges to the received tradition

The received tradition of positive empiricism in the philosophy of science presented a normative or ideal model. According to this view, scientific knowledge starts with the accumulation of sensory facts acquired through neutral observation. The scientists' beliefs, attitudes or subjective state play no part in these observations, providing an objective basis from which universal laws and theories are derived by induction. The truth or falsity of these laws are then evaluated by deducing predictions and testing them against new observations.

This philosophy of science emerged out of seventeenth-century science and, in particular, the science of Galileo and Newton. Galileo was the first to give primacy to observation. In contrast to both religious faith and also to the Aristotelian tradition, which relied on pure reason to work out the laws of physics, Galileo conducted experiments with different weights to discover that they fall at the same rate. Similarly, the telescope enabled Galileo to observe that there were two moons which revolved around Jupiter, not the earth. These observations presented a direct threat to the established orthodoxy showing that the sun, rather than the earth, lay at the centre of the solar system. Furthermore, Newton used these observations as the basis of his laws of motion, which were explicitly stated in his *Principia Mathematica* (Newton, 1685 from Hawking, 1988). The philosopher Francis Bacon, along with his contemporaries, argued that scientific knowledge must be built on observations of the natural world and not on teleological or transcendental explanations. The facts speak for themselves.

The success of scientific theories and, in particular, Newton's theory of gravity which remained unchallenged for three centuries, gave no reason to doubt the positive-empiricist philosophy of science. However, Einstein's general theory of relativity (1915) not only constituted a revolution in theoretical physics but it also challenged the traditional view of science. Newton believed in absolute time which was separate from and independent of space. But studies by Roemer and Maxwell on the propagation of light showed that light travelled at a fixed speed. Einstein was the first to suggest that this implied that there was no such thing as absolute time. Time is not completely separate from and independent of space but is combined with it in space–time (Hawking, 1988). This revolutionized thought on how the world was conceived. In Newtonian physics objects have shape, mass and volume, which can be changed as a result of physical interference. For the general theory of relativity these properties no longer exist but become relations between objects and a reference frame. Furthermore, these relations can be changed without physical interference by changing from one reference frame to another (Feyerabend, 1975; Chalmers, 1982). This is the essence of Mead's notion of social reality discussed earlier which he derived from Einstein's notion of relativity.

This revolution had two related consequences for the philosophy of science. Firstly, if there can be two radically different theories which describe the world of planets and stars, then scientific theories and laws are not pure extensions of observation. This has come to be known as the theory dependence of observation or the underdetermination of theory. Science does not start with observations because they are preceded by theory and because observations are fallible. Observations do not speak for themselves. Secondly, observations are not independent of observers' frames of reference or perspective, that is, they are relative to their positions in space–time. For example, the motion of a ping-pong ball bouncing on a table in a moving train will be different for a person travelling on the train and someone standing on the track. For one, the ball will be bouncing straight up and down; for the other, two consecutive bounces would appear to occur several metres apart. This illustrates the fact that there is no such thing as absolute space. Einstein argued that there was no absolute time either. In other words, objects cannot be observed as independent facts because they are dependent on their relations with other objects. Moreover, the observations of the relations between objects is dependent on the observer's position in space–time. Both the dependence of observation on theory and the significance of perspective contradicts the independence of the known from the knower, a fundamental assumption of positive empiricism.

A further difficulty for the positive-empiricist philosophy of science was presented by Heisenberg's Uncertainty Principle (1926). In order to predict the future position and velocity of a particle, one has to be able to measure its present position and velocity accurately. But, with advances in quantum mechanics, this was shown to be impossible. In order to make these measurements, it is necessary to use at least one quantum of light which disturbs the particle and changes its velocity in a way that cannot be predicted. In other words, the object of observation is affected by the very means of observation in a way that cannot be predicted accurately. Quantum mechanics introduces an unavoidable element of unpredictability or randomness in science (Hawking, 1988).

The underdetermination of theory, the significance of perspective and the uncertainty principle challenged the traditional view of science. Firstly, observation alone does not provide a firm foundation for scientific knowledge. Secondly, there is no absolute reality: objects can only be understood in terms of their relations with each other and not as independent entities. This principle also encompasses the observer, such that the known cannot be independent of the knower. Thirdly, with the loss of certainty, the doctrine of scientific determinism could not be maintained as an ideal goal for science. Science itself is relative. The model of psychology as a branch of natural science was based on a nineteenth-century view of physics – if experimental psychologists took Einstein seriously then *all* of psychology would be a social science since humans are both the agent and object of investigation.

The growth of scientific knowledge

A positive-empiricist philosophy clearly did not correspond to the realities of science. By focusing on the context of justification for universal laws and the rationality of science it failed to realize how scientific knowledge changes. Furthermore, by insisting on the independence of observation, it failed to reflect the very principles of science that it set out to explain. The demise of a positive-empiricist philosophy of science culminated in the development of alternative philosophies which emphasized the growth and transformation of scientific knowledge and took into account background knowledge and historical context.

One of the vanguard philosophers in this movement was Karl Popper. According to Popper (1968, 1969), science progressed through a series of conjectures and refutations. The relative merits of competing theories are assessed not in terms of observational proof but, rather, in terms of their falsifiability and their novel predictions. This approach again provided a normative model of science, the influence of which is still apparent in psychology. But, for the same reasons that scientists cannot prove a theory, they cannot falsify it either. As a philosophy of science it failed to overcome the problems associated with the dependence of observation on theory. Science was still meant to be an objective and rational endeavour, 'a process without a subject', independent of the scientists who made it. Furthermore, although Popper frequently refers to the history of science, his philosophy fails to give an accurate account of the historical transformation of scientific knowledge (Kuhn, 1962, 1970; Chalmers, 1982).

I have mentioned Popper briefly because it would be improper not to do so. But of greater significance in the current context is the work of Thomas Kuhn. Kuhn started his academic career as a physicist but soon turned his attention to the history of science. In so doing, he was confronted by material which radically undermined his basic conceptions about the nature of science. In his book entitled *The Structure of Scientific Revolutions* (1962), Kuhn develops a philosophy of science which is more in keeping with historical evidence.

Kuhn describes the growth of science in terms of successive periods: pre-science leading to normal science, then crisis and revolution, then a new normal science, etc. Pre-science is characterized by numerous theories and total disagreement over fundamental theoretical assumptions as well as the kind of observational phenomena that are relevant. This is replaced by normal science, when a single paradigm structures and directs the activities of a scientific community. As the number and significance of the anomalies relating to this paradigm increase, normal science gives way to a state of crisis. This is resolved with the emergence of an alternative paradigm which attracts the allegiances of an increasing number of scientists and constitutes a scientific revolution. Once accepted, this alternative paradigm structures and directs a new period of normal science. The main features of this work have important implications for our understanding of science.

Firstly, theories are represented as part of a complex structure as opposed to a collection of refutable statements. Secondly, Kuhn adopts a historical and evolutionary approach, describing the progress of science in terms of successive periods. Thirdly, he emphasizes the role of sociological and psychological factors. Together, these portray science as a human endeavour in which people identify and solve problems, construct meanings and change the world.

Paradigms and social representations

Below, I shall describe Kuhn's ideas about the nature and role of a paradigm in normal science. It will be seen that paradigms share many of the features of social representations. Firstly, the tenacity of a paradigm in normal science portrays the prescriptive and conventional characteristics of a social representation. Both constitute a framework or environment of thought which structures a person's observations and guides his or her behaviour. In this case, 'the thinking society' (Moscovici, 1984b) is the community of research scientists rather than that of lay folk. Secondly, initiation of students into the scientific community involves the active learning and application of a paradigm's concepts, laws and theories just as an individual's socialization into society depends upon social interaction and communication. Thirdly, scientific knowledge is transformed through the identification of anomalies and the process of discovery, just as social representations are transformed by 'the unfamiliar' becoming familiar and through innovation. Furthermore, a paradigm is expressed not only in the activities of scientists but also in their structuring of the research environment, and in their textbooks and journals. These correspond to the media that convey social representations. Indeed, Moscovici frequently employs the terms 'paradigm' and 'theory' in his descriptions of social representations, despite his categorical denial of their existence in the 'reified universe'.

Although the nature of a paradigm belies precise definition, its typical components can be described in general terms. These include general metaphysical assumptions, explicit theories and laws which are applied to a variety of situations using standard instrumental techniques. It also contains general methodological prescriptions which guide analysis of the relationship between the paradigm and nature. Within the scientific community, the paradigm provides a framework for the identification of legitimate problems, the employment of appropriate research methods and the interpretation of observable phenomena. Paradigms constitute a consensual view of the world which coordinate and direct the theoretical and experimental activities of the scientists involved in its elaboration. The various components of a paradigm are not always explicitly articulated, but are expressed in the research activities of scientists. Individual scientists thus acquire knowledge of a paradigm by solving standard problems, performing standard experiments and eventually doing research in close association with a skilled practitioner within a given paradigm. Students literally have to learn where to look and what to see through their social interactions with skilled practitioners and with the environment.

Kuhn portrays normal science as a problem-solving activity. Pre-supposition of the paradigm gives scientists the confidence to explore esoteric problems on the assumption that it is capable of sustaining their solution. This having being said, the paradigm will remain sufficiently imprecise and open-ended, leaving room for further research. Moreover, it is able to withstand various unsolved problems and anomalies which do not 'fit'. Before going on to discuss Kuhn's ideas about crises and revolutions it is worth considering anomalies in a little more detail.

An anomaly arises with the awareness or recognition that nature somehow violates the paradigm-induced expectations. Anomalies are thus similar to what Moscovici has called the unfamiliar. Although Kuhn stresses the role of nature while Moscovici stresses the role of sciences in the production of unfamiliar concepts, these two aspects of anomalies are not distinct. Just as Moscovici stresses the interdependence of image and concept, Kuhn emphasizes the interdependence of fact and theory. With reference to our earlier discussions this accommodates the theory-dependent nature of observation. Similarly, just as Moscovici highlights the transformation of scientific knowledge as it enters into the realms of the consensual universe of lay folk, Kuhn stresses the adjustment of the paradigm required to assimilate anomalies. Discovery involves more than the simple addition of a new fact to the conceptual system; it demands the restructuring of conceptual categories such that nature is seen in a different way. There is thus no clear distinction between discovery and invention. Furthermore, discovery and invention cannot be attributed to an individual at a given moment. Rather, it is a complex process which is structured by and restructures the paradigm. 'Anomalies appear only against the background provided by the paradigm' (Kuhn, 1970: 65) and discovery/invention involves both experimentation (interaction with the environment) and assimilation (thinking and restructuring) over time. It entails 'the previous awareness of anomaly, the gradual and simultaneous emergence of both observational and conceptual recognition, and the consequent change of paradigm categories and procedures often accom-panied by resistance' (Kuhn, 1970: 62).

Although a paradigm can withstand a number of anomalies they will eventually lead to crisis and revolution. This will depend on the number of anomalies, their persistence, their association with social needs and their relation to fundamental aspects of the paradigm. The accumulative force of anomalies gives rise to a state of crisis in which there is a loss of confidence in the paradigm and 'pronounced professional insecurity'. As this persists, scientists turn to argument and debate over the fundamental theoretical assumptions and relevant observational phenomena, giving rise to philosophical and metaphysical dispute. The seriousness of a crisis deepens when a rival paradigm emerges. This lack of consensus encourages the articulation of the old paradigm: what was once implicit is made explicit in the face of alternative viewpoints. It is at this juncture that science exhibits extraordinary dynamics and undergoes revolution. The new paradigm, according to Kuhn, 'emerges all at once, sometimes in the middle of the night, in the mind of a man deeply immersed in crisis'. Adherents of the new paradigm undergo a 'religious conversion' or 'gestalt switch' as they change their allegiances from the old to the new paradigm.

This dramatic and discontinuous character of revolution will be challenged in the following chapter but much can be learned about the similarities between science and social representations by looking at the nature of competing paradigms. Kuhn depicts revolutions as changes in world view. After a revolution, scientists are living in different worlds. This does not imply that scientists are transported to a different planet, but that the world is seen as made up of different things. They may look in the same place with the same instruments but they will observe different phenomena. Observations are not fixed by the nature of the environment and perceptual apparatus. They are not given in immediate experience or communicated in a neutral observation language. What a person sees depends not only on what he or she looks at, but also on what he or she looks for. This will depend on his or her paradigm or frame of reference, which is acquired through social interaction and communication. Furthermore, the paradigm legitimizes different problems, makes new kinds of data relevant and suggests different modes of investigation.

Kuhn elaborates on his conception of paradigms as world views by drawing on evidence both from psychology and from the history of science. His examples focus on change in meaning which relate to both perception and conception. It involves both change in relations within the paradigm and the paradigm's relation to the environment. In other words, changing the meaning of one item has repercussions for the meanings of related terms and experience. Although the same terms may be used by competing paradigms their meanings will not be the same. For example, by postulating that the sun was not a planet but a star, the Copernican revolution changed the meaning of 'planet', which had repercussions for the distinction between various celestial bodies. It transformed the conceptual system such that our experience of the solar system was also transformed.

It can be seen that paradigms constitute the social reality for a community of scientists just as social representations constitute the social reality for the lay person. They are a frame of reference in which meaning is defined and in which problems are identified or legitimized and they also constitute the world of things. As such, competing paradigms offer alternative social realities in which scientists do science. This is frequently referred to as the incommensurability of competing paradigms which has important implications for our understanding of science. Firstly, it is not possible to choose between paradigms on the basis of neutral observations. Observation is always structured by and imbued with meaning from the perspective of a given paradigm. Secondly, there are no purely logical grounds on which to make a rational choice between paradigms. Different paradigms embrace different metaphysical assumptions, standards of evaluation, etc. Supporters of one paradigm will not accept the premises of the alternative paradigm and hence do not have to accept its conclusions. Seen in this light, the transformation of science cannot be described within the terms of the 'reified universe' or a positive–empiricist philosophy of science.

Unlike previous philosophies of science, Kuhn's account of 'paradigm shifts' emphasize the importance of psychological and sociological factors in the growth of science. This applies not only to the emergence of new paradigms but also to the processes by which revolutions are resolved and a new normal science instantiated. According to Kuhn, a new paradigm emerges first in the minds of one, or at most, a few individuals. These will be scientists whose attention is focused on crisis-provoking problems and who usually are either so young or so new to the field that they are less socialized and, hence, less committed to the old paradigm. But a scientific revolution requires the abandonment of one paradigm and the adoption of a new one, not just by a minority of scientists, but by the relevant scientific community as a whole. This is achieved through the social processes of argument, debate and persuasion.

Those arguments that appear to be most persuasive depend on the comparative problem-solving ability of the alternative paradigm. This is particularly true if the new paradigm can resolve those anomalies that instigated the crisis. However, these are not the only considerations. It is rarely the case that an emerging paradigm immediately improves on its predecessor. Indeed, those scientists committed to the old paradigm will produce convincing counter-arguments resisting the change to an alternative world view. Furthermore, the incommensurability of paradigms hampers communication and debate between opposing factions. Other considerations which are equally, if not more, influential are less obvious. Scientists may be persuaded by the aesthetic appeal of the new paradigm, being 'simpler' or of 'greater beauty'. The new paradigm may be more applicable to a pressing social need. Scientists may also come to believe that it offers greater potential for future research.

Kuhn's ideas about the emergence of a crisis and the revolution of a science further emphasize the similarity between paradigm and social representations. Paradigm shifts and the transformation of social representations display many of the same characteristics. Both denote 'world views' or 'frames of reference', constituting a social reality for the relevant community; both depend upon psychological and sociological factors which cannot be described in terms of the 'reified universe'; and both are transformed through the social processes of interaction and communication. It may well be that the criteria, values and content of arguments will vary across different sciences and in different spheres of life. But, just as the transformation of social representations is dependent on socio-psychological factors, so, too, is the revolution of scientific knowledge. Many of the major 'scientific revolutions' are discoveries of a social-psychological nature. That 'man' as a species was not created separately from other species (Darwin); that the earth is no longer the centre of the universe (Copernicus); that what is in consciousness is finite in relation to the unconscious (Freud); that space and time are not independent dimensions (Einstein). Furthermore, they all involve a change in the relationship between the knower and the known. The transformation of scientific knowledge is not dependent upon logic or pure observation any more than it is in common sense. Kuhn, like Moscovici, emphasizes the interdependence of individuals, their community and the environment in which they work or live.

THE SOCIOLOGY OF SCIENTIFIC KNOWLEDGE – SUPPORTING EVIDENCE

One of the most important books in the sociology of knowledge has been *The Social Construction of Reality* by Berger and Luckmann (1966). This treatise is concerned explicitly with the social construction of reality in everyday life and shares many features with the general approach expounded by Moscovici in his theory of social representations. Farr (1987b) even suggests that several studies within the field of social representations are themselves empirical contributions to the literature on the sociology of knowledge. For example, in *La Psychanalyse* (1961), Moscovici traces the diffusion and transformation of an existing body of scientific psychology into French culture. Similarly, in *The Age of the Crowd* (1985a) he examines the use of Le Bon's mass psychology by political leaders such as Hitler and Stalin. In so far as these leaders acted on the basis of Le Bon's ideas, his mass psychology was a science which 'created history', transforming the nature of the world in which we live. Furthermore, Moscovici has not been interested exclusively in the diffusion and transformation of scientific psychology as it becomes part of common-sense understanding. He has also examined the origins and impact of theories within science. For example, in *The Age of the Crowd*, Moscovici analyses Le Bon's influence on the development of Freud's second, more social, psychology. Similarly, in the preface to *La Psychanalyse*, Lagache notes that Moscovici was interested in the origins and diffusion of psychoanalysis within the community of psychoanalysts. It was only due to their lack of cooperation that this aspect of the problem was not studied. Some studies, in particular the work of Restivo (1984) and Traweek (1984), have actually employed the concept of representations in studying the dialectic relationships between scientific knowledge and the social environment. Farr (1984) has also argued that the proper place to look for social representations in laboratory studies is at the level of the scientific community. For example, behaviourism, as a social representation, affects the layout of psychology laboratories and structures the social interactions within the research process.

Moscovici himself does not attempt to integrate this work on science with the theory of social representations. This is possibly due to the fact that he wishes to maintain the distinction between the reified and consensual universes. For him, studies of science examine the reified universe whereas studies of common-sense understanding of science fall within the consensual universe. However, studies in the sociology of knowledge discussed below make it clear that these are part of the same enterprise. Rather than entering into the debate on the proper research programme for the sociology of knowledge or the various approaches which have been used, I shall focus on those studies which illuminate the social construction of scientific knowledge. These include studies on the influence of institutions and society more generally; the socialization of novices into the scientific community; and the processes by which scientific knowledge is transformed and diffused within the community.

Many of these studies were inspired by the writings of Kuhn as well as historians of science. A central assumption is that social truths cannot be contrasted with objective rational truth; that culture is not separate from nature; and that science is not, in some way, asocial or ahistorical. The sociology of scientific knowledge, for most of its proponents, is not simply trying to demonstrate the social influences on objective knowledge but, rather, that scientific knowledge is a social construction. By rejecting the traditional distinction between social and scientific knowledge the role of convention, of the social processes of negotiation and argumentation and of the influence of society are shown to be inherent aspects of science. The world of science is also a world of meaning and social significance, dependent on the collaboration of scientists and some degree of consensus with regard to theory, subject-matter, problem formulation, methods of investigation and interpretation. Science is fundamentally a social activity, situated in a cultural and historical context. The roles of tradition and innovation are as important in the transformation of knowledge within the sciences as they are in the transformation of common-sense understandings.

Perhaps the first and most traditional approach in the sociology of scientific knowledge is concerned with the influence of society in general and social institutions in particular upon the development of scientific ideas. For example, the work of MacKenzie (1981) and Restivo (1984) discussed in Chapter 5 demonstrate the influence of social goals on the creation and acceptance of scientific theories.

> social interests affect (scientific knowledge) at the organisational level, as well as at the *most basic level of the development and evaluation of theories and techniques*. Scientific knowledge is *constitutively social* because science is goal-oriented and because the goals of science are *socially sustained*.
>
> (Restivo, 1984: 73, emphases in original)

Others have focused on the institutional and organizational influences on the development of scientific knowledge. For example, Ben-David and Collins (1966) investigated the social factors in the origins of psychology as a new scientific discipline. The fundamental ideas for experimental psychology had been available in Germany and elsewhere for some time. However, its development did not occur until there was both an intellectual interest *and* the potential for gaining intellectual identity. As a physiologist, Wundt was unable to achieve recognition and, accepting the philosophy chair in Leipzig, integrated the methods of physiology with the problems of philosophy.

The sociology of knowledge has not restricted its interest to the influence of society on science. More recently, there has been an increasing focus on the social processes by which scientific knowledge is constructed (e.g. Latour and Woolgar, 1979; Barnes and Edge, 1982; Knorr-Cetina and Mulkay, 1983). Much of this work adopts a similar approach to that adopted in the theory of social representations. Scientific knowledge is portrayed as systems of representations which are products of, sustained by and embody social practices. These practices 'integrate psychological and biological states and processes, social relations and activities, and material things and processes' (Restivo, 1984: 86). In other words, scientific knowledge is a product of the organism–culture–environment system. For example, Traweek (1984) indicates how physicists' conceptions of time and space are interdependent with their social realities, from the mechanical functioning of the detectors, to the social relations and beliefs in the scientific community and on to the wider cultural and physical environment.

The organism–culture–environment system is also evident in discussions of socialization into the scientific community. This is emphasized by Barnes (1983) in his writings on the conventional character of scientific knowledge. Socialization involves interacting with competent members of the community and the environment, in both formal and informal settings. Meanings and conceptual networks are established through communication with authoritative teachers in conjunction with the indications of experience in the physical environment. For example, a learner classifies an object or event as C, whereas the teacher classifies it as C2, a concept not yet available to the learner. Through instances of object or event A and the corresponding indications of the teacher, the learner comes to distinguish between C and C2. In this way, the learner is introduced to the conventions of the community and is taught how to make original contributions within the limits of its cognitive, technical and social norms (representations).

Furthermore, socialization is a dynamic and an ongoing process which continues to be effective throughout a scientist's career. This is evident from studies that have approached science as a social system. These focus on the social relations and social norms which structure scientific activity (Hagstrom, 1965; Mulkay, 1972). Scientific behaviour is seen in terms of gifts or social exchange in return for recognition. Scientists present papers at conferences, send them to colleagues, publish articles in journals and write books as a means of communication and diffusion of their work. This is done in order to receive recognition from the relevant scientific bodies through citations, invitations to lecture, invitations to edit journals, honorary degrees, society membership, prizes and eponymy (Merton, 1957). Recognition is allocated in accordance with the evaluated quality of the research which, in turn, is dependent upon the representations shared by the community. This encourages the selection of problems, methods and solutions which conform to the status quo.

The transformation of scientific knowledge similarly depends upon social processes in the scientific community. Innovation, negotiation and communication depend upon the social relations among scientists in conjunction with their interactions in the environment. Hagstrom (1965) and Mulkay (1972) elaborate Kuhn's framework by emphasizing the role of social exchange and recognition in both maintaining social control (conventional and prescriptive characteristics) and encouraging innovations. In particular, Mulkay argues that intellectual migration and modification of existing techniques and theories to different problem areas have brought about some of the most radical innovations in science. For example, the migration of Delbruck and others from physics, which lacked opportunities for development, into biology, led to the emergence of molecular biology, a successful and innovative field, that encountered little opposition (Mullins, 1972).

Mulkay's account of the social process of innovation focuses on social control and social relations within and between scientific networks. In so doing, he underplays the role of the environmental context and the actual research process in the social construction of innovations and the transformation of scientific knowledge. Scientific research is an important aspect of innovation and is in many ways similar to socialization. Within the research process scientists indicate to others the problem and proposed solution, adjusting their representations to accommodate new relations with objects or events in the environment. However, in the frontiers of research the conventions have not been pre-established. Scientific observations, the conduct of research and theoretical interpretation must be negotiated through the rhetorical processes of argument and persuasion.

Consensus, at whatever level, is a social accomplishment (Knorr-Cetina and Mulkay, 1983). For example, Collins (1982) identifies the disagreement and negotiations involved in the replication of experiments on gravity waves. The establishment of facts is only achieved through the linguistic, conceptual and social interactions of the scientists concerned. Similarly, Kuhn (1982) argues that measurement is not as precise as the textbooks suggest, but is dependent upon 'reasonable agreement' as to what is and is not acceptable. The rhetoric of science is perhaps more apparent at the level of theoretical and meta-theoretical debate. Martin (1979) shows how the technical assumptions, selective use of evidence, selective use of results, and the style of reference are associated with the scientists' general perspective and presuppositions. These relate both to the scientific community itself and to the concerns of the wider society as a whole.

Negotiation takes place through the face-to-face interactions of scientists working together on research projects, at informal meetings and at lectures and conferences. Negotiation also occurs through the medium of written communications, be they letters, journal articles or books. Such forms of communication are often described in terms of the diffusion of scientific knowledge. However 'diffusion' is not a simple process of contagion, whereby information is shared. Rather, it is part of the social construction process, in which meanings are negotiated and consensus continually challenged, established and reconfirmed (Knorr-Cetina and Mulkay, 1983). In order to understand the growth of scientific knowledge some sociologists have focused on the use of scientific literature and the patterns of communication. An analysis of citations reveals the 'life' of papers and gives some indication of their impact on the community. In particular, innovations which have been accepted by the community can be identified and their history of diffusion analysed. Also, citation patterns reveal the structure of scientific communities, 'problem networks' (Mulkay, 1972) or 'invisible colleges' (Crane, 1972), and the extent of cross-fertilization between research groups, or between different fields. Crane (1972) adopted this approach in her study of 'invisible colleges' and found that the pattern of diffusion reflected the structure of the scientific community, the perspectives adopted by 'problem networks' and the social processes involved in the growth of scientific knowledge. Although, in itself, this method is extremely restricted, it provides a useful addition to the above-mentioned qualitative studies which focus on the content of scientific knowledge and the social processes by which it is transformed.

These studies, taken together, illuminate the social construction of scientific knowledge. The influence of society, the processes of social-ization, the role of convention, the social processes of exchange and negotiations are inherent aspects of science. The world of science is a dynamic world of meanings and social interactions, of consensus and disagreements, of tradition and innovation. In short, science is essentially cultural. It does not consist of a reified universe, divorced from history, culture and social beliefs. Science is carried out by scientists who are social beings interacting in, learning and creating a social world.

There is only one sense in which science can be considered to be reified and this is as the end product of social construction. Berger and Luckmann (1984) describe the reification of social reality as

> the apprehension of the products of human activity, *as if* they were something other than human products – such as facts of nature, results of cosmic laws, or manifestations of divine will. Reification implies that man is capable of forgetting his own authorship of the

human world and, further, that the dialectic between man, the producer, and his products, is lost to consciousness.

(Berger and Luckmann, 1984: 106, emphasis in original)

Moscovici has ironically reified this process of reification to create a universe. But this ignores the social construction of reality in science. Scientific facts are constructed through scientists' social activities. Even when scientists apprehend the world in reified terms they continue to produce it (Latour and Woolgar, 1979). Reification is but the final stage in the social construction of reality and does not differentiate science from society. The similarities between science and other cultural enterprises far outweigh their differences.

CONCLUSION

Both the philosophy of science and the sociology of knowledge suggest that science should be conceived as a human and social endeavour in which knowledge is socially constructed. The growth of scientific knowledge is not characterized by the accumulation of facts through objective observation, the induction of universal laws and the deduction of testable hypotheses. In order to understand the transformation of paradigms, theories and research, it is necessary to adopt a historical and evolutionary approach which takes into account the sociological and psychological factors in the production of scientific knowledge. The work involved in science is carried out by people working in a scientific community which itself is located in a cultural and historical context. The products of science cannot be divorced from the producers; nor can people, in their capacity as scientists, be divorced from the products of the scientific community. Scientists are social individuals who actively engage in the perpetuation and transformation of a social reality which is at once prescriptive and dynamic. The world of the scientist is imbued with meanings which are learned, sustained and changed through social interaction and communications. Scientific knowledge is not distinguishable from scientists' beliefs, which themselves are an expression of the ongoing interdependence between scientists, their cultural context and their environment.

The theory of social representations provides a social psychology of knowledge which is manifestly appropriate for the study of scientific knowledge. Social representations constitute a reality which is constructed through the social activities of individuals interacting and communicating within a historical and cultural context. This reality is essentially social and dynamic, both in its conventional and prescriptive character and in the origins and diffusion of innovations. Furthermore, social representations are not simply consensual beliefs about the world, rather they embrace individuals' beliefs, people's actions and interactions with the world, and the cultural products of those interactions.

8

TOWARDS A SOCIAL
PSYCHOLOGY OF SCIENCE

Moscovici developed social representations theory in order to describe and explain the transformation of common-sense knowledge as the innovations and discoveries of science diffuse within society. In so doing, he made a sharp distinction between the reified universe of science and the consensual universe of social representations. However, in the preceding chapters we have seen that this distinction is, at least, problematic and, at worst, totally unfounded. It creates considerable difficulties both in defining the relationship and interaction between the two universes and in demarcating the boundaries of the reified universe. Moreover, the theory as a whole embraces two antagonistic and contradictory epistemologies: the positive empiricism of the reified universe is antithetical to the social constructionism of the consensual universe. By examining developments in the philosophy of science we have seen that Moscovici's description of the reified universe reflects a 'traditional view' of science. This view was challenged by significant advances in physics in the early part of this century which gave rise to alternative philosophies. In particular, Kuhn (1962, 1970, 1974) propounded a historical, cultural and social psychological approach to the transformation of scientific knowledge. This bears many similarities to the consensual universe within social representations theory. Furthermore, research in the sociology of knowledge identifies parallels between social representations and science. The influence of institutions, the processes of socialization and the processes of transformation and diffusion within the sciences bear witness to the social construction of scientific knowledge. This led us to the conclusion that social representations theory constitutes a social psychology of knowledge that is not only applicable to the transformation of common sense but also to science itself.

Many of the theoretical arguments, clarifications and elaborations that I have presented so far have been directed, at least in part, by the conflicts and ambiguities that are created by applying the theory to science. In order to account for the dynamics of scientific knowledge it was necessary to consider and understand the relationship between knowledge and the environment (i.e. the object of study); between the individual (i.e. the scientist) and his or her community; and between common sense and science. Moreover, in conducting the research that is reported in Part IV it became apparent that further theoretical developments were required. In order to understand the dynamics of social representations, be they within science or common sense, it is essential to restructure the theory and elaborate the principles of transformation. In particular, the familiarization of the unfamiliar, although attractive in its simplicity, is totally inadequate as a conception of the transformation of social representations. If social representations theory is to provide an adequate framework within which to understand the dynamics and evolution of scientific knowledge, or, for that matter, common sense, then it will be necessary to describe not only anchoring and objectification but also the social construction of the unfamiliar; not only assimilation but also the accommodation of elements in a social representation; and not only a single social representation but, rather, systems of social representations.

In the first section of this chapter I shall focus on the processes of transformation, using examples drawn from common sense to illustrate my arguments. In the second section I shall focus my attention on the transformation of science, drawing on recent developments in the philosophy of science that emphasize the dynamic and cultural nature of scientific knowledge. In the final section I shall vivify my perspective with reference to the social construction and diffusion of Darwin's theory of evolution. In sum, by applying social representations theory to science we can simultaneously develop social representations theory and move towards a social psychology of science.

PROCESSES OF TRANSFORMATION

The social construction of the unfamiliar

Moscovici describes two social processes of transformation: anchoring and objectification. These processes transform the unfamiliar into the familiar by making the meaningless meaningful and by making the abstract real respectively. In each case the unfamiliar object, event or idea threatens the stability of our social representations, challenging our conventions, blurring distinctions and disrupting the continuity of social interaction. In so doing it initiates the social activities involved in anchoring and objectification.

Given that the unfamiliar constitutes a vital component of the theory it is surprising that it has not, as yet, received the attention it deserves. In part this is due to Moscovici's definition of the unfamiliar: 'the unfamiliar is there without being there; perceived without being perceived' (Moscovici, 1987: 526). Such a definition mystifies, rather than clarifies, the notion of the unfamiliar. It is also due to the original location of the unfamiliar in the reified universe. As we have already seen, Moscovici states that scientists working in a universe of objective observation and pure facts produce unfamiliar concepts and objects which lay people must then assimilate into their consensual universe of social representations. Regardless of the arguments presented in the previous chapters against the notion of the reified universe, this separation of the unfamiliar and familiar is unwarranted. The unfamiliar and the familiar are not worlds apart.

Firstly, the unfamiliar cannot be totally unfamiliar. If social representations constitute our social reality and if all thought and perception acquire an order in our social representations, then the unfamiliar cannot be set apart as something outside our reality. Our very awareness of something unfamiliar means that it must be associated with our social representations in some way. This can be illustrated with reference to the diffusion of science into common sense. Common-sense knowledge does not act as a sponge that soaks up scientific innovations indiscriminately. Rather, we select those scientific ideas and objects which, in one way or another, are useful to us in everyday life. That is, they have some connection with what we already know or do, or they impinge on our lives in such a way that we are forced to take notice. This can be seen in Moscovici's own study of psychoanalysis (1961), its diffusion being dependent both on its association with Catholicism and its ability to describe socially significant behaviour that was unusual yet familiar.

Secondly, the unfamiliar arises within the consensual universe of social representations. What was once familiar becomes unfamiliar. Indeed, this is the role that Moscovici has given science in modern society. But the unfamiliar arises within common sense and within science, as well as through the diffusion of science. A lay person as well as a scientist may be a discoverer or innovator, may find a new solution to an old problem, or may be confronted with a peculiar problem which requires resolution. For example, changing the social representation of women in sport has largely involved breaking the boundaries between femininity and masculinity. Change is brought about by the introduction of novel connections between what we already know within the consensual universe rather than something totally unknown from a different reality.

The familiar at once defines what is unfamiliar and is changed by it. Simultaneously, the unfamiliar emerges out of the familiar and is familiarized by it. In my opinion, the unfamiliar needs to be reconceptualized. In order to understand the dynamics of social representations, the unfamiliar cannot be treated as a given, as something that requires no further explanation. Rather, the theory must embrace the unfamiliar within its historical and evolutionary framework such that it incorporates the social construction of the unfamiliar as well as the perpetuation of the familiar. It must encompass both tradition and innovation in all their aspects, both within common sense and within science.

Assimilation and accommodation

I have argued that social representations theory must deal with the social construction of the unfamiliar as well as the familiarization of the unfamiliar. Here, I shall argue that it must also deal with the accommodation of the familiar. Only then are we in a position to describe the dynamics and evolution of social representations.

By focusing on how the unfamiliar becomes familiar the processes of anchoring and objectification are restricted to the assimilation of unfamiliar objects, events or ideas into our social representations. Neither process describes the accommodation of familiar social representations to the unfamiliar. As a consequence, priority is given to the prescriptive and conventional character of social representations, undermining the significance of their dynamic nature. The balance of past and present must be readdressed by specifying the processes of accommodation as well as those of assimilation. These two aspects of transformation are simultaneous and inseparable (Flavell, 1963). Every assimilation of an object to a social representation simultaneously involves an accommodation of the social representation to the object. Conversely, every accommodation of a social representation involves an assimilatory modification of the object to the social representation. This may occur at any point in the organism–environment–culture system. For example, if the physical abilities of a person change, the environment must be modified accordingly and people's beliefs and interactions adjusted to the new circumstances. Alternatively, new ideas or values may instigate changes in people's interactions and their impact on the environment.

It should always be remembered that transformation in social representations involve not simply changes in beliefs but rather changes in social reality involving people's interactions and communications and their cultural environment. It is equally important to bear in mind that we are talking not about one person's beliefs but about the social realities of different groups or communities. The unfamiliar is both created and made familiar through the processes of assimilation and accommodation throughout the system. What is familiar in one social representation will be unfamiliar in the context of another. Similarly, what is familiar to one person or group will be unfamiliar to another. The assimilation of a new object, either from another social representation or from another group's social representations will, itself, create unfamiliar associations and accommodations. This, in turn, will be assimilated by people or groups, changing the significance of the object, people's interaction with that object and people's relations with each other.

Social representations systems

Once it is accepted that the transformation of social representations involves not only the assimilation of the unfamiliar into the familiar, but also the social construction of the unfamiliar and the accommodation of the familiar then it becomes necessary to consider these ongoing dynamics within a *system* of social representations. All too often, empirical research on social representations has focused on a single target, such as health, the body or the city. This isolates a particular social representation from others with which it is related (Breakwell, 1993). But it is the relations or interconnections between social representations which lies at the heart of their transformation. The organism–environment–culture system encompasses numerous social representations which overlap to a greater or lesser extent, and the meaning or social significance of any object, event or idea is dependent on the network of relationships within and between these social representations. Changing the relations or meaning of any one element will create novel associations and conflicts which may have repercussions for the whole system. New associations or links made between two or more elements, either within or between social representations, may eventually lead to the restructuring of a whole network of relations within the social representations system, thus transforming social reality.

The nature of the system and its evolutionary transformation can be clarified with an example. In recent years, our social representation of the environment has changed considerably as the impact of human beings on the world ecosystem has been increasingly recognized. This has restructured diverse systems of social representations in all their aspects, transforming relations within the organism–environment–culture system. It has affected our beliefs, our values, our social interactions and our relationship with the environment itself. This has involved the creation of unfamiliar associations and conflicts between particular elements of relevant social representations; the accommodation of established social representations; and changes in the relations among groups and nations.

For example, trees constitute one element in the social representation of the countryside but they have also become an element in the world ecosystem and a commodity in the form of timber or paper. The destruction of the Amazon rain forest emphasizes their association. Trees are involved in conflicting social representations which must somehow be reconciled. They are no longer simply part of the countryside but are part of a natural balance upon which the very air that we breathe is dependent. This enters our daily lives, not only through media coverage and communication but also in the growing concern for unnecessary waste and for the use of recycled paper. Similarly, the globe no longer consists of discrete countries and oceans with particular climates, but is an ecosystem in which all the parts are interdependent.

The transformation of these social representations are dependent upon earlier transformations associated with air and river pollution from industrial waste. These forms of environmental hazards were both more local and visible. As such, they inspired the creation of a relational representation of the environment; that is, the deterioration of the environment was related to industrial waste. This representation could then be extended to less tangible issues including acid rain, nuclear waste and the ozone layer. These new social representations are expressed and transformed in our daily activities, from the boardroom to the petrol station. Moreover, 'green' is no longer just the colour of grass. It is a political, social and environmental revolution.

In abstract terms, as an element from one social representation is assimilated into another social representation, it will change the network of relations (accommodation) and hence transform the meaning of all the elements involved. This creates a route or form in which similar yet novel associations and conflicts are created. Eventually they transform the social representation as a whole, such that previous meanings are forgotten. Social representations systems are conceived here in terms of an evolutionary process within an environmental and cultural context. Assimilation and accommodation within social representations systems are inextricably interwoven with transformations in the organism–environment–culture system.

Once this is realized the prescriptive and conventional nature of social representations goes hand-in-hand with the transforming and evolutionary nature. Tradition and innovation are complementary aspects in the dynamics of social representations, embracing not only their perpetuation but also their generation in the organism–environment–culture system.

THE TRANSFORMATION OF SCIENCE: A SOCIAL CONSTRUCTIONIST PERSPECTIVE

In the previous chapter I identified fundamental similarities between social representations and paradigms. However, my account of the transformation of social representations presented above conflicts with Kuhn's account of the growth of scientific knowledge. Critics within the philosophy of science have suggested modifications that bring the two accounts closer together. Furthermore, the writings of philosophers such as Kuhn, Lakatos and Feyerabend have encouraged the development of a new approach in the philosophy of science. This approach focuses on the processes of science from the perspective of the scientist in a historical and evolutionary framework. Rather than restricting philosophy to the 'context of justification' this approach also embraces the 'context of discovery', with all its historical and psychological concomitants (Nersessian, 1987b). It is concerned not only with the products of science but also with how knowledge is produced (Shapero, 1987). Such a philosophy requires both a historical overview and a detailed analysis of the development and transformation of science (Nersessian, 1987b; Kuhn, 1988). Only then can we understand the processes by which problems are structured, theories formulated and solutions accepted or rejected by the community. Only then can we understand the processes by which meanings are established and changed. This approach to the growth of scientific knowledge embraces the social constructionist perspective that I have been propounding in this book.

Kuhn's writings proclaim a special regard for science which distinguishes normal and revolutionary science from pre-science and, for that matter, from common sense. This separates tradition and innovation into successive periods or phases. The main distinguishing characteristic of normal science is that a single paradigm guides and coordinates the activities of scientists. It provides a single framework for communication and interaction within the community of scientists, who share the same world view. Alternative paradigms emerge only once a crisis is well established. This contrasts with pre-science in which different and incommensurate world views proliferate, hindering communication and coordinated research activity. Given the primacy of a single paradigm in normal science, extraordinary or revolutionary science is conceived in terms of a dramatic and discontinuous event.

While Moscovici left the construction of the unfamiliar to science, Kuhn leaves the construction of new paradigms to individual scientists who mystically achieve an alternative world view. His exposé fails to give any clear idea of how alternative world views are created. I have argued that Moscovici's account leaves us with an inadequate understanding of evolving social representations in common sense. Philosophers of science, most notably Lakatos and Musgrave (1974) and Feyerabend (1970) have presented parallel critiques of Kuhn's description of evolving paradigms in science. The history of science cannot be divided into successive periods of tenacity and proliferation. Alternative paradigms do not emerge only after a crisis is established. Rather, they are always present and play an important part in the growth of scientific knowledge. It is not the central paradigm alone that determines the problem-solving activities of scientists, but also the clash of ideas between alternative views. These may come from within the discipline or from other fields, sustaining critical discussion and argument as a normal part of scientific activity. This adjustment to Kuhn's original thesis integrates the role of tradition and innovation in the development of scientific knowledge and further emphasizes the similitude of paradigms and social representations.

In his more recent work, Kuhn (1988) has identified two aspects of historical analysis both of which are essential to the philosopher. Historical narratives of changes in scientific knowledge provide a source of data from which philosophers construct an understanding of science. However, prior to this, it is necessary to 'regain the past', to re-establish the meanings and concerns confronting the scientists involved. In other words, it is necessary to adopt the perspective of the scientist to re-discover the intellectual tradition, to reconstruct the contradictions or problems, and to research the scientists' solutions.

Similarly, Giere (1987), Nersessian (1987a), Shapero (1987) and others have argued that philosophers have tended to contrast former conceptualization with later versions without analysing the periods of transition between theories. In order to understand the transformation of science, it is necessary to examine how new concepts emerge and are subsequently altered, raising new problems to be resolved, in a gradual process of theory change. The creation of a scientific concept takes place within frameworks or beliefs in response to specific problems which are theoretical, experimental, methodological and metaphysical. The meaning of a new concept is thus always founded in the meaning of its predecessors and is better understood in the dynamics of meaning-change

and its context of use rather than in the necessary and sufficient conditions of a static definition. This evolutionary approach applies both to
the substantive issues addressed by a particular theory and to the broader
notions of observation, explanation, criteria for evaluation, methodology
and the goals of a scientific discipline.

By including the scientist in the process of science and by focusing on
beliefs, meaning and creativity, these philosophers narrow the gap between
our understanding of science and our understanding of cognition, and the
achievement of knowledge more generally. To quote Nersessian

> The cognitive mechanisms at work in the meaning-making
> dimensions of science cannot be fundamentally different, i.e.
> different in kind, from those we employ in non-scientific and
> science-learning contexts . . . any adequate science of cognition
> must also take the data from the analysis of science into account in
> its formulation and this has not been done to any significant extent.
>
> (Nersessian, 1987a: 164)

Science is conceived as a human endeavour in which individuals, who
have internalized the language and beliefs of their community, contribute
to and evaluate knowledge. Science, like any other activity, is a culturally
and historically situated activity which is ongoing and open-ended,
always open to revision and change. This does not imply an extreme
relativism or extreme social constructionism. Such a position could not
explain the phenomenal success of the sciences, nor could it explain the
transformation of science. Rather, it expresses a reality which is founded
in the organism–environment–culture system. This is expressed in the
philosophical writings by terms such as 'historical realism', 'contextual
objectivity', 'evolutionary naturalism', 'relative objectivity', etc. It is a
human reality founded in the biological and cultural inheritance of the
species: a reality which does not separate the internal, subjective world
from the external objective world. The cultural environment is not
distinct from the natural environment, nor the mental from the material
world. It is a form of social reality that embeds the individual in culture;
the scientist, like any other individual, is 'a personification of nature
through participation in, and an expression of, a culture' (Grene, 1987:
73). The conception of science as a cultural phenomenon makes it no less
real. In fact, it includes the scientist and the scientific community in that
reality. Science is a human endeavour and, far from being a reified
universe, it is a culturally and historically situated activity. Scientists, as
scientists, are both the product and the producers of science just as
individuals are both the product and the producers of culture.

SCIENCE AND SOCIAL REPRESENTATIONS

The understanding of science will necessarily require a multi-disciplinary approach including sociology, anthropology, psychology, history and philosophy. As yet, social psychology has made little contribution to such a science of science. However, following the theoretical developments that I have elaborated here, social representations theory provides us with the opportunity of making considerable progress in this direction. Social representations theory, as an expression of the social constructionist paradigm, constitutes a framework in which to develop a social psychology of science.

With the insights provided by the work of Moscovici, on the one hand, and writings in the philosophy and sociology of science on the other, I have attempted to reveal the similarities between the adult's active reconstruction of the social world and the scientists's creation of a new perspective in science. Indeed, social representations theory illuminates the transformation of knowledge, which is the hallmark of science, while, simultaneously, philosophical and sociological studies on the transformation of scientific knowledge can inform social representations theory. Below, I shall illustrate and vivify this perspective with reference to a particular example of scientific creativity which has had a profound effect on contemporary reality. For this purpose I have selected Darwin's theory of evolution and we shall examine its origins in Western thought, its creation by Darwin, its subsequent transformation in scientific communities and its diffusion into common sense.

Gruber (1981) illuminates the origins and development of the Theory of Evolution in his highly readable book entitled *Darwin on Man: A psychological study of scientific creativity*. In this book he specifically rejects two popular approaches to the explanation of innovation. The first focuses on the societal forces and objective conditions which bring about innovations. An individual's thoughts and actions are seen simply as a reflection of society. This approach externalizes and depersonalizes creativity such that the individual plays no active role, being wholly determined by the prevailing *Zeitgeist*. The second approach focuses on the individual and tends to attribute innovations to unconscious and non-rational thought. By ignoring the influences of society, this approach internalizes and de-socializes creativity. In contrast, Gruber argues for an approach which integrates the societal and individual aspects of creativity. Throughout his study, Gruber reveals the interdependence between Darwin and his social and intellectual milieu. The creative process cannot always be conceived in terms of a single act, a sudden insight or the solution to a single problem. Scientific creativity, more often than not, involves the gradual construction of an alternative perspective. Gruber shows how the theory of evolution emerged through the gradual development of a new perspective as Darwin continually adjusted and reconstructed his beliefs. He was 'a person striving to construct a new synthesis, a new way of looking at many problems, a new point of view' (Gruber, 1974: 4). Furthermore, this creative process 'must be seen as rooted in its total human context' (Gruber, 1974: 6), in the relationship between the individual, the environment and the social and intellectual milieux.

Gruber schematizes Darwin's changing world view in terms of five stages, as shown in his diagram (Figure 1). This transformation of Darwin's evolutionary thought was related to the environment and to his intellectual and social context. Rather than giving a general historical survey, Gruber explores this in the personal terms of Darwin's life. In his adolescent years, he assimilated the 'family *Weltanschauung*' and, in particular, ideas from his grandfather, Erasmus. Those which were most significant refer to the conception of nature, struggle, adaptation and change; to the nature of scientific work, invention and education; and to social and ethical issues. These were elaborated upon through his education at Edinburgh and Cambridge where he was influenced by a number of teachers.

The gradual emergence of a new perspective was founded in the context of his family and university education, but required a further one and a half decades to reach publication. These years were taken up by the integration of his experiences on the *Beagle* voyage and his observation in the archipelagos; the assimilation of Lyell's ideas on geology and, in particular, the conception of the physical world as continuously changing over a period of two million years; and the development of what Gruber refers to as the conservation schema and the equilibration schema. In particular, the conception of a changing world populated by well-adapted but unchanging organisms posed a dilemma which was not resolved until Darwin, inspired by the writings of Malthus [1826], transformed ideas of natural selection from a conservative to an evolutionary force. Darwin's active search and enquiry, his social and intellectual context and his experiences in the world all played an essential role in the creative process.

The ideas of evolution and natural selection with which Darwin was working were well established, at least within his immediate circles. But, as Darwin searched, selected and reorganized his material, these ideas appeared and reappeared in slightly different forms, taking on a new

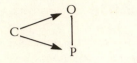

A. 1832 and before: The Creator has made an organic world (*O*) and a physical world (*P*); *O* is perfectly adapted to *P*.

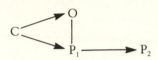

B. 1832–1834: The physical world undergoes continuous change, governed by natural laws as summarized in Lyell's *Principles of Geology*. In other respects, *B* resembles *A*.

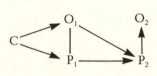

C. 1835: The activities of living organisms contribute to the evolution of the physical world, as exemplified by the action of the coral organism in making coral reefs. In other respects, *C* resembles *B*.

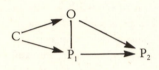

D. 1836–1837: Changes in the physical world imply changes in the organic world, if adaptation is to be maintained; the direct action of the physical milieu induces the appropriate biological adaptations. In other respects, *D* resembles *C*.

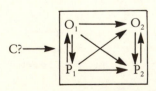

E. 1838 and after: The physical and organic worlds are both continuously evolving and interacting with each other. The Creator, if one exists, may have set the natural system in being, but He does not interfere with its operation, standing *outside* the system.

Figure 1 Gruber's diagram: Darwin's changing world view.
(Reproduced with permission from Gruber, 1981.)

significance within the changing structure of his argument. That which is important is not so much an original idea, but the creative syntheses of various ideas into a coherent and intelligible system of representations.

While his family and teachers played an important role in initiating the creative process there were other societal and personal factors which restrained the construction of a novel perspective. In particular, Darwin was aware that his ideas challenged religious orthodoxy and, from the experience of others who had violated the majority view of the world, had reason to fear persecution if his ideas on evolution became known. On the one hand, this repressed the free exploration and expression of his early evolutionary ideas; on the other hand, it also served to encourage the search for further materials to support his argument. Similarly, the difficulties encountered by Darwin in communicating a novel and ill-defined perspective encouraged the development of a coherent and justifiable theory.

Following the publication of *The Origin of Species* (1859), the diffusion of Darwin's evolutionary perspective gave rise to 'a revolution in every mode of thought and feeling'. It transformed our thinking about the animal and plant kingdoms, about the place of human beings in the world and about 'the scheme of things' in the cosmos. Oldroyd (1980) illuminates the breadth and depth of influence on intellectual thought in his comprehensive book entitled *Darwinian Impacts: An introduction to the Darwinian revolution*. In particular, he explores the consequences of 'Darwinism' from the public reception of *The Origin of Species* to its diffusion into various spheres of thought. Not only has it radically changed biological theory but it has also transformed areas of sociology, politics, theology, philosophy, psychology, anthropology, literature and music.

Beyond this, the evolutionary perspective has entered into our common-sense understandings in many spheres of life. This refers not so much to lay knowledge of the theory of evolution, but to people's understanding of the natural world, of social and political phenomena and of how things change. As Farr has suggested (personal communication), the Darwinian revolution is an apt subject for investigation within the framework of the theory of social representations. The mistake which has been made in the theory of social representations, and which has frequently been made elsewhere, is the distinction between the creative process and the diffusion of that which has been created. Rather, the creation of a theory and its subsequent diffusion are part and parcel of an ongoing process of transformation. In terms of Einstein's relativity theory the distinction depends upon one's point of reference in time–space. There is always a tendency to select points of radical and influential change as the node of creativity and then to conceive of any subsequent transformation in terms of that creation. However, just as Gruber argues that there is no one step which is more crucial than any other in the development of Darwin's evolutionary perspective, so too, there is no one point which can be selected out in a continual process of change, when we consider the transformation of social representations.

This can be illustrated by taking different points of reference within the Darwinian revolution. If I select Darwin as my point of reference I would describe ideas on natural selection, evolution and the creation of the natural order in terms of social and intellectual influences. I would then go on to describe the influence of the theory of evolution in terms of its diffusion and subsequent transformation. However, if I take as my point of reference a later stage in the continual process of change, the world of Darwin becomes part of the social and intellectual influences. It is important to realize here that those who are influenced by the theory of evolution are also creative in constructing new syntheses which assimilate and transform Darwin's ideas. Each individual, within and as a part of his or her environment, must go through the creative process of breaking with what is known and reconstructing his or her perspective (Markova, 1987).

In some ways, this is precisely Moscovici's point when he emphasizes the creative and transformative character of social representations as the products of science diffuse into common sense. What he fails to realize is that the psychologist or anthropologist or, for that matter, Darwin himself, are at least as creative as the lay person in the construction of a new perspective. Both Gruber (1973) and Piaget (1974) liken the creative process in science to the child's active construction and reconstruction of the social world. In both spheres, a new perspective is created through interacting with and changing the environment. The theory of social representations highlights the same constructive and transformative processes in the social world of the adult lay person.

The domain of social representations has been one of the major issues addressed in this book. For Moscovici, social representations are science made common. However, closer examination of the theory and associated research has shown this restriction to be ill-founded. In Chapter 2, it was argued that the theory applied to the dynamics of common sense regardless of its association with science. Social representations of scientific theories or concepts cannot be distinguished from social representations of socially significant, non-scientific objects. This applies to their dynamic nature, to the roles of convention and experience, to the various modes of communication and to the processes of transformation. In

Part III, I have argued that the theory also applies to the dynamics of scientific knowledge. Science, like common sense, constitutes a social reality that is constructed by social individuals in a historical and cultural context. The theory of social representations thus provides a social psychology of knowledge that applies to the dynamics of both common sense and science. Moreover, the interactions between science and common sense can only be understood if they are conceived in the same terms. In conclusion, the social constructionist paradigm and social representations theory provide a framework in which to study the social psychology of science.

Part IV

THE TRANSFORMATION OF SOCIAL REPRESENTATIONS

9

A CASE STUDY IN SOCIAL PSYCHOLOGY

INTRODUCTION

In Part I, I presented the theory of social representations and discussed some of the conflicts and contradictions that became apparent on close examination of its central tenets and related research. In particular, there was an incongruence between the force of society and the potency of the individual in the dynamics of social representations.

In Part II, I traced this antithesis to the individualistic and mechanistic principles of the Cartesian paradigm and suggested that the evolutionary and constructionist principles of the Hegelian paradigm provide a more suitable framework for the integration of the individual and society. By representing the individual as a social being and redefining social reality in terms of an organism–environment–culture system, I showed how people's identities and social interactions are interrelated essentially with the maintenance and transformation of social representations.

In Part III, I concentrated on the relationship between science and common sense, arguing that social representations theory is applicable not only to the diffusion of science into common sense but also to the transformation of science itself. Developments in the philosophy of science and in the sociology of scientific knowledge are used to dismiss Moscovici's problematic notion of the reified universe and to present a social constructionist account of scientific knowledge that is in keeping with social representations theory as a whole.

The main purpose of Part IV is to elaborate and vivify these arguments by presenting my research on the transformation of social representations in social psychology. This research reflects the cultural and historical perspective of the theory focusing, firstly, on the dialectic relationship between individuals and their culture and, secondly, on the evolution and transformation of social representations. Adopting a self-reflexive

129

stance, it should be realized that this research played a significant part in directing and shaping the construction of the social representations system presented in this book. That is, the book itself can be seen as an example of the creative evolution of a social representations system, involving conflict, active research and personal involvement embedded in a particular intellectual, social and cultural context.

Choosing a science

Choosing which science to investigate is an important decision that should be supported by theoretical and methodological considerations. Psychology and, in particular, social psychology is an appropriate choice for a number of reasons. Firstly, social representations are most accessible during periods of conflict and change. Psychology, as a scientific discipline, has seen frequent and heated debates about the most appropriate paradigm from empiricism to rationalization to constructivism; about appropriate methodologies for the study of mind and behaviour from introspection to experimentation to participant observation; and about the relative strengths of theories that provide antagonistic explanations of both specific and general psychological phenomena. Secondly, as a participant in the research process, it is advantageous to be able to draw on implicit knowledge and personal experience. Psychology is relatively accessible to me with regard to its data sources, its concepts and its methods. Moreover, it furthers my own interest in conflicts and alternative perspectives within psychology.

Thirdly, few in-depth investigations of psychology have been carried out. The philosophy of science has been notorious in selecting illustrative examples from the natural sciences and, in particular, from physics. Similarly, the vast majority of studies in the sociology of knowledge have focused on the natural sciences, and it is only recently that the biological sciences have attracted increasing attention. While there have been a number of 'internal histories' of psychology (e.g. Boring, 1959; Miller, 1966; Hearnshaw, 1986), books on the history of behaviouristic (Mackenzie, 1977) and cognitive (Gardner, 1985) approaches and numerous reviews of particular fields, there are few studies which present a detailed analysis of the transformation of a psychological theory and its related fields of research. Miller's book on the obedience experiments (1986) and Cartwright's analysis of the risky-shift experiments (1973) are two exceptions, although both focus on research controversies. Historians and philosophers of science are beginning to take an increasing interest in the human sciences, including psychology (Shotter, 1975;

Mackenzie, 1977; O'Donnell, 1979; Ash, 1983). Furthermore, psychologists are becoming more aware of their own past. The celebration of psychology's centenary in 1979 instigated a look-back into the role of psychology in the past and speculation about its possible futures (Koch, 1985). An increased awareness of where psychology has been, its successes and its limitations, provides guidance and direction for the future development of the discipline.

Designing the research

The style or design of the investigation is also an important issue. It is not sufficient to examine a single social representation or the similarities and differences between two or more social representations. It is necessary to trace the continuities and discontinuities in the evolution of social representations systems over time. Neither is it sufficient to construct a 'history of meanings': it is also necessary to make explicit the role of individuals in maintaining and transforming social representations. On the basis of these considerations it was decided to conduct an in-depth historical analysis of the transformation of social representations in a specific field of study, focusing on the contributions of an influential scientist in relation to his or her scientific community and the broader society. On the basis of results from an exploratory questionnaire the research focused on Henri Tajfel's contribution to the psychology of groups and the emergence of a new perspective in social psychology. This permitted a detailed analysis of the dynamic interrelationships within the organism–environment–culture system during a period of substantial change.

It might be argued that this research strategy is in danger of individualizing social representations: by focusing on the contribution of a single scientist the research endorses a 'Great Man' theory of science. This would be an oversimplistic interpretation of the research strategy and antithetical to my thesis. The study deals explicitly with the socialization of the individual and the creativity of individuals; with the influence of society on the individual and the influence of the individual on society; in sum, with the dialectics of the individual and his or her culture.

It might be argued, also, that a study focusing on the contribution of a single scientist, in a particular field of study, will tell us little about the processes of science or the processes of social representations. Such a critique, however, is founded on the Cartesian principles of universals, particulars and generalization (Markova, 1982). Generalizations are universal, unrestricted and stable scientific laws which ignore particular variations. However, within the Hegelian paradigm particulars are expressions of universals and generalizations are always indeterminate, unstable and relative to the social and historical context. For this reason, it is appropriate to conduct a detailed case study which investigates the interdependent relationships among the elements of a system of social representations within a particular social and historical context and examines their transformation over time. Emergent generalizations would be those that engender understanding within the theoretical framework. Comparative studies with the dynamics of social representations in other sciences and in common sense would show how far these generalizations are transferable to other contexts. Such comparative studies are outside the scope of this book. They require the coordinated activity of scientists working within the same general framework and would be the product of the relevant research community as a whole.

Conducting the research

The investigation of social representations in all their complexity and diversity requires the coordinated employment of complementary research methods. This current research adopts a largely qualitative and interpretative approach in order to analyse the historical and cultural transformation of social representations, while preserving the integrity of the system as a whole. The evolution of the social representations system and the changing pattern of relations among elements of the organism–environment–culture system only becomes apparent gradually. Firstly, the content and structure of the social representations system is analysed in terms of successive phases in its development. By examining the similarities and differences among these phases and the continuities and discontinuities across time the pattern of relations within the social representations system is made explicit. Secondly, the functions and consequences of the social representations system are examined. This combines both the emergence of problems and the construction of solutions within the social representations system with the changing pattern of relations within the organism–environment–culture system.

The aim of this analysis is to describe and explain the transformation of social representations, not by the invocation of general laws, but by constructing a legitimate and fruitful account of a dynamic system. Firstly, this requires the construction and communication of a coherent understanding which is internally consistent with and takes account of the available data in all its richness and diversity. This is facilitated by making explicit a number of theoretical principles that identify different processes involved in the transformation of social representations systems. Secondly, this account should generate fresh solutions to problems in the field of social representations that assist in the investigation of other social representations systems.

While a variety of data sources were used, including in-depth interviews with prominent social psychologists, books and chapters on the psychology of groups and the Social Science Citation Index, the research focused on articles, chapters and books either written or edited by Henri Tajfel. These scientific publications constituted excellent documentary material for a historical and cultural analysis. These documents were authentic, accessible, historically sequenced, of low cost and of high quality, permitting a detailed examination of stability and change over extended periods of time. The historico-interpretative analysis of these documents involved reading and rereading the publications, moving backwards and forwards in time, following up initially vague ideas, dropping others and continually structuring and restructuring the material.

Within social psychology, methods of documentary research are rarely discussed in any detail. In recent years, however, there has been an increasing interest in content analysis (Weber, 1985; Kerlinger, 1986) and also in discourse analysis (Potter and Wetherell, 1987) the latter being frequently used in the study of science (e.g. Potter and Mulkay, 1982; Gilbert and Mulkay, 1984). Such forms of analysis are justified within the theoretical and methodological commitments of social representations theory which explicitly incorporate the cultural products of human activity. Social representations are expressed not only in what people say or do but also in what people write or produce. Moreover, the articles, chapters and books which scientists write form an essential component in the social process of science. They constitute one of the most important forms of creativity, communication and social interaction within the community.

This perspective contrasts with that of discourse analysis which focuses on the account or document itself; on the context, variability and constitution of accounts; and the role of language or 'linguistic repertoires' in the active construction of diverse social worlds. While this approach takes accounts seriously, it inadvertently reflects the Cartesian dualism between mind (language) and reality, in this case adopting a behaviouristic or positivistic perspective on language! This appears to me to be a peculiar perversion. Discourse analysis separates what scientists say or write from that which they are talking or writing about, and focuses on the former. But, if discourse is active in constructing social worlds and in social interaction, then it must refer to objects, events, situations and actions in reality. Indeed, this is what language is for. Meaning is not simply dependent upon systems of relations within language but on relations within the organism–environment–culture system. This is particularly important when we wish to understand and explain transformations of social representations. Changes in meaning and language usage do not occur through rhetoric alone but through interactions with the physical, social and cultural environment. Within the theoretical context of social representations the form and content of scientists' written or oral accounts cannot be separated from the scientists' actions and beliefs relating to the object of study.

Clarifying the processes of transformation

The emergence of a new, more social, perspective in the psychology of groups involved the gradual reconstruction of a social representations system through the processes of assimilation and accommodation. Here, I shall present an outline of the various forms of assimilation and accommodation that I was able to identify during the research. Numerous examples of these processes will be found in the following narrative account (Zukier, 1986) of social representations and their transformation.

It will be remembered that Moscovici defines anchoring in terms of classification and naming where classification may involve both generalization and particularization. All three processes of transformation are frequently found in the construction of a theory of intergroup relations. Generalization refers to the application of a set of ideas within the social representations system to a new object or second set of ideas that frequently lies at the periphery of the system. This is achieved through emphasizing or accentuating the similarities between the two fields of concern. This is frequently accompanied by *re*naming relevant components of the system in order to signify their changing meaning and role within the system as a whole. Particularization can be construed as the opposite process whereby the differences between two fields within the social representations system are accentuated, distinguishing one field from the other. Frequently, I refer to this process as differentiation. This is usually accompanied by naming: the use of new labels or terms of reference to identify those features in the social representations system that have been particularized.

These are not the only processes involved in the transformation of social representations. In order to provide an accurate description of social representations and their transformation it is necessary to consider a number of other processes. Firstly, the social representations system is often expanded by creating links with other social representations systems and including new fields from the latter into the former. This process of inclusion is not the same as generalization: it does not involve applying one set of ideas to another object. Rather, it involves linking two or more distinct fields that are in some way complementary. Although it rarely occurs in the present study, the opposite process of exclusion should also be considered. This would involve the rejection or expulsion of a particular field from the social representations system.

Inclusion is often stimulated by the process of discovery whereby anomalies in the social representations system are identified. This can arise when interactions with objects in the environment do not conform to the social representations system and people are confronted by unfamiliar and unexpected phenomena. Alternatively, contradictions within or between social representations may reveal gaps or anomalies in our understanding of the relevant phenomena.

Finally, inclusion is usually followed by a process of integration whereby fields within the social representation are transformed in such a way as to make them independent. This may be achieved by emphasizing particular components that link the different fields; by restructuring the relationships among fields within the social representations system; or by transposing a pattern of relationships from one set of fields to another, related, set of fields.

Vivifying the organism–environment–culture system

Above, I have described the processes by which social representations are transformed. However, it is their function in the social construction of reality that is of greatest significance. These processes only occur through the concatenation of an organism–environment–culture system. It is this latter aspect of social representations theory that distinguishes it as a form of societal psychology. Within the realm of the social sciences the organism–environment–culture system embraces the individual, both as a scientist and as a member of society; it embraces the object of study in the research setting as well as in society and everyday life; and it embraces the community of scientists as well as the broader culture. The dialectics of individuals, their environment and their culture, is manifest in Tajfel's relationship with the community of psychologists and with the broader European culture in the emergence of a social perspective.

It will be seen that the conventions of a community act as a prescriptive force that shapes and directs individuals' activities, imposing restrictions on ways of thinking and ways of interacting with objects, both physical and social. The power of these social representations systems is achieved through socialization processes whereby individuals learn and assimilate ways of viewing the world. In so doing individuals themselves achieve an identity that locates them in society and defines their relations with others. This is achieved through interaction and com- munication at various levels; through personal relations with others; through personal experiences of and active involvement with a particular phenomenon; or through the experiences of others in diverse social realities. Communication and interaction do not only function as prescriptive forces: they also function as innovatory and creative forces. People break with convention simultaneously transforming their social representations systems and their identities. This involves not only coordination of activities and collaboration among members of a community but also conflict and disagreement, argument and debate and the negotiation of identities and social realities. From one generation to the next the transformations become established as reality through the process of objectification. It is this relationship between people and knowledge that is expressed in the notion of objectification, whereby individuals and groups identify so completely with a social representations system that it becomes their reality.

Introducing group psychology

In the final part of this introduction I shall give a synopsis of the background to group psychology. In the years preceding Tajfel's initiation and involvement in group psychology it had become increasingly individualistic in orientation. Following the atrocities of World War II, the deteriorating economies and the subsequent nationalistic and class antagonisms, the interest in group processes and group dynamics increased. However, little attention was given to social or ethnic groups, their historical development, their cultural traditions and their changing political and economic relations with other groups. This was left largely to sociologists and anthropologists. In psychology, the study of groups was reduced to the study of interactions between two people (dyads) with little or no reference to their social context (Deutsch, 1949; Cartwright and Zander, 1953, 1960, 1968; Kelley and Thibaut, 1954, 1969; Thibaut and Kelley, 1959).

> Because the existence of the group is based solely upon the participation and satisfaction of the individuals comprising it, the group functionalism becomes an individual functionalism. The

ultimate analysis then is in terms of the vicissitudes of individuals as they try out various adaptations to the problems confronting them.

We assume that if we can achieve a clear understanding of the dyad we can subsequently extend our understanding to encompass the problems of larger and more complex social relations.

(Thibaut and Kelley, 1959: 5–6)

This reductionist argument was by no means unusual. It was a perspective that remained ignorant of a social group's history, its relative position in society and the ideologies (or social representations) extant in society. Little attention was given to sequences of collective action, to membership of social groups or to the creativity of individuals in groups. Two major exceptions were Kurt Lewin (1935, 1948) and Muzafer Sherif (1967), both of whom attempted to integrate psychological and sociological approaches to groups, arguing that it was necessary to see individuals as members of social groups. However, the individualistic perspective in social psychology continued to dominate, such that the group was not seen as theoretically distinctive from individuals. Once again, with the work of Henri Tajfel on intergroup relations, there has been a re-emergence of the social or societal dimensions. In my view his most significant achievement was to integrate explicitly the psychological processes of individuals with the social realities of society. But Tajfel's career in the scientific discipline of psychology did not commence with the study of intergroup relations. Rather he began in psychophysics, studying the effect of value on the perception of size.

Introducing Henri Tajfel

Tajfel had a wealth of social and cultural experience before coming to psychology at more than thirty years of age. During his early years in a semi-fascist Poland, Tajfel's life was shaped by his Jewish background. Although he was an agnostic from an early age, his experience as a member of an extremely discriminated-against minority stayed with him throughout his life. At the outbreak of World War II he became a member of the French army, having moved to France to study chemistry. He was taken prisoner in the 'great débâcle' of June 1940, and spent the next five years as a prisoner-of-war in Austria and Germany. During his imprisonment the life-or-death significance of his Jewish identity was further pressed upon him: his life was in danger, not for anything that he, himself, believed or had done, but simply because he was a Jew. Liberated in 1945, he returned to Paris to find only four of his relatives left alive. He spent the next six years working for various international organizations on the rehabilitation of children and adults who had become refugees as a consequence of the war. This work took him to Paris, Brussels and north-west Germany.

At this time, Tajfel began to nurture an interest in psychology, which he envisaged as an applied field of endeavour to do with helping people and he took a *'certificat'* at the Sorbonne and a diploma in educational sciences in Brussels. It was not until 1951 that Tajfel came to England for the express purpose of studying psychology at Birkbeck College. Working during the day and studying during the evening, he graduated with one of the two best First Class Degrees in the University of London that year, before being appointed research assistant at the University of Durham in 1955.

Tajfel's formal education at Birkbeck is notable for three reasons. Firstly, during his years as an undergraduate he wrote an essay entitled 'Prejudice' which won an award from the Ministry of Education for a mature student scholarship. Secondly, he was influenced by one of his teachers, Richard Peters, the philosopher, who together with Tajfel wrote an article entitled 'Hobbes and Hull – metaphysicians of behaviour' (Peters and Tajfel, 1957). In it they argue against reductionism and against any hypothetico-deductive oversimplifications which attempt to reduce human action to motion, with no regard for the rules, conventions, criteria and canons of human social behaviour. While physiological and mechanical principles may be necessary, they can never be sufficient to explain complex rule-following. Thirdly, he developed an interest in cognition and perception, the field in which he immersed himself for the first few years of his academic career.

I
FROM PERCEPTUAL OVERESTIMATION TO STEREOTYPES: PARTICULARIZATION, GENERALIZATION AND NAMING

Tajfel's initial interests (Tajfel, 1956, 1957) focused on the relationship between motivation and perception and, in particular, on perceptual overestimation, the vogue topic of research among the 'New Look' perceptionists in America. In 1947, Bruner and Goodman had published a paper entitled 'Value and need as organizing factors in perception'. The article itself did little more than demonstrate the existence of a 'peculiar' or unfamiliar phenomenon. In contrast to traditionalists who assumed an invariant relationship between stimulus and perception, they argued that individuals' subjective needs produced distortions. This initiated a controversy in the study of perceptual phenomena and, with it, a new research endeavour.

By the time Tajfel came to the field the New Look in perception was already well established with numerous psychologists conducting experimental research and producing theoretical explanations and critiques. However, there continued to be confusion in interpreting a variety of findings. Firstly, the association of value with a physical object did not always lead to perceptual overestimation in comparison to neutral stimuli or objective measures (Carter and Schooler, 1949; Lambert *et al.*, 1949; Klein *et al.*, 1951). The discovery of these negative instances provided the basis for Tajfel's distinction between relevant and irrelevant dimensions. Perceptual overestimation would only occur when value was linked with changes in the physical dimension on which the object was being judged. For example, large coins tended to be associated with a higher value but the physical dimension of size is not relevant to the value of a swastika. By particularizing physical dimensions that were relevant to the perceptual judgment of objects associated with value, Tajfel made sense of these unfamiliar or problematic findings.

Secondly, distortions in perception were not always unidirectional. The association with value did not always lead to overestimation on the physical dimension. For example, Carter and Schooler (1949) noted that larger coins were overestimated and smaller coins were underestimated in size. This created conceptual problems for a purely motivational account of perceptual overestimation. Tajfel presented an alternative, functional account of the 'accentuation of differences'. Accuracy of perception *per se* was unimportant; what was important was the ability to distinguish between valued objects by sharpening their relevant distinctive features. The idea that it was not simply a mysterious process of perceptual overestimation was already emerging in others' interpretation of their research. Erikson and Hake (1955) had discussed the functional role of perceptual shifts in increasing the accuracy of discrimination; McCurdy (1956) had argued that exaggerating differences between coins can be considered a 'good error'. However, while Dukes and Bevan (1952) had previously employed the term 'accentuation' to describe shifts in perceptual judgments, Tajfel was the first to coin the phrase 'accentuation of differences', a name that subsequently came to be accepted and employed by others.

Thirdly, Tajfel differentiated interserial and intraserial perceptual judgments. Most experiments had confined their interest to comparisons between a value series (coins) and a neutral series (disks). However, it had already been suggested that subjects' perceptual judgments might be based on comparisons within a series (Dukes and Bevan, 1952; Hochberg, 1957). What Tajfel made clear was that perceptual judgments must be seen in terms of comparisons between stimuli rather than a direct relationship between a single stimulus and response.

In all three instances it can be seen that unfamiliar findings are anchored into the social representations by particularization and naming. The unfamiliar is socially constructed within the organism–environment–culture system of the research community and is then familiarized by negotiating an alternative account of perceptual phenomena. In each instance Tajfel builds on others' empirical and theoretical research, making explicit what was already implicit in their work by creatively restructuring elements in the social representations and by providing labels that identify and communicate significant features of the research problem. Naming can also be used to circumvent problematic definitions. For example, Tajfel consistently employs the term 'perceptual judgment' to avoid the confusion within the 'New Look' between perception on the one hand and judgment or cognition on the other.

Tajfel soon turned his attention to the perception of social, as opposed to physical, objects. By generalizing the principles of perceptual judgments, the social phenomena of stereotypes and prejudice could be anchored within the cognitive framework of social perception. In order to justify this generalization it was necessary to emphasize the similarities between the two spheres. Tajfel focuses on the dimensional or comparative nature of both spheres while dwelling on the transitional case where stereotypes are based on the physical features of people. A line is shorter or longer than other lines just as a person is shorter or taller than other persons. For example, the overestimation of the size of coins is not, in principle, different from the accentuation of differences in skin colour between blacks and whites. For both, a physical attribute varies concurrently with value. In this way, perceptual judgment and perceptual stereotypes are integrated within the same theoretical framework centring on the accentuation of differences. Furthermore, he adopts a reductionist stance, whereby the problems of social stereotypes and prejudices are, in principle, reducible to the cognitive processes involved in perceiving the length of lines or the sizes of coins.

Such generalization was by no means unusual. For example, within this particular field, Hochberg (1957) argued that prejudice and stereotypes were no more than the inescapable tendencies of cognitive processes. Although greater attention has been paid to social factors in perception (psychophysics), the same principles may also apply to perception of the social environment. In this way the distinction between physical perception and social perception is obviated. Specifically, the judgmental effects of value could be generalized to the perception of social objects and events. A similar reductionist perspective was also common in other fields, including attitude change (Hovland and Sherif, 1952), personal involvement in social issues (Sherif and Hovland, 1961) and strength of personal views (Manis, 1960). Tajfel draws on these examples to bolster his claim that the accentuation of differences can be generalized to the perception of social phenomena. Furthermore, methodological developments in the field both permit and support this generalization. The development of experimental methods employing rating, ranking and paired comparisons meant that it was not essential to know the physical dimensions which corresponded to the dimensions of experience as it had been in classical psychophysical methods. This allowed the quantification of stereotypes and the perception of social objects comparable to research procedures employed in psychophysics.

The significance of the work of others in the field goes beyond theoretical and methodological arguments for generalization. The inclusion of others' research on stereotypes and prejudice within the explanatory domain led to a much greater emphasis on classification. The influence of value which changes concurrently with a physical dimension was apparent from the studies on perceptual judgment of physical objects. This corresponds directly to prejudice. Prejudiced subjects accentuate differences in skin colour more than non-prejudiced subjects (Secord *et al.*, 1956; Allport and Kramer, 1946). However, these studies also highlighted the influence of classification in stereotyping. Skin colour is a continuous physical dimension super-imposed by a discontinuous classification, distinguishing groups of stimuli, in this case whites from coloureds. This classification has a greater emotional or value relevance for prejudiced subjects. Skin colour provides a cue to the valued classification, and hence judgments exhibit shifts which accentuated the differences between the classes.

By assimilating prejudice and stereotypes into the social representation of perceptual phenomena it was also necessary to accommodate the latter to the peculiarities of the former. This is achieved, firstly, by identifying, defining and naming the role of classification and, secondly, by including classification in the experimental studies on social perception of physical objects. For example, the use of linguistic labels to classify the lengths of lines was found to have a significant effect on perceptual judgments (Tajfel and Wilkes, 1963a).

What emerges is a predictive framework (Tajfel, 1959a) that embraces all possible combinations of three factors in social perception, namely physical dimensions, value differentials and classifications. This was a significant achievement. The predictive framework allowed previous research findings to be explained, suggested further experimental research and gave rise to new research hypotheses. It specified the impact of value and classification on the perceptual judgment of physical (or social) dimensions and provided a unified explanation for research findings on perceptual overestimation, perceptual stereotypes and prejudice.

Its prescriptive power can be seen in the conversion and re-analysis of previous research findings (e.g. Bruner and Goodman, 1947; Carter and Schooler, 1949; Klein *et al.*, 1951; Bruner and Rodrigues, 1953) and its persistence in the face of subsequent research findings that did not clearly support its predictive hypotheses (e.g. Tajfel and Wilkes, 1963b). This is because it provided a functional and cognitive explanation which resolved inconsistencies in the research literature, integrated related fields of concern and suggested a number of theoretical extensions. Perhaps the most significant extension was the inclusion of abstract (as opposed to physical) dimensions such as beauty, pleasantness or intelligence that are frequently associated with value superimposed by a classification. On the basis of a burgeoning body of research on shifts and biases in perception (e.g. Razran, 1950), Tajfel argued that judgments on abstract continua would also show the effects of classification (stereotypes) and value (prejudice). This extension caused Tajfel to move from the realm of social perception into the realm of social cognition.

II
A REDUCTIONIST PERSPECTIVE:
SOCIALIZATION IN THE CONVENTIONS OF A
DISCIPLINE

The prescriptive nature of social representations extends well beyond the boundaries of the predictive framework. Given Tajfel's social background, his work with refugees and the influence of Peters in his formative years in psychology, it is difficult to understand how he became enmeshed in the highly technical and esoteric problems of perceptual judgment and why he should have adopted a reductionist stance on the issues of social perception. As early as 1958 he was aware that his interests lay in 'the effects of social and cultural milieux in which an individual lives on the way he looks at the world' (Tajfel in Cohen, 1977: 297). This can only be explained with reference to the established conventions and institutions of the academic psychology community.

The ivory towers, more solid than they are now, had a way of smothering one with their benevolent warmth and comfort. Very soon, first briefly in Durham and then in Oxford, I was talking a new language. I learned a new jargon and discovered 'problems' which I never knew existed. The academic psychology took full hold of me.

(Tajfel, 1981a: 2)

Tajfel was socialized into a well-established culture with its own language and values, its sets of legitimate problems, its methods of research and its criteria for acceptable solutions. Tajfel's earliest research adopted the standard experimental procedures and hypothetico-deductive rationale along with the canons of confirmation and refutation. It explored the established problem of the perceptual judgment of physical magnitude associated with value. His first published research examined the effect of value (experimentally manipulated using paper bonuses) on the perceptual judgment of weight (using a series of ten weights). These experiments were conducted while Tajfel was still at Durham and fell well within the conventional bounds of psychophysics.

This process of socialization into the academic community depends upon interpersonal relationships. Most notable, at this time, was the influence of Jerome Bruner. His earliest research addressed the problem that Bruner and his colleagues created. However, Bruner's influence extends well beyond this. Tajfel visited Harvard, Cambridge (Massachusetts) in 1958 and his early publications on social perception owed much to the encouragement and advice of Bruner. He also worked with Bruner on individuals' use of 'broad' and 'narrow' categories. This led Tajfel into the research on individual differences in social perception (Bruner and Tajfel, 1961; Tajfel et al., 1964a, b; Tajfel and Bruner, 1966). In this particular respect, Bruner's influence led to one of the major discontinuities in Tajfel's intellectual career but it is associated also with some of the major continuities (Tajfel, 1980a). Firstly, Bruner was a functionalist (Bruner, 1980), a perspective that is evident throughout Tajfel's works, being closely associated with the comparative or relative perspective. Secondly, Tajfel's understanding of classification and differentiation owes much to Bruner's work on cue utilization and categorical identity. Thirdly, Bruner's work emphasizes the social context in which cognitive mechanisms function; that is, the social determination of perceptions as opposed to the perception of social stimuli. It provided an established and respected perspective for the study of social phenomena that interested Tajfel.

143

In 1956 Tajfel was given a lectureship at Oxford in the Department of Social and Administrative Studies. Despite the fact that Tajfel's interests broadened to encompass issues of social perception and the cognitive processes involved in stereotyping, his research continued to use the traditional techniques of psychophysics. These included the study of value and the accentuation of judged differences using a series of coins (Tajfel and Cawasjee, 1959), and the study of classification and its effect on quantitative judgments using a series of lines varying in length (Tajfel and Wilkes, 1963a). Although his theoretical framework relates these to social classification and stereotyping, Tajfel continued to examine the perceptual judgment of physical objects with limited social relevance.

Secure in the 'New Look' approach to the problems of perception, his work characterized an orthodox and reductionistic perspective. Whereas in 1957 the phenomenon of perceptual overestimation was considered to be a special case of social perception, by 1959 the problems of social perception could be reduced to principles of perception of the physical environment – the simplest case. Furthermore, it met with the scientific canons of the Oxford community. Although the interests of this community were varied, there was considerable social pressure to conduct 'good science', such that psychology would be accepted by other disciplines as a 'bona fide' natural science. These conventions placed severe restrictions on the development of social psychology and, in particular, on the development of a more social approach to the problems of social perception and stereotyping.

The prescriptive force of these conventions is reflected further in the format, style and language of his experimental reports, consisting of a brief introduction, followed by a detailed presentation of method and results, and a relatively brief discussion. Even in his review papers there is no explicit consideration or discussion of the proper content and function for social psychology or of appropriate methodologies for research. The conventions of the research community are accepted without question.

However, in order to understand the prescriptive and conventional power of social representations we must also look at the individual's relations to the groups that propagate and sustain them. Tajfel was both an immigrant to Britain and new to the profession of academic psychology. One can only assume that it was important for him to establish an identity within the community in which he found himself. This he achieved by making a distinctive contribution within the system of social representations that was already established. Rather than challenging the fundamental principles of these social representations and thereby excluding himself from the community with which he had chosen to belong, Tajfel focused on particular problems within the system of social representations, developing a perspective that drew upon and integrated the work of others within the field of social perception. Furthermore, Billig (personal communication) has suggested that there were personal and social constraints outside the academic realm. Given the intensity and pain of his experiences during the Holocaust, Tajfel, like others, found it difficult, if not impossible, to look at the issues directly. Both within and outside psychology there was a lack of social opportunities to speak about the emergence and consequence of intergroup conflict.

Despite some delay, Tajfel eventually shifted his research activities to the social perception of people. In 1959 Tajfel had employed his cognitive theoretical framework, centring on the accentuation of differences, to reinterpret and explain unexpected findings from the research of Lambert and Klineberg (1959) on national stereotypes and group evaluations (Tajfel, 1959c). They had found that English subjects evaluated English speakers more favourably than French speakers on seven of fourteen traits, as expected, but that French subjects favoured English speakers on ten traits. That is, they were not ethnocentric. Tajfel explained this in terms of value or relevance in situations of intergroup conflict such that attributes associated with socio–economic class were highly valued by the French.

However, it was not until 1963 that Tajfel published his own research on the social perception of people. Initially, in collaboration with Wilkes, he employed traditional research methods using photographs of people to elicit descriptive categories and perceptual judgments on abstract dimensions (Tajfel and Wilkes, 1963b). This was constructed within the previously developed theoretical framework. Of greater interest is the research conducted in collaboration with Sheikh and Gardner (Tajfel *et al.*, 1964c) on social stereotypes. This research was conducted on a visit to Ontario, Canada, and was associated with previous work conducted by Lambert, Sheikh and Gardner.

Tajfel's personal involvement in research on real groups in the social environment and his personal relations with other psychologists introduced him to new methods of research, to new but related ideas and to new research problems. Although this research involved the standard procedure of ratings on semantic differential scales, the 'stimuli' comprised two interviews conducted in front of subjects from different ethnic groups. Furthermore, the experiment attempted to demonstrate that specific individuals of an ethnic group were actually attributed traits which form part of the stereotype concerning that group.

145

This research led to the principles of accentuation of differences and classification to be developed and transformed. The former was renamed 'polarization' in order to mark the tendency to make more extreme judgments towards the poles of the continuous dimensions that have a value significance for the subjects. 'Polarization' further emphasizes the bi-directional nature of these shifts in judgment (Tajfel and Wilkes, 1963a, b). Classification is more precisely defined in terms of minimization and maximization of difference. When judgments are made on dimensions that are associated with a classification (stereotype), in order to distinguish the two groups, differences among stimuli belonging to different groups will be maximized (Tajfel and Wilkes, 1963a; Tajfel et al., 1964c). In this way, the social representations of social perception were accommodated to assimilate and identify distinctive features of the research results.

Other aspects of the research on social stereotypes were not so easily accommodated within the social representations system. Conducting research on perceptual judgments of the social attributes of people highlighted important differences between the two domains. Perceptual judgments of physical attributes are characterized by a high consensus and, furthermore, they can be compared to objective measures. In contrast, perceptual judgments of social attributes display a low consensus or greater subjective variability. Social attributes have different connotations and different subjective values for different individuals. The difficulty of identifying the variables concerned is overcome by employing a method developed by Hastorf, Richardson and Dornbusch (1958) whereby the salience of various descriptive attributes is measured in terms of frequency and sequence. Thus, at this stage, the social representations system is maintained by emphasizing the similarities between perception of the physical and social environments; by locating problems at the methodological level; and by arguing for the integration of sophisticated experimental research with sound theory.

However, research on social stereotypes demonstrating a lack of ethnocentricity within the social representations system was substantially more difficult to assimilate or accommodate. No explanation is given as to why particular dimensions are relevant, or as to why particular ethnic groups do or do not make ethnocentric perceptual judgments. Rather it was necessary to draw on notions external to the social representation of perceptual judgments, in order to maintain the legitimacy of a reductionist stance. For example, polarization only occurred on dimensions which formed part of a group's stereotype and were influenced by the relative socio-economic positions of the different ethnic groups.

Tajfel's collaboration with Lambert and his colleagues and the anomalies presented by their research had a significant influence on the future direction of his work. Lambert and his associates had been concerned with the origins and development of national stereotypes (Lambert and Klineberg, 1959) and with children's views of foreign peoples (Lambert and Klineberg, 1967), addressing issues and employing methodologies which Tajfel was later to adopt in his own work.

III
BEYOND COGNITION IN THE STUDY OF PREJUDICE: DIFFERENTIATION AND INCLUSION

The next phase of Tajfel's intellectual career marks a transition between his early work in psychophysics and his later work on intergroup relations. In the first phase he developed a cognitive perspective in order to address problems within the study of the social perception of the physical environment. By the end of Phase II, he had established the role of value and of categorization in perceptual judgments of both the physical and social environments. Moreover, he had become increasingly concerned with cultural differences and the influence of social groups on perception (Tajfel, 1969b). In the third phase, Tajfel focused explicitly on the phenomenon of prejudice in the context of intergroup relations (Tajfel, 1969a). In 1965, Tajfel edited a volume with Dawson which contained a number of essays on 'the colour problem' written by African, Asian and West Indian students visiting Britain. These essays highlighted, for Tajfel, the very real effects of stereotypes, prejudice and discrimination. For the first time since his initiation into the academic world Tajfel 'stepped out' of the ivory towers to take on board the existence of problems in society at large. It also brought with it an awareness of the relationship between psychology and the social and economic factors in their historical and political context.

His theoretical focus shifts from the technical problems of social perception to the wider social realities and to an analysis of the conflicts apparent in various societies. His writings, here, reveal a passionate concern for intergroup prejudice in its various manifestations, both explicitly and also implicitly in the free use of examples drawn from the 'real world'. These include colonialism and slavery, social class, conflicts in South Africa, and prejudice in Nazi Germany. Moreover, Tajfel's own experience in society as a member of a discriminated-against minority predisposed him towards the pursuit of an understanding of large-scale intergroup relations and of the etiology of intergroup conflict and hostility. These large-scale social problems had by no means diminished since World War II. Confrontation between groups, the emergence of national identities and the existence of minority groups in the minds of members of dominant groups were prevalent in the various societies of the world. These issues had not been totally ignored by psychologists. Well-founded theories of interpersonal behaviour had been extrapolated to encompass large-scale social issues. But these tended to provide purely trait or motivational explanations of stereotypes, prejudice and inter-group relations. They provided neither a means of understanding his own past experience as a Jew nor an understanding of genocide. In particular, they did not explain the large-scale uniformities which characterize prejudice and intergroup relations.

Tajfel's previous work in the field of social perception provided the ground on which to explore the cognitive aspects of these social pheno-mena. However, as it stood, this social representations system required considerable modification and elaboration. For the first time, Tajfel demonstrates his imaginative and creative abilities to integrate diverse strands of his own experience, of social psychological knowledge and of real social issues. What was familiar in one context was unfamiliar in another context. For example, his own and others' experiences of wide-spread prejudice could not be explained purely in terms of the cognitive and evaluative principles of classification and polarization. Nor could it explain the insidious effects of national and cultural stereotypes evident from various studies of children's views of foreigners and children's lack of ethnocentricism in particular social contexts (Clark and Clark, 1947; Goodman, 1964; Vaughan, 1964; Morland, 1966). The assimilation of prejudice in the context of intergroup relations into the social represen-tations system involved the accommodation of both aspects, simul-taneously creating a new understanding of prejudice and transforming the social representations system.

In contrast to the previous phases, social perception of the social environment is differentiated from social perception of the physical environment in order to assimilate the particular attributes of prejudice. Categorizations of the social environment are more rigid and resistant to change. This is explained in terms of the paucity of clear negative feedback from social phenomena. Not only is the social environment more ambiguous, but also the preservation of social categories is self-rewarding as it maintains the associated value differentials between one's own and other groups. The impact of the social context on an indivi-dual's propensity to categorize groups is explained in terms of identi-fication with his or her own group.

While the principle of 'classification' is generalized across domains the changing symbolic significance is stabilized and communicated, at least in part, by providing new labels or terms of reference, first to 'categorization' and then to 'social categorization'. Social categorizations not only simplify and organize the social environment; people are also members of those social categories. This is an important insight that clearly differentiates the physical from the social domain, the implications of which are only gradually made explicit over the next decade. This having been said, their initial exploration leads to the inclusion or incorporation of new dimensions into the social representations system. In particular, attention is given to the assimilation of social values by children, and the identification of a child with his or her own group in a multi-group context. The assimilation of social values by individuals is dependent upon their social context and, in particular, upon the relative positions of groups within the structure of society. Devaluation of the child's own group would arise when there is conflict between the individual's identification with his or her own group and the social values which are prevalent and socially transmitted in society.

If Tajfel had simply applied the cognitive and evaluative principles developed in the field of social perception to the social issue of prejudice, his theoretical analysis might well have stopped here. But Tajfel's intellectual horizons now broadened to address the social issues and real world problems of various societies and he explicitly locates the phenomenon of prejudice within the wider context of large-scale intergroup relations. In order to understand these phenomena, Tajfel has to examine the role of people's beliefs and views about the causes of social events. How do individuals react to specific intergroup situations and how do they come to understand the continual changes in these situations?

These questions led to the inclusion of research literature on causal attribution, a field well established in its own right but yet to be applied to prejudice and intergroup relations. The social representations system is transformed by integrating principles of social categorization and attribution in order to explain why causal attributions are made in terms of the inherent and immutable characteristics of large-scale groups. Explanations in terms of groups not only provide greater simplicity. They also avoid conflict with prevailing values and beliefs and facilitate the preservation of personal integrity and the individual's self-image. In other words, in order to preserve their self-image and to avoid a conflict of values and beliefs, individuals will find or create explanations for social events in terms of the relations between groups.

In this instance transformations in the social representations system were directed not so much by interpersonal communication and interaction or direct collaboration within the scientific community, but by the diffusion and assimilation of research and theoretical ideas through the medium of academic publications. Tajfel draws on the work of others within the same field of study as well as developing links among related fields in his bid to address the issues and problems associated with large-scale prejudice. Allport (1954), among others, had elaborated extensively on the role of stereotypes in simplifying and ordering the social environment. Bruner (Bruner, Postman and Rodrigues, 1951) and the 'New Look' had emphasized the greater ambiguity in the perception of people and social situations. Piaget had worked extensively on the cognitive process of assimilation. Furthermore, there was a growing theoretical belief in social psychology of the pivotal role played by personal consistency and the individual's self-image (Sherif and Sherif, 1969). Finally, attribution theory provided much of the material for conceptualizing the role of belief systems in intergroup relations. In this way, the perspective offered by the social representations system is broadened and developed.

This transformation of the social representations system provided a novel and unfamiliar view of prejudice. Prejudice and intergroup behaviour were no longer simply due to an individual's motivations, either in terms of the unconscious or in terms of animal instincts and the evolutionary past of the species. Prejudice and intergroup behaviour can be conceived as the products of rational and cognitive processes, influenced by the concepts, values and beliefs held by individuals and shared within a particular group or society at a given historical time.

Tajfel indicates and emphasizes the significance of his own contribution by explicitly challenging and rejecting the accepted explanations of prejudice founded in a 'blood and guts' model of social phenomena. By propounding an alternative cognitive perspective he is forced to confront the conventions of the field. While a rational model of man had been adopted in individual psychology its adoption in social psychology had to be justified. The legitimacy of cognitive explanations of large-scale social phenomena is justified by its use in anthropology and other fields of psychology. Interest in the cognitive aspects of various psychological and social psychological phenomena had come to dominate the general perspective in the discipline (Gardner, 1985). Its application in the context of intergroup relations is justified in terms of both its scientific credibility and its use in social action. Not only is a cognitive explanation more parsimonious and testable than a motivational account but also the examination of people's cognitions and beliefs is far more promising in planning any form of social change than attempting to alter their motives.

His disenchantment with purely motivational and individualistic accounts, and his alacritous endeavour to address the cognitive aspects of large-scale social phenomena, arose from a firm belief that social psychology could offer something positive to society and from a desire to remain true to the principles of social psychology while simultaneously remaining true to his own experiences (and those of others) in social life. Significantly, his interest in politics and social change brought him to consider the possible role of institutional and social policy in alleviating intergroup conflict and discrimination. This shift in perspective did not occur in a social vacuum. The constraints of convention were ameliorated, at least in part, by Tajfel's rising status in the field of social psychology and a change of working environment.

IV
NATIONAL AND SOCIAL IDENTITIES: THE TRANSITION TO A NEW PERSPECTIVE

In 1968, Tajfel was appointed Professor of Social Psychology in the Department of Psychology, University of Bristol. By this time, his reputation was well established. He had published a series of articles in the field of social perception which had advanced the understanding of cognitive processes and established a theory of social judgment which had initiated and stimulated a whole field of research. His standing in the field is confirmed, furthermore, by the fact that he was asked to produce the review for the *Handbook of Social Psychology* on 'Social and cultural factors in perception' (Tajfel, 1969b). This gave Tajfel a new-found freedom to address a range of issues and gradually to develop a more explicitly social perspective. However, it is highly unlikely that this, alone, could have radically transformed his whole approach. Two related events were also highly significant: these were the 'crisis' in social psychology and the establishment of the European Association of Experimental Social Psychology. The transformation of Tajfel's thinking, the broader crisis in social psychology and the origins and characteristics of the European Association were all part and parcel of the same general movement in social psychology.

In the post-World War II period, European social psychology was dominated by the orientation, research problems, methods and theories developed and sustained in the United States of America. Although European countries had their own distinctive schools of psychology, the national and linguistic barriers severely restricted communication and cooperation within Europe. As a consequence, there was often a greater association with what was going on in American social psychology than with developments in neighbouring countries within Europe.

It was not until the early 1960s that cooperative attempts by both American and European social psychologists led to the establishment of a European 'centre' for the development of social psychology. Those directly involved included L. Festinger, Keekebakker, J. Lanzetta, S. Moscovici, M. Mulder, R. Pages, R. Rommetveit, H. Tajfel and J. Thibaut. With funding from the American SSRC and the Ford Foundation a series of 'unofficial meetings', exchange visits, seminars, summer schools and plenary conferences were organized all over Europe. These led to, and were facilitated by, the establishment of the European Association for Experimental Social Psychology in 1966. The principle aim of the association was

> to encourage and investigate communication in Europe, to create a milieu of social psychologists which would become a breeding ground for more research, more training and more inventiveness in what was being done.
>
> (Tajfel, 1972c: 309)

The Association was not simply an organization: it involved the progressive creation of an actively interacting community of people; the creation of mutual contacts; an awareness of an intellectual basis for social psychology in Europe; and the creation of new cross-currents of thought and controversy that stimulated a variety of new research developments. It was, in effect, a European community of social psychologists, however diverse in its social and political perspectives.

Tajfel was a highly prominent figure in this European Association and expended a great deal of energy in encouraging and controlling its development. Eminently well qualified, given his European background, his facility with several European languages, and his prior experience in international cooperation, he was involved from its inception and he continued to play an extremely active role until his death. It was this European Association with which Tajfel identified, providing a network of friendships and communications, both personal and intellectual. Furthermore, the transformation of his own outlook and the emergence of a new perspective in social psychology was co-terminous with the emergence of a European social psychology community.

One of the earliest research programmes undertaken by this community was an international study of the development of national stereotypes and attitudes in children. While the research was coordinated by Tajfel it involved a series of studies conducted in England, Scotland,

Belgium, Italy, Austria and Israel and the collaboration of no less than ten other European psychologists including N.C. Barbiero, J.D. Campbell, G. Jahoda, J. Jaspars, N.B. Johnson, M.B. Middleton, C. Nemeth, Y. Rim, M.D. Simon and J.P. van der Geer (Tajfel and Jahoda, 1966; Tajfel *et al.*, 1970, 1972). The synergy of these scientists required good communication and convergence of interests which were interdependent with the growing awareness of a European community of social psychologists and the establishment of the European Association. It also required a common theoretical framework. The principles of value and categorization were translated into the conventional language of the three component model of attitudes, being consistently referred to as the affective and cognitive components respectively. The primary focus of the research was to examine the developmental relationship between the affective and cognitive components in large-scale intergroup relations. Significantly, the research findings presented a number of anomalies, findings that were unfamiliar or difficult to explain within the theoretical framework itself.

This stimulated the expansion and reformulation of the social representations system as a whole. Firstly, in general, consensual preferences for one's own nation develop *before* children possess any detailed knowledge about other nations or countries. Children differentiate between nations on the basis of the countries' names (nominal realism) in the absence of physical or behavioural cues. Furthermore, even though evaluative differentials tended to decrease with age, preferences for one's own nation continued to be found in older children. Tajfel and his collaborators suggest that the early intervention of value judgments results in a lack of cognitive empathy with other large-scale groups. These research findings highlighted the essential role of assimilation, social influence and the mass media of communication. Children assimilated the social and cultural values prevailing in their own societies.

Secondly, differences among cultures in the relationship between the cognitive and affective components of attitudes were found. With the plurality of nations and cultures Europe provided an ideal context for a cross-cultural study of national attitudes. However, the cross-cultural differences to emerge could not be explained within the three-component model of attitudes. It was necessary also to consider the social context as it played a significant role in the development of national attitudes and intergroup relations.

Thirdly, unexpected results in Louvain and Glasgow demanded post-hoc explanation. In Louvain it was found that preference for one's own nation increased with age. This was explained in terms of the city's bi-nationality (Belgian and Flemish), influencing the development of both affective and cognitive components. In Glasgow children showed no preference for their own nationality. Devaluation of the ingroup is often found in minority or underprivileged groups but it is surprising here, where the Scots are not a minority and there was no overt conflict between the English and Scottish. In both cases, the results indicate children's high degree of sensitivity to their social context and to the value systems of their societies and to subtle aspects of social influence.

Many of the emergent problems and questions remained unanswered at this stage. It was still necessary to explain children's sensitivity to the social context and the variations across cultures; to understand the role of preferential differentiations in intergroup relations; and to explain the devaluation of one's own group in situations where there was no overt conflict. These were findings in search of a theory. While the research is shaped by the theoretical framework it also confronts the framework with specific problems. Research is not purely a rhetorical device for justifying theoretical claims but, rather, the observation of and inter-action with the environment or object of study constitutes an essential component in the evolution and construction of social representations. The discovery of anomalies challenges central components of the social representations system or highlights the significance of factors which lie at its periphery. In either case, the social representations system must be adapted to accommodate the object of study.

The development of national attitudes could not be explained in purely cognitive terms, demanding the inclusion of the social context and the assimilation of social values. However, the ensuing development of the social representations system was not presented in the research reports themselves. Rather, it is only in Tajfel's chapter entitled 'The formation of national attitudes: a social-psychological perspective' (Tajfel, 1969c) that the ideas were properly developed. While neither the research nor the chapter received much public acclaim, I believe it to be of great significance in the development of the social representations system. New questions were asked, be they implicit at the time, about the social psychological processes involved in large-scale intergroup conflict (Tajfel, 1981a) and many of the ideas developed in Phase VI were first introduced into the social repre-sentations system at this stage. Furthermore, its lack of recognition has resulted in an overemphasis on the minimal group experiments (Phase V) which are frequently given an overstated significance as the foundation for the theory of intergroup relations (social identity theory).

Encouraged by his general interest in politics, cultural history and social movements, Tajfel is liberated from the constraints of conventional perspectives in social psychology. By drawing on diverse readings in history, political science, anthropology and sociology he is able to elaborate and communicate an alternative approach to large-scale social phenomena within social psychology. Firstly, he draws together various ideas from diverse disciplines to construct the following definition of nationalism, which he later adapted to define groups:

> nationalism is an attitude displayed by a body of people who are a nation because they feel that they are a nation. Nationalism as an attitude implies some conception of a nation of which one is a member; an emotional significance given to that membership; and the sharing of these conceptual and emotional identifications by large masses of people.
>
> (Tajfel, 1969c: 141)

Secondly, Tajfel began to make explicit his vision of social psychology by differentiating it from the other social sciences. Studies of nationalism in other social sciences had examined its historical determinants, its role as a causal factor in political action and the connection between various conditions for, and characteristics of, political movements. All these writings, in one form or another, referred to nationalism as an attitude shared by large masses of individuals, but remained highly speculative as to the social and psychological processes by which individuals came to identify with national groups. It was left to social psychologists to provide a description of these features; to consider the psychological functions of the cognitive and emotional components of nationalism in relation to their contextual social variables; and to examine the psychological and social pressures responsible for their widespread diffusion into society. Tajfel, more than any other social psychologist, took up this challenge. But the challenge was not set by psychologists; it was set by social scientists in general and by a desire, on his own part, to understand the large-scale social processes that had dominated his own life and which, more than ever before, were such a prominent feature of contemporary society.

Thirdly, this gave Tajfel an alternative perspective from which to construct a critique of traditional psychological approaches to the topic; to clarify outstanding issues or questions and to identify useful and less useful concepts in the foundation of a new account of large-scale social phenomena. In this way social psychology as a scientific discipline became a topic of concern in its own right. Although the social representation of social psychology was always on the periphery, differentiation from other social sciences and conflicts within social psychology brought it to the fore. As such, it came to have a major influence on the structure and integration of the social representations system as a whole. The transformations involve a dynamic interplay between the new and the old, between an emerging perspective and the established view, between accommodation of tradition and assimilation of innovation. At any point in the construction of Tajfel's theory of intergroup relations, the transformation of social representations involves the dynamic inter-dependence of stability and change in the course of communication and interaction. This is demonstrated by the dynamics of the social representations system in Phase IV.

Biological and pseudo-biological approaches, which explain an individual's national affiliation in terms of instinct or inheritance, could be rapidly dismissed as neither tended to be taken very seriously by the academic community. Theories of personality functioning in relation to social structure presented more of a problem. Founded on the work of Freud, psychodynamics continued to be used by social scientists and to be developed by psychologists in an attempt to explain large-scale social phenomena. This includes a vast literature on national character (e.g. Erkison, 1953) used by political scientists (e.g. Pye, 1961, 1962; Greenstein, 1965), the work of Adorno et al. (1950) on the authoritarian personality and Campbell and LeVine's research (1961) on ethno-centrism. The main problem with these theories is that they assume, rather than explain, cultural uniformity and they are too dependent upon outgroup hostility as the cause of social affiliation. Theories arising from small group research similarly adopted the orthodox position whereby nationalism or ingroup affiliation arises as a result of outgroup hostility. In this case, the latter results from an individual's perception of a threat which applies directly to him or her and which is shared by other members of the group.

Perhaps the most famous study in this field is Sherif's Robbers' Cave Experiment (Sherif et al., 1961; Sherif 1966). Without going into too much detail, this experimental field study of intergroup relations created real ethnocentrism, real stereotypes and real hostility between two 'camps' of eleven-year-old boys on a three-week summer camp. Group affiliation was crucially intensified in the second week when the two groups were brought into direct competition with each other. However, even during the first week of the study, independent group activities resulted in the formation of group affiliations. Tajfel suggested that groups with a long history of common goals, activities, norms, distinctive patterns of behaviour and sets of values developed and shared for a long time, may achieve strong group affiliation without any intervention of acute conflict with an outgroup. Tajfel was not the only one to criticize these experimental studies. Others, such as Deutsch (1966), noted how the absence of any long-term unifying processes and a stable starting point of group integration created the need for outgroup hostility and artificially supported the 'crisis' version of nationalism. Furthermore, studies by Pettigrew *et al.* (1958) and Campbell (1965), as well as the international studies on the development of national attitudes in children, showed that national identification was not limited to ethnocentrism or to situations of intergroup conflict.

While rejecting certain aspects of Sherif's approach, his work on intergroup relations provided the background and legitimization for Tajfel's own work on intergroup relations within social psychology. Sherif and Sherif (e.g. Sherif and Sherif, 1953, 1969; Sherif and Wilson, 1953) had devoted much of their academic careers to the problems of intergroup relations and social change. They were, in effect, well ahead of Tajfel in claiming this field to be part of the discipline of social psychology. Moreover, Tajfel adopts Sherif's definition of intergroup behaviour and the role of identification.

> whenever individuals belonging to one group interact, culturally or individually, with another group or its members in terms of their group identification, we have an instance of intergroup behaviour.
>
> (Sherif, 1966: 12)

Tajfel's approach differed in that he was directly concerned with large-scale social phenomena and that he did not accept the high profile given to intergroup conflict and hostility. The traditional focus on motivational factors and outgroup hostility, which intensify group affiliations, had resulted in an ignorance of previously existing structures of beliefs and systems of values (cognition and preferences) in the creation of large-scale group affiliations. The significance of belief systems in intergroup relations was evident to Tajfel from his own experience as a Jew in pre-war Poland and from his broad reading in social history and political movements of others' experiences. Their significance was also evident to Tajfel from research in social psychology on ethnocentricity and the development of national attitudes. The study of nationalism forced Tajfel to take his analysis beyond the individual cognitive mechanisms that had dominated his earlier work. Furthermore, it gave him the opportunity to weld his various interests together. In order to explain children's sensitivity to their social context, the assimilation of social values and the devaluation of one's own group in situations which lacked overt conflict it was necessary to include the diffusion of belief systems and social values and the patterns of social communication and social influence. Once again this had not been ignored by other social psychologists but nor had they been applied to intergroup relations.

There was a vast literature on social influences in small group research which had identified normative (motivational) and informational (cognitive) sets of factors. Festinger's theory of social comparison processes (1954) provided a synthesis of these factors centring on 'the drive for self-evaluation'. Similarly, Tajfel draws on the work of Deutsch (1966) on social communication, Fishman (1968) on linguistic categories, and Barbichon and Moscovici (1965) on simplification and applies it directly to the large-scale phenomena of national attitudes. By so doing he is able to address not only the cognitive and affective components of national attitudes but also the formation of relevant belief and value systems through the process of social influence and identification. In particular, it is here that Tajfel first introduces the notion of social identity. Depending upon the systems of social communication and the processes of social influence, an individual acquires a national social identity by making evaluative social comparisons between social or national categories. Furthermore, in contrast to social perception *per se*, in the context of intergroup relations, differences between groups or nations are not only perceived, accentuated or generalized but also created or eliminated.

By assimilating ideas developed in related fields of study Tajfel is able to create a new conception and understanding of the phenomena being studied. The ideas by no means represent, at this stage, a coherent social representation but they set the agenda and provide the foundation for a comprehensive theory of intergroup relations. Such transformations take time. A fully fledged theory of intergroup relations is not constructed as soon as the principles of social perception are applied to prejudice and national attitudes. It takes time for the problems or conflicts between the different social representations within the system to emerge and then to be made explicit. And it takes time to assimilate related ideas and accommodate the established framework. This involves not simply the discovery and identification of links between the social representations or the inclusion of novel ideas into the social representations system but also the creative integration and transformation of related components within the system.

V

SOCIAL CATEGORIZATION AND INTERGROUP BEHAVIOUR: THE EMERGENCE OF ANOMALIES

The collaborative research on the development of national attitudes in children and Tajfel's theoretical analysis of nationalism which, as we have just seen, drew on a wide literature in the social sciences, both posed the same question. What factors, other than intergroup conflict, would produce intergroup discrimination? Research on the developmental relationship between the cognitive and affective components of attitudes suggested that categorization (nominal realism) and value (preferences) might be sufficient to produce intergroup differentiation in situations where there was no overt conflict. However, the nature of these studies meant that many other variables were also involved in shaping the children's responses, not least the historical context of the relations between the relevant groups. It was still necessary to establish the base-line conditions leading to a differentiation between groups. In some respects this problem had already been addressed in the experimental investigations of Rabbie and his associates (Rabbie and Wilkens, 1968; Rabbie and Horwitz, 1969; Rabbie and Wilkens, 1971). This European group of researchers had focused their investigations on social influence and interdependence, suggesting that the mere anticipation of future interaction between and within groups was sufficient to produce intergroup discrimination.

In contrast, Tajfel (1970a, 1978c), together with Flament, Billig and Bundy (Tajfel et al., 1971), employed an innovative experimental design that either controlled for or eliminated all variables other than social categorization and value. On the basis of their theoretical framework, in the initial experiments they hypothesized that social categorization, on its own, would not produce intergroup discrimination. Only in situations where the categorization was evaluative would intergroup discrimination occur. To their surprise, it was found that subjects discriminated in favour of the ingroup in both conditions and that there was no significant difference between the two. That is, value did not need to be associated with the categories in order to create intergroup discrimination. Further experiments confirmed that social categorization on its own was sufficient to produce intergroup discrimination. This was true even when groups were established purportedly on such irrelevant grounds as subjects' preferences for paintings by two modern painters (Tajfel et al., 1971) or alternatively on the toss of a coin. Subjects acted in favour of their own group in situations where there was no benefit to the individual. Furthermore, their choices tended towards maximum differentiation between the ingroup and the outgroup even at the cost of forfeiting maximum gain for the ingroup. Subjects' behaviour could not be explained purely in terms of economic gain.

How were these experimental results to be accommodated by the social representations system? In some senses, the initial explanations abandoned the progressive expansion of the social representations system that had been achieved by integrating relevant work both from psychology (Phase III) and from related disciplines (Phase IV). The experimental investigations (Phase V) had focused attention on relatively narrow and specific research questions that addressed only a subsection of the system taken as a whole. Furthermore, the research findings presented anomalies that had arisen through the direct interaction of scientists with the object of study. This led to a shift in emphasis or a restructuring of the social representations system. Greater emphasis was given now to social categorization combined with a withdrawal from 'value' as a distinct theoretical principle in understanding intergroup relations. Tajfel *et al.* (1971) argued that social categorization, whereby the social environment is categorized in terms of social criteria, is inherent in all intergroup behaviour, involving divisions between ingroups and outgroups. This guides social action in situations where alternative guidelines for actions are unclear.

However, it was still puzzling as to why social categorization alone should produce intergroup discrimination. Surprisingly, the concepts of personal integrity, social comparison and social identity that had been introduced into the social representations system during the study of the cognitive aspects of prejudice and the development of national attitudes, were not applied to this problem. Rather, Tajfel and his colleagues re-endorse the social reality which is expressed in the conventions of social psychological theory and research. This applies to the problems investigated, the research conducted and the interpretation of results. The reasons for this are not entirely clear but a combination of factors may be suggested.

Firstly, value and the assimilation of value systems had been a significant element of the social representations system but the experiments showed that value associated with a social category was not a necessary condition for intergroup discrimination. This inevitably created a gap between theory and research which proved difficult to bridge. Secondly, the experimental research followed the methodological conventions, with specific hypotheses and rigorously controlled conditions. As a consequence, factors associated with the social context that had previously emerged as significant were purposefully eliminated. By concentrating on the minimal conditions sufficient to produce intergroup discrimination the research was intentionally acultural and ahistorical. This focused attention solely on the cognitive processes (i.e. social categorization) of individuals in group situations. Thirdly, the unexpected results required a clear and definite response: Tajfel's theoretical ideas were not, as yet, well structured or integrated and would not have provided a convincing explanation. What was needed was a widely accepted conceptual framework with explanatory power that would simultaneously provide a context for the research and highlight the novelty of the results. Sherif's work on intergroup relations and the normative and informational aspects of social norms from small group research provided just such a context. Tajfel and his colleagues proposed a generic group norm whereby subjects classified the social situation of the experiment as one in which social categorization ought to lead to intergroup discrimination. In some respects this explanation, in terms of social norms, reintroduces the social context into the social representations system despite the fact that it was not a feature of the research design or experimental hypotheses.

Within the community of social psychologists the proposed explanation was unlikely to be accepted without question. Rather, the transformation of social representations involves negotiation and justification; alternative interpretations of the results need to be proposed, challenged and dismissed. Firstly, in order to explain the particular pattern of subjects' choices a social norm of fairness was also proposed, mitigating against extreme cases of differentiation. Secondly, Tajfel *et al.* (1971) argued that Rabbie and his associates had failed to create a group in their control condition. Thirdly, they argued that alternative interpretations of the results were inadequate. These included subjects responding in accordance with experimenters' expectations (experimenter effect); subjects' expectations of reciprocity; or anticipation of future interaction between the groups. In each case, it would still be necessary to construct an explanation of subjects' expectations. Fourthly, further experiments were conducted that both replicated the original results (e.g. Deutsch *et al.*, 1971; Doise and Sinclair, 1973) and negated alternative explanations in terms of perceived similarity or familiarity among group members (e.g. Doise *et al.*, 1971; Billig and Tajfel, 1973; Tajfel and Billig, 1974). This was by no means an end to the debate. Rather, the minimal conditions in which groups will discriminate against each other and the theoretical explanation of intergroup differentiation became a burgeoning field of research and a topic of continued theoretical controversy. Frequent use of the experimental design gave rise to the name 'minimal group paradigm'. Similarly the label 'ingroup favouritism' indicated both the differentiation between groups and its direction.

While social categorization and social norms continued to be used as an explanation for some time it was soon realized that it left some important questions unanswered. As Tajfel himself reflected, 'Rather than providing answers to certain crucial problems of intergroup behaviour, they highlighted some crucial questions and suggested directions of future theorizing and research.' (Tajfel, 1978b: 10). Why should subjects choose the social norm of grouping in this particular situation in preference to any other? What are the psychological processes involved in intergroup discrimination on the basis of social categorization? Furthermore, it ignored the questions raised by the previous research and that of others on nationalism and ethnocentricity. How are variations across cultures and the impact of the social context on personal preferences to be explained? What is the role of preferences and of differential evaluations in a situation of real intergroup conflict? Why do people devalue their own group in relation to other groups, even in situations where there is no obvious conflict?

Solutions to these problems emerge slowly in the form of an elaborate and comprehensive theory of intergroup relations. An initial outline of these developments was already in evidence by 1969, in both *The Cognitive Aspects of Prejudice* and Tajfel's theoretical chapter on *The Formation of National Attitudes*. The research findings of Phases IV and V, as well as a desire to understand conflicts between large-scale groups in society, provided the stimulus for and directed the evolution of this social representations system. However, these developments did not occur 'overnight'. It was only through the painstaking theoretical work undertaken during the early period of Phase VI that the theory of intergroup relations in all its complexity came to be established by 1978 (Tajfel, 1978a). Furthermore, it presented a new perspective in social psychology, one which was to challenge the conventional boundaries of the discipline.

VI
A NEW PERSPECTIVE IN SOCIAL PSYCHOLOGY

A theory of intergroup relations: a collaborative affair

The transformation of social representations systems, the construction of a theory of intergroup relations and the conduct of research is a collaborative enterprise founded in the interdependence of people, their environment and their culture. This is nowhere more evident than in the explicit elaboration of a novel and exciting perspective in social psychology: a perspective that gave primacy neither to the individual nor to society; that integrated strands of experience, ideas and purposeful investigations; that created a coherent and extensive system of understanding.

The centre of activity for these innovations was at Bristol University where Tajfel was, without question, a prominent figure: a powerful personality who both energized and directed the research activities of others. Here there was a group of scientists who worked together for several years on the same problems: who designed, constructed and interpreted research, exchanged ideas and discussed or debated relevant issues. As Tajfel commented in the Preface to the 1978 volume:

> it is very difficult (and also quite unimportant) to know at the end who was the initial 'owner' of one idea or another, who has been the first to formulate a useful hypothesis, or to push us in a new direction.
>
> (Tajfel, 1978a: vii, parentheses in original)

Tajfel had moved to Bristol in 1968. He was shortly joined by a group of young and enthusiastic researchers including Michael Billig and Dick Eiser and later Jonathan Turner and Glynis Breakwell, all of whom were initially PhD students under his supervision and went on to become prominent social psychologists in their own right. Tajfel took the lead in creating an environment that simultaneously focused and coordinated research and debate without imposing obtrusive restrictions. The focus was provided by an explicitly anti-individualistic approach that integrated theory and research in order to develop a social psychology that addressed important social issues in modern society. The freedom was created by encouraging debate and disagreement, cross-disciplinary reading and diverse research programmes.

In 1974 Tajfel submitted a successful research proposal on 'Social identity, social categorization and social comparison in intergroup behaviour' to the Social Science Research Council (SSRC). The research grant was of paramount importance. Under the leadership of Tajfel, it provided the finances for a comprehensive research programme, attracting other psychologists to Bristol, and supporting exchange visits and conferences in Europe. In particular, Rupert Brown, originally as a PhD student, Howard Giles, a psychologist, and later on Jennifer Williams, joined the team. Others who were actively involved in research meetings and discussions included Anthony Agathangelou, Richard Bourhis, Brian Caddick, Fred Ross, Suzanne Skevington and Philip Smith, with Donald Tyler from Canada and Graham Vaughan from Auckland, who were long-term visitors. The financial support and involvement of a relatively large number of people in one place meant that research efforts could be both coordinated and diverse. Experimental research was complemented by field studies while Giles and Bourhis applied the same theoretical principles to language and linguistic differentiation.

Furthermore, the nucleus of researchers in Bristol developed strong links with other European centres of research. Firstly, research teams in Paris and Geneva were working on closely related issues. While these centres had their own history of development and their own distinctive style of research and theoretical work, there were many overlaps. Moscovici and Paicheler (Paris) had been working on processes of identification; Lemaine, Kastersten and Personnaz (Paris) were working on social differentiation; and Deschamps, Doise and Meyer (Geneva) continued to work on social categorization and accentuation in inter-group relations. Secondly, with the administrative support and funding offered by the Fondation de la Maison des Sciences de l'Homme together with the SSRC, it was possible to develop working relationships with others in Europe. Tajfel spent some time at the Ecole des Hautes Etudes en Sciences Sociales in Paris, where he worked on and discussed his ideas with Moscovici and others. Ties with The Netherlands were established in some joint research on status differences, comparative relevance and intergroup relations by Ad van Krippenberg, John van de Geer and Henri Tajfel. Similarly, brief exchange visits between Bristol (England), Paris (France), Geneva (Switzerland) and Gronigen (The Netherlands) and three research conferences in Paris and Bristol, encouraged and facilitated the exploration of new ideas and new research departures.

The psychological processes: restructuring established principles

Each person has his or her own story but here I shall concentrate on Turner's contribution, which was to prove the most significant in the early stages of developing a social psychology of intergroup relations. Turner joined the research group at Bristol after the minimal group experiments had been completed, but quickly demonstrated a keen ability to ask precise and direct questions about the processes involved. Embarking on his PhD (1975) on social categorization and social com-parison in intergroup relations, Turner was looking for something to do and designed a series of experiments that, firstly, varied the salience of the group and, secondly, allowed individuals to respond not only by distri-buting money or 'points' between other ingroup members and outgroup members but also directly to self versus an anonymous 'other'. This was supplemented by a questionnaire designed to find out how subjects perceived their choices in the experimental situation.

The research results were to lead to important developments in the social representations system as they could not be explained purely in terms of social categorization and a generic group norm. Not all conditions led to intergroup differentiations. In some conditions, individuals acted in terms of self as opposed to their group membership. In other conditions, subjects displayed a balance between individual gain and ingroup gain. This showed that perception of an ingroup–outgroup dichotomy does not alone result in intergroup discrimination: social categorization *per se* does not promote social conflict. Rather, it depends upon a process of identification with one's own group as a means of self-expression.

This led to the whole issue of intergroup discrimination within a minimal group context being reappraised (Tajfel, 1974a, b, 1978d; Tajfel and Turner, 1979). The experimental research conducted at Bristol served as a point of departure for new insights and new directions for an understanding of intergroup relations. Most significantly, the influence of social norms and social values came to be expressed in terms that were directly relevant to the individual. This involved four interdependent forms of transformation in the system of social representations. Firstly, drawing on the ideas that had been developed previously in Phases III and IV, a motivational element at the individual level was reintroduced into the system and integrated with the other psychological processes. A subject's behaviour was assumed to be an expression of his or her ubiquitous tendency towards self-evaluation (Festinger, 1954) and self-definition. Social categorizations not only provide a system for organizing and simplifying the social environment, they also provide a system of orientation in which individuals locate and define themselves. Once denied the opportunity to evaluate or define themselves as individuals they will do so as members of their group. Social categorizations within the experimental set-up are comparable to the complex network of groupings in society. The problem of self-definition within society underlies the process of identification with a group or social category.

Within the social representations system the construction of an individual's self-image through group membership becomes a central tenet. This is expressed in terms of 'social identity', an identity derived from an individual's attempt to find, create and define his or her place in society in terms of group memberships and intergroup relations. While the role of social categorization had been long established, the process of social identity was constructed from the notions of group identification and self-image. Furthermore, the integration of social categorization and social identity gave greater prominence to the process of social comparison. Social comparison is the comparative principle which links social categorization with social identity. An individual's self-evaluations and self-definitions made in terms of group memberships (social identity) only acquire meaning in relation to, or in comparison with, other groups or social categories.

The interrelated psychological processes of social categorization, social identity and social comparison provide an integrated explanation of why individuals differentiate between their own group and other groups. Individuals acting in terms of their own group or social category will discriminate against the other group. This either maintains or creates a differentiation between their own group and other groups so that social comparisons afford a positive social identity. This set of interrelated principles also integrates the cognitive and affective components in the development of national attitudes and begins to explain children's sensitivity to their social context. It specifies the psychological motivation for and the processes by which intergroup relations are established and maintained.

Secondly, it might appear that this restructuring of the social representations system abandons the notion of value completely. This is not the case. Value still plays a prominent, if more diffuse, role. Value differentials are associated with categorizations of the social environment; evaluations are made through the process of social comparisons; and a positive social identity is derived from the value significance of the individual's membership of various groups and his or her psychological distinctiveness. All three aspects relate directly to the system of social values in society. Individuals, as members of a group, will attempt to claim as their own those characteristics which are valued positively by society. These transformations involved restructuring elements previously established within the social representations system.

Thirdly, the application of pre-established ideas such as social comparison theory to intergroup relations and their accommodation into the social representations system required modifications of those ideas being assimilated. In particular, it was necessary for Tajfel to take issue with some of the assumptions and restrictions adopted by Festinger in association with this comparative principle. Festinger maintains that intergroup comparisons may be made on a fantasy level, but rarely in reality. Furthermore, he limits the employment of social comparison processes to situations in which objective, non-social means of comparison are not available and focuses his discussion on individuals comparing themselves with other individuals in terms of their similarities. Challenging these assumptions, Tajfel argued that social comparisons are frequently made between groups and have very real consequences. Objectivity depends upon a high social consensus concerning the nature of phenomena such that social comparisons between groups will be made whenever there is an awareness of alternative definitions and evaluations. Furthermore, in the context of intergroup relations, comparisons are made in terms of the differences rather than the similarities between groups.

Fourthly, within the social representations system the developing theoretical framework could also be differentiated from Sherif's realistic group conflict theory. In his first article, Turner (1975) made clear the distinction between social competition and economic or realistic competition, simultaneously locating and differentiating their theory within the social psychology of intergroup relations. By using abstract dimensions of evaluation for social comparisons, as opposed to monetary rewards, Turner showed that intergroup differentiations were not dependent upon a conflict of group interests over monetary rewards, but were dependent on an individual's identification with a group. The main point of departure from Sherif's perspective on intergroup relations was that identification with a group (group affiliation) occurs *prior* to any intergroup conflict. That is, an individual's sense of belonging to a group is acquired prior to the perception of threat or competition with an outgroup. The centrality of this process is expressed in the concept of social identity.

The crisis in social psychology: constructing a future

While these transformations were important in the development of a theory of intergroup relations they were not, perhaps, the most significant in the development of a new perspective in social psychology. This rested in Tajfel's firm belief that if social psychology was to have any impact on the social issues confronting society its theories must take into account and be applicable to the social realities of the contemporary world. In his chapter entitled 'Experiments in a vacuum' Tajfel was highly critical of experimenters who extrapolated from the behaviour of subjects in a laboratory context to social conduct in natural settings without an examination of the social context (Tajfel, 1972a). This included modelling experiments in Game Theory; simulation experiments, such as Sherif's, on the emergence of social norms (autokinetic effect); and his *own* experiments on social judgment (Phase II). Others have even argued that the minimal group paradigm experiments themselves failed to examine the social context. It was left to his students and collaborators to design and conduct research which examined the social context of social behaviour and intergroup relations. Tajfel now argued that experimental situations should be viewed as caricatures of or hints about social reality. He was intolerant of research without theory and critical of pure experimentation. Good experimental research depends upon both good theory and good *cultural analysis*.

By 1972 Tajfel was arguing vociferously for a social psychology that went beyond the psychological processes of inter-individual behaviour to examine their interrelations with the social conditions of society. The discipline should adopt a level of enquiry and explanation that attempts to determine the relationship between the wider social and cultural context and certain 'basic' psychological processes which shape the individual's understanding of, and actions in, his or her social environment.

> Social psychology can and must include in its theoretical and research preoccupations a direct concern with the relationship between human psychological functioning and the large-scale social processes and events which shape this functioning and are shaped by it.
>
> (Tajfel, 1981a: 7)

Tajfel did not achieve this change of perspective in an intellectual and social vacuum. While an individual's creative abilities are essential to the transformation and evolution of social representations they are also dependent upon the social milieu of which the individual is a part. Firstly, within the community of social psychologists, widespread dissatisfaction with their achievements gave rise to a crisis in the discipline. Secondly, it is likely that this crisis was related to developments in other disciplines and social movements in society as a whole. Thirdly, Tajfel was intimately involved with the European Association of Experimental Psychology which provided a social and intellectual context for public debate over the central issues of the crisis. The emergence of a new perspective was dependent upon Tajfel's location within this context: his work is inseparable from the people that surrounded him and the culture in which he was embedded. It is also inseparable from his own identity, both as an experimental social psychologist and as an emigré Jew, passionately concerned about large-scale social conflict.

It is difficult to define and identify the various elements in the crisis. Frequently, it is referred to in inverted commas, denoting some uncertainty as to what it actually was, but also a common awareness of its existence. This is not the place to explore the origins and development of this crisis but it is worth reviewing some of its more salient characteristics. Not least of these was the lack of confidence within the community as to the validity and social relevance of various endeavours. Research and theorizing were by no means paralysed but a considerable number of publications, both books and articles, posed questions about methodology and challenged the theoretical and philosophical assumptions governing research in social psychology. There was widespread debate regarding what social psychology was, or should be, about. Moreover, there was a common consensus that such debate was legitimate.

As early as 1959, Koch had expressed considerable dissatisfaction with the achievements of psychology in his epilogue to *Psychology: A study of a science*. Nowhere was this more severely felt than in social psychology. Problems with the use of experimental methodology first emerged into public awareness with the publication of Orne's paper on demand characteristics (1962) and Rosenthal's book on the experimenter effect (1966). The initial response focused on methodology with the design of unobtrusive measures and non-reactive research methods (e.g. Webb *et al.*, 1966). However, continued concern with the external validity and the triviality of much experimental research in both laboratory and field settings, as well as questions regarding the ethics of social research, shifted the focus of doubt to the whole 'enterprise' of social psychology (e.g. Ring, 1967; Kelman, 1968; Smith, 1972).

Dissatisfaction with a positivistic science was expressed in many critiques of and blueprints for social psychology, especially in Europe. These addressed not only issues of methodology but also the substance of social psychology; its problems and theories, its inherent values, its models of human kind and its style of explanation (Mixon, 1972; Harré and Secord, 1972; Israel and Tajfel, 1972; Gergen, 1973; Elms, 1975; Shotter, 1975; Gauld and Shotter, 1977; Stroebe, 1979, etc.). That this represented a major shift is evidenced by books such as *Reconstructing Social Psychology* (Armistead, 1974) and *Social Psychology in Transition* (Strickland *et al.*, 1976a).

It is likely that the 'crisis' within the community of social psychologists was associated with social movements in society and with developments in other disciplines. Kuhn's 1962 thesis on *The Structure of Scientific Revolutions* and other critiques of positivistic and hypothetico-deductive philosophies of science have had, no doubt, an impact on the social sciences. Nor has sociology been entirely free from some turbulence (e.g. Gouldner, 1970). Moreover, the student movement of the late 1960s, changes in attitude of society towards science and general trends in the style of thought (Capra, 1983) constituted a wider social context amenable to the crisis within social psychology.

The European Association was closely involved in the articulation of the crisis. This is nowhere more clearly seen than in the contents of the second European Monograph in Social Psychology edited by Israel and Tajfel, with contributions from Moscovici, Tajfel, Israel, Rommetveit, Asplund, Janousek, Wiberg, Von Cranach, Flament and Harré who were based in Scandinavia, France, Germany, England or Czechoslovakia. The book originated from the 1969 plenary conference of the Association where a 'complex and conflicting collective state of mind' (Israel and

Tajfel, 1972: 2) became evident. The conflict was between a respect for the well-established traditions, ideas, theories and associated experimental research on the one hand and a general dissatisfaction with the social, scientific and philosophical assumptions on which these were based on the other. This raised questions as to the nature of theory, the adequacy of methods, the unstated assumptions, values and presuppositions and the relevance of research in social psychology and its relationship to the natural sciences. These issues were further discussed in a small working group and eventually were published under the title of *The Context of Social Psychology: A critical assessment* (Israel and Tajfel, 1972). This book has probably been highly influential in various strands of European Social Psychology and is still relevant to the continuing debate. But, even if this were not the case, it is an expression of the ideas and concerns which were prevalent in the European Social Psychology community during the early 1970s.

In his own contribution, Tajfel presents his case for continuing to employ experimental research in social psychology. While others, such as Harré and Secord (1972), were pronouncing that experimental methodology was not suited to the exploration of social psychological phenomena and could never provide the proper foundation for a science of social behaviour, Tajfel did not wish to abandon the experimental tradition. In some respects, this is not surprising. Throughout his academic career he had worked within the experimental tradition of social psychology. All the research with which he had been directly involved was experimental. In this respect, Tajfel remained an active proponent of the orthodox, and he remained unconvinced by arguments proclaiming the greater value of other methods. Tajfel's faith in the experimental tradition was not only evident in these theoretical debates. During the formative years of the European Association there were heated discussions and disagreements over the most suitable name for the association. Eventually, it was named the European Association of *Experimental* Social Psychology, a name which Tajfel had advocated strongly.

While others were arguing that social psychology must develop a new methodology, Tajfel advocated the case for experimental research (Tajfel, 1972a, 1979d). Such debates about the appropriate methodologies were closely associated with conception of the individual. Tajfel advocated a social model of 'homo' which recognized the lack of individual autonomy and their lack of independence from social conditions. This was related to his primary interest in large-scale uniformities in social behaviour. The vast majority of theories in social psychology were basically about individual or inter-individual behaviour since their explanations of social behaviour are founded in individual motives and cognitions. Theories of aggression, of inter-individual and small group competition and cooperation, of judgments, stereotypes, attitudes and beliefs about ingroups and outgroups, and of the genesis of prejudice (including Tajfel's own work in Phase II and, in some respects, Phase III) reduce social behaviour to the pre-social or asocial aspects of 'homo'. This approach is epitomized by Berkowitz (1962) in his statement that

> Dealings between groups ultimately become problems of the psychology of the individual. Individuals decide to go to war; battles are fought by individuals and peace is established by individuals . . . Ultimately it is the single person who attacks the feared and disliked ethnic minority group.
>
> (Berkowitz: 167, quoted in Tajfel, 1972a: 95)

This passage, along with Harré's claim for the autonomy of individuals (Harré and Secord, 1972; Harré, 1979), must have incensed Tajfel in its denial of his own experience as a Jew and the experience of many other minority peoples. When it came to large-scale interrelations between groups such a view was clearly untenable. The psychology of the individual, or even of inter-individual behaviour, could not be simply extrapolated to explain the social uniformities. This required a different perspective on the relationship between the individual and the social. Individuals feel, think and behave in terms of their social identities which are determined, to a large extent, by the relations between the groups to which they belong. The social setting of intergroup relations contributes to making individuals what they are and they, in turn, produce the social setting in a symbiotic relationship of development and change. Social psychology must encompass the social and cultural context as well as the psychological processes and provide an understanding of their dialectic relationship (Tajfel, 1977, 1979a, c).

> It is because of the socially derived, shared, accepted and conflicting notions of appropriateness of conduct, because of the social definition of the situations to which they apply, and of the social origin of their manner of changing and of relating to one another, that individual and inter-individual psychology cannot be usefully considered as providing the bricks from which an adequate social psychology can be built. The derivations used must be in the opposite direction.
>
> (Tajfel, 1972a: 104)

This new perspective was born out of Tajfel's burning ambition to understand the genocide of the war years and to ensure that it would never happen again; to find, and to remove, the causes underlying the discrimination against, and the persecution of, millions of people on the basis of their ethnic identity; and eventually to create a psychology of social conflict that addressed the social-psychological processes and the cultural and political conditions which produced such large-scale uniformities in social behaviour. Social psychology could then provide important and indispensable insights into the world of real conflict between real social groups. His interests were in political phenomena, in social and cultural history, in the history of art and of political and social movements, but these interests did not enter explicitly into his social psychology until the 1970s. While they were implicit in the shift from the study of social perception *per se* to the study of prejudice and intergroup relations it was not until Phase VI that Tajfel was able to integrate his profession as a psychologist, his interests in social and cultural phenomena and his life experience as a Jew before, during and after the war. While his early work had been shaped by the conventions of a North American social-psychological culture his interest and reading outside the discipline and his own distinctive cultural background stimulated, directed and encouraged the development of an alternative perspective.

Tajfel had asked different questions and, in so doing, had developed and elaborated a new perspective. The primary focus of his theory was to explain large-scale uniformities in intergroup behaviour and the existence of social movements and social change. Furthermore, although this perspective was at odds with the viewpoint of some members of the social-psychology community, it was also in alignment with others. Most notable of these is Moscovici's discussion of society and social psychology (Moscovici, 1972) and his work on social representations and minority influence, both of which were, by then, well established in France. Also, Rommetveit's perspective on social communication, meaning and language similarly stressed that social interaction requires an analysis that goes beyond individual behaviour.

The development of a new perspective and the European Association provided the context for conferences, working parties and summer schools in which dissent from traditional orientations in social psychology could be voiced. That other Europeans were thinking the same way and talking the same language was absolutely vital to the development of a new perspective in group psychology and to social psychology in general. It also provided the context in which to establish friendships, academic networks and an identity which distinguished members from their North American counterparts. Equally important was the establishment of *The European Journal of Social Psychology*, in April of 1971. This provided a new medium for the publication and communication of research and the development of theory. Similarly, the series of European Mono-graphs provided another means by which to draw together, diffuse and stimulate developments in European social psychology. Together these became the main publishing outlets for work on intergroup relations.

Social realities and social change: integrating individuals and culture

The interrelationships among social categorization, social identity, social comparison and psychological distinctiveness were presented, firstly, in the Katz–Newcomb lectures. This gave Tajfel the opportunity to develop his theoretical position on the psychological processes and functions of social behaviour in intergroup relations (Tajfel, 1972b, 1974a, b). It was also here that he elaborated and made explicit his ideas on the social-psychological aspects of the social conditions in which intergroup conflict will arise. Common sense and everyday experience illustrate clearly that not all social interactions are examples of intergroup behaviour. There are many occasions in which social interactions are not directed primarily by our social identities and group memberships. The expression of social identity is thus, in part, dependent upon the con-ditions in which the social interactions occur.

Turner's experiments had demonstrated that the expression of group membership in social behaviour is dependent upon the social situation. Individuals can act in terms of self or purely in terms of their group membership. This was re-conceived or re-presented in terms of a con-tinuum that differentiated interpersonal behaviour from intergroup behaviour. In the former, social interactions are determined largely by the people's personal relationships and individual characteristics. In the latter, they are determined wholly by their membership of different social groups or categories. These ideas were developed later with reference to work on relative deprivation in sociology and political science and, in particular, Gurr's 1970 volume on *Why Men Rebel* (Tajfel, 1978c). In order to distinguish the psychological processes involved at the two poles of the continuum, Tajfel and Turner differentiated between personal identity and social identity respectively.

However, these principles needed to be elaborated and applied beyond the social vacuum of the minimal group paradigm to describe the social conditions in which the different forms of social interaction would occur, taking into account groups' histories, their social contact and the wider context of multi-group relations. These relate to the social realities of a particular society, to the economic, historical and political structures. This is consonant with the dialectic nature of intergroup behaviour emphasized by Tajfel. The expression of subjective group membership in social behaviour is interrelated with the social context. What are the social conditions in which individuals will behave in terms of their subjective group membership? When does an individual's social identity become the primary motivational force directing his or her social behaviour?

Already in Phase III Tajfel was concerned with how individuals came to understand the constantly changing relations between groups. There, he focused his attention on individuals' cognitive structures and causal attributions. By Phase VI his interest in social change at the societal level became more explicit. One of the striking characteristics of intergroup relations is their dynamic character. Social conflict, social movements and social creativity are all salient features in today's society. The central problem was to relate the large-scale social, political, economic and technological transformations in society to everyday changes in an individual's life. The individual must create change, resist it, adapt to it or prepare for it. In order to understand social uniformities in intergroup behaviour and the dynamics of social change it was necessary to consider not only the psychological processes involved but also the social-psychological aspects that relate directly to the structure of society.

Rather than leaving these issues in the realm of other disciplines such as sociology, politics and economics, the structure of society is transformed into the realm of social psychology in terms of consensual belief systems. Whether someone interacts at the interpersonal end of the continuum or at the intergroup pole will depend upon their beliefs about the structure of society. Here, a second, parallel, continuum is employed to distinguish between societal conditions of social mobility and of social change (Tajfel, 1975, 1976a, 1978c; Tajfel and Turner, 1979). In conditions of social mobility people believe that there are flexible boundaries between groups and that individual movement from one group to another is relatively easy. Such conditions promote interpersonal behaviour. In conditions of social change people believe that the boundaries between groups are sharply drawn and immutable, making it extremely difficult or impossible to move between groups. In order to achieve a positive identity it is necessary to maintain or change the image, position or circumstances of the group as a whole, promoting intergroup behaviour. The system of shared expectations, beliefs and evaluations must be changed, or the environment must be changed to preserve them. This creates a symmetry and integration of the psychological and societal levels of explanation, the former, interpersonal–intergroup continuum, being interdependent with the latter, social mobility–social change continuum.

These ideas were developed by drawing on the work of Hirschman on *Exit, Voice and Loyalty* (1970). Tajfel met Hirschman while visiting Harvard and realized the congruence between their ideas. Hirschman was himself an economist who had been influenced by theories in political science. His thesis focuses on the use of 'exit' – leaving an organization – and 'voice' – expressing dissatisfaction to management, etc. – as ways of dealing with institutional problems. Hirschman's analysis related directly to social mobility and social change with some implications for the social psychology of intergroup relations. But it largely addressed an individual's exit or voice in organizations in response to decline. This had to be transposed to, or integrated with, the inter-individual–intergroup continuum (Tajfel, 1976a). Firstly, the contrast between social mobility and social change could be conceived as a continuum which involved a transposition from individual exit to group voice. Secondly, the use of group voice could serve as a powerful force working towards the maintenance of the status quo as well as towards the implementation of change under conditions of social change.

However, this is only a partial answer. It establishes the *potential* for intergroup behaviour but it does not specify the conditions in which intergroup behaviour *will actually* occur, nor does it distinguish between the various forms of intergroup behaviour to be found in society (Tajfel, 1978i). Examples of intergroup relations, the activities of minority groups and the emergence of social movements in society played a formative part in the specification of the conditions for social change to occur and the various forms of social creativity employed by groups in the maintenance and creation of intergroup differentiations.

Firstly, examples extant in society demonstrate that the 'objective' conditions of social change do not necessarily lead to social action in terms of group membership and social identity. The ancient caste system in India constituted a social system in which individual mobility was impossible and group boundaries were well defined but this did not, in itself, bring about social change. Social systems in which some groups exhibit ingroup devaluation and negative social identities can persist for a long time. This problem is overcome by specifying two social-psychological attributes of the consensual belief systems. These refer to the perceived *legitimacy–illegitimacy* and the perceived *stability–instability* of the social system. Social movements will arise when the social system is perceived by one or more groups as illegitimate and/or unstable. These social movements will aim either to create or to prevent social change.

Similarly, the existence of shared cognitive alternatives is necessary for large-scale social action to be undertaken.

Secondly, an examination of relations between consensually inferior and consensually superior groups highlighted a diversity in forms of social action. Groups may reinterpret or re-evaluate group attributes such as being black, their cultural traditions, and their accents or dialects, etc.; they may intensify and justify group differences as in the case of Jews in pre-war Germany; or they may create new conditions, ideologies and attributes as in the rise of Welsh nationalism.

Unfortunately, within the social representations system, the form, content and role of consensual belief systems does not achieve the same degree of lucidity as that of the psychological processes involved in intergroup relations. Moreover, there is little discussion concerning communication processes, social influence and the diffusion of social beliefs. This was due, in part, to the relatively recent inclusion and elaboration of these issues within the evolution of the system. However, it also reflected the lack of research and theoretical debate within social psychology that directly addressed issues related to large-scale social phenomena and, in particular, to the positional relations among groups and the widespread beliefs or ideologies of a culture or society (Doise, 1986). This was explained by applying the social representations system to the social context of social psychology as a discipline. The focus on interpersonal relations within the dominant tradition of social psychology was related to the shared beliefs in social mobility within American culture. Within European cultures the belief in individual mobility was not so strong, creating a second cultural base in which to develop a social psychology of intergroup relations and social change.

VII
THE DIFFUSION OF SOCIAL IDENTITY THEORY

In subsequent years intergroup relations was to become an established field of study within social psychology. Numerous journal articles, books and edited volumes were devoted to the subject (e.g. Billig, 1976; Giles, 1977; Tajfel, 1978a; Austin and Worshel, 1979; Hamilton, 1981; Turner and Giles, 1981; Ng, 1982; Tajfel, 1982a, c; Brewer and Kramer, 1985; Hewstone and Brown, 1986; Wilder, 1986; Pettigrew, 1989); the *Handbook of Social Psychology* included a chapter on intergroup relations (Stephan, 1985); and books on group psychology or social psychology more generally have chapters or sections on intergroup relations (Deaux and Wrightsman, 1984; Tajfel, 1984b; H. Brown, 1985; R. Brown, 1986; Hewstone *et al.*, 1988; Howitt *et al.*, 1989). Tajfel's impact on these and related developments was substantial. It is reflected in the diffusion of his ideas on social identity, social change and intergroup relations; in the many authors who refer to his influence and encouragement in prefaces and acknowledgments; in the growth of the social dimensions in social psychology; and in the flourishing of a European community of social psychologists.

In particular, there are two distinctive trends in the diffusion of social identity theory. The first is epitomized by Turner and his colleagues (Turner *et al.*, 1987; Hogg and Abrams, 1988) whereby the psychological processes associated with social identity are applied to fields other than intergroup relations, including psychological group formation, group cohesion, social attraction, social influence and conformity, social co-operation, group polarization, crowd behaviour and attribution theory. At the heart of this work lies the conviction that the concept of social identity can furnish social psychology with a better understanding of both intra- and intergroup processes. In order to address those problems in social psychology which have been consensually accepted as legitimate and worthy of study, it was necessary to emphasize particular features of the social representations system. On the one hand, our understanding of intragroup processes is now transformed by giving priority to the processes of social identification (self-categorization) and treating the group as a theoretically distinctive entity. On the other hand, it focused attention on the more conventional, psychological processes of the social representations system and failed to sustain its more radical or novel aspects. In particular it ignored the role of consensual beliefs and the relative status of groups and thus failed to provide an account of the historical evolution of groups, the social creativity of groups or the processes of social change.

In part, this was due to the conventional reliance on experimental methodology for legitimate evidence. While the functions of the psychological processes had been clearly demonstrated within the laboratory, the large-scale social dimensions within the social representations system were more apparent by examining social realities. The role of examining naturally occurring events in the development and evolution of scientific knowledge is frequently underestimated. While experimental research can serve as a means to evaluate particular issues in a controlled environment an examination of phenomena in all their complexity may reveal interrelations among components not yet considered and may serve as an important stimulus in the genesis and evolution of comprehensive theories. We cannot hope to set up a society in the laboratory, just as natural scientists cannot auspicate the global system within the confines of a laboratory.

In contrast to the work on intragroup relations, the second trend sustains the original extent of the social representations system, examining the relationship between the psychological processes and consensual beliefs systems as well as elaborating ideas on power relations between groups. Interestingly, this applies to research and theorizing that continued to focus on intergroup relations (e.g. Mugny, 1982; Ng, 1982, 1984; van Krippenberg, 1984; Brown, R. J. 1988a, b) and also on the social psychology of language (e.g. Ball *et al.*, 1984; Giles, 1984; Giles and Street, 1985). These were closer to the original object of study, allowing the social representations system as a whole to be sustained and developed. Furthermore, as emergent topics of interest within social psychology there was greater scope for defining new problems and adopting innovatory approaches.

SUMMARY

In the course of Part IV we have immersed ourselves in the evolution of a social representations system that culminated in a new field of study and a new perspective in social psychology. From our location in the ongoing stream of transformation these subsequent developments may be considered as the diffusion of an established social representations system. However, it is important to realize that this depends upon our position in space–time. From a different point of view, focusing on the contribution of a different scientist in a different institution, these developments would be construed as the ongoing reconstruction of the social representations system, through the processes of assimilation and accommodation within the organism–environment–culture system.

We have seen that, while Henri Tajfel remained a social psychologist throughout his academic career, the content and form of social psychology which he espoused underwent a radical transformation. His approach retained its functional and comparative components but, as the object of study changed, the locus of explanation shifted from individual cognition towards the social psychological concomitants of people's location in society. This is accompanied by a shift away from an overriding concern with method and experimental research towards the development of theory and its application to social reality.

These transformations are stimulated and guided by the emergent conflicts and anomalies within the social representations system. These conflicts emerge within the organism–environment–culture system, relating to people's interactions with the environment, both physical and social, and their communications with each other. Within the scientific community this includes collaboration with others in conducting research and the theoretical and research publications of others working in the same or related fields. Beyond the scientific community it refers to stereotypes, prejudice and intergroup relations in society as an object of study and to society more broadly as an influence in the process of science.

The influence of culture, both within the scientific community and in society more generally is effected through the expression of people's identities. In this case, Tajfel's identity, both as an emigré Jew and as a European social psychologist, plays a profound role in directing changes and shaping the social representations system. His cultural history and his experiences both in childhood and through World War II gave him an acute awareness of the power and reality of intergroup relations. The expression and flowering of this awareness within societal psychology was initially suppressed by the institutions and conventions of the discipline. However, his involvement in the growth of a European community of social psychologists created an environment in which he could bring together his life experiences as a Jew before, during and after the war, his interest in cultural phenomena and social movements and his profession as a social psychologist.

In years to come, it may well be that the social representations system constructed in the social sciences diffuses into other sectors of society. This, in turn, would involve the reconstruction of interrelated social representations systems through people's interactions and communications in particular environmental, cultural and historical contexts. In this way, social reality itself is transformed.

BIBLIOGRAPHY

Abric, J.-C. (1971) 'Experimental study of group creativity: Task representation, group structure and performance', *European Journal of Social Psychology* 1(3), 311–26.

—— (1984) 'A theoretical and experimental approach to the study of social representations in a situation of interaction', in R.M. Farr and S. Moscovici (eds) *Social Representations*, Cambridge: Cambridge University Press.

—— (1987) *Cooperation, Competition et Representations Sociales*, Crousset: Delval.

Abric, J.-C. and Kahan, J.P. (1972) 'The effects of representations and behaviour in experimental games', *European Journal of Social Psychology* 2(2), 129–44.

Ackermann, W. and Rialan, B. (1963) 'Transmission et assimilation des notions scientifiques: une étude de la représentation de quelques faits scientifiques chez des ouvriers de l'industrie chimique', *Bulletin du CERP*, 22, 1–2.

Adorno, T.W., Frenkel-Brunswick, E., Levinson, D.J. and Sanford, R.N. (1950) *The Authoritarian Personality*, New York: Harper.

Allport, F.H. (1924) *Social Psychology*, Boston: Houghton-Mifflin.

Allport, G.W. (1954) *The Nature of Prejudice*, Cambridge, Mass.: Addison-Wesley.

Allport, G.W. and Kramer, B.M. (1946) 'Some roots of prejudices', *Journal of Psychology* 22, 9–39.

Armistead, N. (ed.) (1974) *Reconstructing Social Psychology*, Harmondsworth: Penguin.

Asch, S.E. (1956) 'Studies of independence and submission to group pressure: a minority of One against a unanimous majority', *Psychological Monographs* 70(9), no. 416.

Ash, M.G. (1983) *The Emergence of Gestalt Theory: Experimental psychology in Germany 1890–1920*, New York: University Microfilms International.

Austin, W.G. and Worshel, S. (eds) (1979) *The Social Psychology of Intergroup Relations*, Monterey, Cal.: Brooks/Cole.

Ball, P., Giles, H. and Hewstone, M. (1984) 'Second language acquisition: The intergroup theory with catastrophic dimensions', in H. Tajfel (ed.) *The Social Dimension: European developments in social psychology* (vol. 2), Cambridge: Cambridge University Press.

Barbichon, G. and Moscovici, S. (1965) 'Diffusion des connaissances scientifiques', *Social Science Information* 4, 7–22.

Barnes, B. (1983) 'On the conventional character of knowledge and cognition', in K.D. Knorr-Cetina and M. Mulkay (eds) *Science Observed: Perspectives on the social study of a science*, London: Sage.

Barnes, B. and Edge, D. (eds) (1982) *Science in Context*, Milton Keynes: Open University Press.

Ben-David, J. and Collins, R. (1966) 'Social factors in the origins of a new science: the case of psychology', *American Psychological Review* 31, 451–65.

Berger, P.L. and Luckmann, T. (1966; 2nd edn 1984) *The Social Construction of Reality: A treatise in the sociology of knowledge*, London: Allen Lane.

Berkowitz, L. (1962) *Aggression: A social psychological analysis*, New York: McGraw-Hill.

Billig, M. (1976) *Social Psychology and Intergroup Relations*, London: Academic Press.

——— (1982) *Ideology and Social Psychology: Extremism, moderation and contradiction*, Oxford: Blackwell.

——— (1987a) *Arguing and Thinking: A rhetorical approach to social psychology*, Cambridge: Cambridge University Press.

——— (1987b) *The Concept of Social Representations: Particular and universal aspects*. Unpublished manuscript.

——— (1988) 'Social representation, objectification and anchoring: A rhetorical analysis', *Social Behaviour* 3, 1–16.

Billig, M. and Tajfel, H. (1973) 'Social categorisation and similarity in intergroup behaviour', *European Journal of Social Psychology* 3, 27–52.

Billig, M., Condor, S., Edwards, D., Gane, M., Middleton, D. and Radley, A. (1988) *Ideological Dilemmas: A social psychology of everyday thinking*, London: Sage.

Boring, E.G. (1959) *A History of Experimental Psychology*, New York: Appleton-Century-Crofts.

Breakwell, G. (1987) 'Widespread beliefs: Some methodological problems'. Paper presented at ESRC Empirical Approaches to Social Representations, Surrey University.

——— (1993) 'Integrating paradigms, methodological implications', in G. Breakwell and D. Canter (eds) *Empirical Approaches to Social Representations*, Oxford: Oxford University Press.

Breakwell, G. and Canter, D. (eds) (1993) *Empirical Approaches to Social Representations*, Oxford: Oxford University Press.

Brewer, M.B. and Kramer, R.M. (1985) 'The psychology of intergroup attitudes and behaviour', *Annual Review of Psychology* 35, 219–43.

Brown, Hedy (1985) *People, Groups and Society*, Milton Keynes: Open University Press.

Brown, R. (1986) *Social Psychology*, 2nd edn, New York: Free Press.

Brown, R. and Taylor, D.M. (1979) 'Towards a more social social psychology', *British Journal of Social and Clinical Psychology* 18, 173–80.

Brown, R.J. (1984) 'The role of similarity in intergroup relations', in H. Tajfel (ed.) *The Social Dimension: European developments in social psychology*, Cambridge: Cambridge University Press.

——— (1988a) *Group Processes: Dynamics within and between groups*, Oxford: Blackwell.

——— (1988b) 'Intergroup relations', in M. Hewstone, W.W. Stroebe, J.-P. Codol and G.M. Stephenson (eds) *Introduction to Social Psychology: A European Perspective*, Mass.: Blackwell.

Bruner, J.S. (1980) 'Afterword', in D.R. Olson (ed.) '*The Social Foundations of Language and Thought*', *Essays in Honour of J.S. Bruner*, London: W.W. Norton.

Bruner, J.S. and Goodman, C.C. (1947) 'Value and need as organizing factors in perception', *Journal of Abnormal and Social Psychology* 42, 33–44.

Bruner, J.S. and Rodrigues, J.S. (1953) 'Some determinants of apparent size', *Journal of Abnormal and Social Psychology* 48, 17–24.

Bruner, J.S. and Tajfel, H. (1961) 'Cognitive risk and environmental change', *Journal of Abnormal and Social Psychology* 62, 231–41.

Bruner, J.S., Postman, L. and Rodrigues, J.S. (1951) 'Expectation and the perception of color', *American Journal of Psychology* 64, 216–27.

Campbell, D.T. (1965) 'Ethnocentric and other altruistic motives', D. LeVine (ed.) *The Nebraska Symposium on Motivation*, Lincoln, Neb.: University of Nebraska Press.

—— (1967) 'Administrative experimentation, institutional records and non-reactive measures', in J.C. Stanley (ed.) *Improving Experimental Design and Statistical Analysis*, Chicago, Ill.: Rand McNally.

Campbell, D.T. and LeVine, R.A. (1961) 'A proposal for cooperative cross-cultural research on ethnocentrism', *Journal of Conflict Resolution* 5, 82–108.

Campbell, D.T. and Stanley, J.C. (1963) 'Experimental and quasi-experimental designs for research on teaching', *Handbook of Research on Teaching*, Chicago, Ill.: Rand McNally.

Capra, F. (1983) *The Turning Point: Science, society and the rising culture*, London: Fontana.

Carter, L.F. and Schooler, K. (1949) 'Value, need and other factors in perception', *Psychological Review* 56, 200–7.

Cartwright, D. (1973) 'Determinants of scientific progress: The case of research on the risky shift', *American Psychologist* 222–31.

Cartwright, D. and Zander, A. (eds) (1953; 2nd edn 1960, 3rd edn 1968) *Group Dynamics: Research and theory*, London: Tavistock.

Carugati, F.F. (1990) 'Everyday ideas, theoretical models and social repre-sentations: The case of intelligence and its development', in G. Semin and K.J. Gergen (eds) *Inquiries in Social Construction*, London: Sage.

Chalmers, A.F. (1982) *What is this Thing called Science?*, 2nd edn, Milton Keynes: Open University Press.

Chombart-de-Lauwe, M.-J. (1971; 2nd edn 1979). *Un monde autre: L'enfance. De ses représentations a son mythe*, Paris: Payot.

—— (1984) 'Changes in the representation of the child in the course of social transmission', in R.M. Farr and S. Moscovici (eds) *Social Representations*, Cambridge: Cambridge University Press.

Clark, K.B. and Clark, M.P. (1947) 'Racial identification and preference in negro children', in T.M. Newcomb and E.L. Hartley (eds) *Readings in Social Psychology*, New York: Holt.

Codol, J.P. (1974) 'On the system of representations in a group situation', *European Journal of Social Psychology* 4(3), 343–65.

—— (1975) 'On the so-called "superior conformity of the self" behaviour: twenty experimental investigations', *European Journal of Social Psychology* 5, 457–501.

—— (1984) 'On the system of representations in an artificial social situation', in R.M. Farr and S. Moscovici (eds) *Social Representations*, Cambridge: Cambridge University Press.

Cohen, D. (1977) *Psychologists on Psychology*, London: Routledge & Kegan Paul.

Cole, M. (1987) Cultural psychology. Unpublished manuscript.

Collins, H.M. (1982) 'The replication of experiments in physics', in B. Barnes and D. Edge (eds) *Science in Context*, Milton Keynes: Open University Press.

Cranach, M. and Harré, R. (eds) (1982) *The Analysis of Action*, Cambridge: Cambridge University Press.

Crane, D. (1972) *Invisible Colleges: Diffusion of knowledge in scientific communities*, London: University of Chicago Press.

Danziger, K. (1979) 'The positivist repudiation of Wundt', *The Journal of the History of the Behavioural Sciences* 15, 205–30.

Darwin, C. (1859) *The Origin of Species by Means of Natural Selection: Or, the presentation of favoured races in the struggle for life*, London: Murray.

Deaux, K. and Wrightsman, L.S. (1984) *Social Psychology in the 80s*, 4th edn, Monterey, Cal.: Brooks/Cole.

Deutsch, K.W. (1966) *Nationalism and Social Communication: An enquiry into the foundations of nationality*, 2nd edn, Cambridge, Mass.: Massachusetts Institute of Technology Press.

Deutsch, M. (1949) 'A theory of cooperation and competition', *Human Relations* 2, 129–52.

Deutsch, M., Thomas, J.R.H. and Garner, K. (1971) 'Social discrimination on the basis of category membership'. Unpublished MS, Teachers College, Columbia University.

Deutscher, I. (1984) 'Choosing ancestors: Some consequences of the selection from intellectual traditions', in R.M. Farr and S. Moscovici (eds) *Social Representations*, Cambridge: Cambridge University Press.

Dewey, J. (1896) 'The reflex arc concept in psychology', *Psychological Review* 3, 357–70.

Dickson, D. (1979) 'Science and political hegemony in the seventeenth century', *Radical Science Journal* 8, 7–37.

Di Giacomo, J.-P. (1980) 'Intergroup alliances and rejections within a protest movement (analysis of the social representations)', *European Journal of Social Psychology* 10, 329–44.

Doise, W. (1978) *Groups and Individuals: Explanations in social psychology*, Cambridge: Cambridge University Press.

—— (1986) *Levels of Explanation in Social Psychology*, Cambridge: Cambridge University Press.

Doise, W. and Sinclair, A. (1973) 'The categorization process in intergrouip relations', *European Journal of Social Psychology* 3, 145–57.

Doise, W., Tajfel, H. and Billig, M. (1971) 'Expectations about the decisions of others in money allocation', in M. Billig, *Social Categorization and Intergroup Relations*. Unpublished PhD thesis, University of Bristol.

Douglas, M. (1975) *Implicit Meanings: Essays in Anthropology*, London: Routledge & Kegan Paul.

Dukes, W.F. and Bevan, W. (1952) 'Size estimation and monetary value: A correlation', *Journal of Psychology* 34, 45–53.

Durkheim, E. (1915) *The Elementary Forms of Religious Life* (trans. J.W. Swain), London: Allen & Unwin.

Duveen, G. and Lloyd, B. (1986) 'The significance of social identities', *British Journal of Social Psychology* 25, 219–30.

Duveen, G. and Lloyd, B. (1987) 'On gender as a social representation'. Paper presented at Symposium on Developmental Reconstructions of Social Representations at Annual BPS Conference, University of Sussex, April 1987.
—— (eds) (1990) *Social Representations and the Development of Knowledge*, Cambridge: Cambridge University Press.
Eiser, J.R. (1986) *Social Psychology: Attitudes, cognition and social behaviour*, Cambridge: Cambridge University Press.
Elms, A.C. (1975) 'The crisis of confidence in social psychology', *American Psychologist* 30, 967–76.
Emler, N. (1987) 'Socio-moral development from the perspective of social representations', *Journal for the Theory of Social Behaviour* 17(4), 371–88.
Emler, N. and Dickinson, J. (1985) 'Children's representations of economic inequalities: The effects of social class', *British Journal of Developmental Psychology* 3, 191–8.
Emler, N., Ohana, T. and Dickinson, J. (1990) 'Children's representations of social relations', in G. Duveen and B. Lloyd (eds) *Social Representations and the Development of Knowledge*, Cambridge: Cambridge University Press.
Erikson, C.W. and Hake, H.W. (1955) 'Multidimensional stimulus differences and accuracy of discrimination', *Journal of Experimental Psychology* 53, 153–60.
Erikson, E.H. (1953) *Childhood and Society*, 2nd edn, New York: W.W. Norton.
Farr, R.M. (1981) 'The social origins of the human mind: A historical note', in J.P. Forgas (ed.) *Social Cognition: Perspectives on everyday understanding*, London: Academic Press.
—— (1983) 'Wilhelm Wundt (1832–1920) and the origins of psychology as an experimental and social science', *The British Journal of Social Psychology* 22, 289–301.
—— (1984) 'Social representations: Their role in the design and execution of laboratory experiments', in R.M. Farr and S. Moscovici (eds) *Social Representations*, Cambridge: Cambridge University Press.
—— (1985) 'Traditions of social psychology: Their variety and diversity'. Unpublished manuscript, London School of Economics and Political Science.
—— (1987a) 'Self/Other relations and the social nature of reality', in C.F. Graumann and S. Moscovici (eds), *Changing Conceptions of Conspiracy*, 203–17, New York: Springer-Verlag.
—— (1987b) 'Social representations: A French tradition of research', *Journal for the Theory of Social Behaviour* 17(4), 343–70.
—— (1989) 'From cognitive science to folk psychology: The role of culture in modern psychology'. Unpublished manuscript, London School of Economics and Political Science.
—— (1990) 'Social representations as widespread beliefs', in C. Fraser and G. Gaskell (eds) *The Social Psychological Study of Widespread Beliefs*, Oxford: Oxford University Press.
—— (1991a) 'The waxing and waning of interest in forms of societal psychology', in H. Himmelweit and G. Gaskell (eds) *Societal Psychology*, London: Sage.
—— (1991b) 'Causal attribution – from cognitive processes to collective beliefs', *British Journal of Social Psychology* 30, 89–93.
—— (1991c) 'The long past and the short history of social psychology', *European Journal of Social Psychology* 21, 371–80.

Farr, R.M. (1991d) 'Individualism as a collective representation', in A. Deconchy and E. Lipiansky (eds), *Idéologies et Representations Sociale*, Cousset: Delval.

—— (1993) 'Theory and method in the study of social representations', in G. Breakwell and D. Canter (eds) *Empirical Approaches to Social Representations*, Oxford: Oxford University Press.

Farr, R.M. and Moscovici, S. (eds) (1984a) *Social Representations*, Cambridge: Cambridge University Press.

—— (1984b) 'On the nature and role of representations in self's understanding of others and of self', in M. Cook (ed.) *Issues in Person Perception*, 1–27. London: Methuen.

Faucheux, C. and Moscovici, S. (1968) 'Self-esteem and exploitative behaviour in a game against chance and nature', *Journal of Personality and Social Psychology* 8(1), 83–8.

Festinger, L. (1954) 'A theory of social comparison processes', *Human Relations* 7, 117–40.

—— (1957) *A Theory of Cognitive Dissonance*, Evanston, Ill.: Row, Peterson.

Feyerabend, P.K. (1970) 'Consolations for the specialist', in I. Lakatos and A. Musgrave (eds) *Criticism and the Growth of Knowledge*, Cambridge: Cambridge University Press.

—— (1975) *Against Method: Outline of an anarchistic theory of knowledge*, London: New Left Books.

Fielding, N.G. and Fielding, J.L. (1986) *Linking Data: The articulation of qualitative and quantitative methods in social research*, Beverly Hills: Sage.

Fishman, J.A. (1968) *Language Loyalty in the United States*, The Hague: Mouton.

Flament, C. (1984) 'From the bias of structural balance to the representation of the group', in R.M. Farr and S. Moscovici (eds) *Social Representations*, Cambridge: Cambridge University Press.

Flavell, J.H. (1963) *The Developmental Psychology of Jean Piaget*, New York: Van Nostrand.

Foucault, M. (1974) *The Order of Things: Archaeology of the human sciences*, London: Tavistock.

Fraser, C. and Gaskell, G. (eds) (1990) *The Social Psychological Study of Widespread Beliefs*, Oxford: Oxford University Press.

Gadfield, W.T., Glee, H., Bourhis, R.Y. and Tajfel, H. (1979) 'Dynamics in ethnic-group relations', *Ethnicity* 6(4), 373–82.

Gardner, H. (1985) *The Mind's New Science: A history of the cognitive revolution*, New York: Basic Books.

Gauld, A. and Shotter, J. (1977) *Human Action and its Psychological Investigation*, London: Routledge & Kegan Paul.

Gergen, K.J. (1973) 'Social psychology as history', *Journal of Personality and Social Psychology* 26(2), 309–20.

—— (1978) 'Experimentation in social psychology: A reappraisal', *European Journal of Social Psychology* 8, 507–27.

—— (1982) *Towards Transformation in Social Knowledge*, New York: Springer-Verlag.

—— (1984) 'An introduction to historical social psychology', in J.K. Gergen and M.M. Gergen (eds) *Historical Social Psychology*, 3–36, London: Lawrence Erlbaum Assocs.

—— (1985a) 'Social constructionist inquiry: Context and implications', in K.J.

Gergen and K.E. Davis (eds) *The Social Construction of the Person*, New York: Springer-Verlag.

Gergen, K.J. (1985b) *The Social Constructivist Movement in Modern Psychology*, New York: Springer-Verlag.

Gergen, K.J. and Davis, K.L. (eds) (1985) *The Social Construction of the Person*, New York: Springer-Verlag.

Gergen, K.J. and Gergen, M.M. (1984) *Historical Social Psychology*, London: Lawrence Erlbaum Assocs.

Gergen, K.J. and Morawski, J. (1980) 'An alternative metatheory for social psychology', in L. Wheeler (ed.) *Review of Personality and Social Psychology*, Beverly Hills, Calif.: Sage.

Gergen, M. (1989) 'Induction and construction – teetering between worlds', *European Journal of Social Psychology* 19, 431–7.

Giere, R.N. (1987) 'The cognitive study of science', in N.T. Nersessian (ed.) *The Process of Science*, Dordrecht: Martinus Nijhoff.

Gilbert, G.N. and Mulkay, M. (1984) *Opening Pandora's Box: A sociologist's analysis of scientists' discourse*, Cambridge: Cambridge University Press.

Giles, H. (ed.) (1977) *Language, Ethnicity and Intergroup Relations*, London: Academic Press.

—— (1984) 'The dynamics of speech accommodation', *International Journal of the Sociology of Language* 46, special issue.

Giles, H. and Street, R.L. (1985) 'Communicator characteristics and behaviour', in M.L. Knapp and G.R. Miller (eds) *Handbook of Interpersonal Communication*, London: Sage.

Gilmour, R. and Duck, S. (1980) *The Development of Social Psychology*, London: Academic Press.

Goodman, M.R. (1964) *Race Awareness in Young Children*, revised edition, New York: Collier.

Gould, S.J. (1981) *The Mismeasure of Man*, New York: Norton.

Gouldner, A.W. (1970) *The Coming Crisis in Western Sociology*, New York: Basic Books.

Graumann, C. (1986) 'The individualization of the social and the de-socialization of the individual, Floyd A. Allport's contribution to Social Psychology', in C.F. Graumann and S. Moscovici (eds) *Changing Conceptions of Crowd, Mind and Behaviour*, New York: Springer-Verlag.

Greenberg, J. and Folgar, R. (1988) *Controversial Issues in Social Research Methods*, SSSP. New York: Springer-Verlag.

Greenstein, F.I. (1965) *Psychological Aspects of Politics*, Stanford: Centre for Advanced Study in Behavioural Sciences (Mimeo).

Grene, M. (1987) 'Historical realism and contextual objectivity: A developing perspective in the philosophy of science', in N.J. Nersessian (ed.) *The Process of Science*, Dordrecht: Martinus Nijhoff.

Gruber, H.E. (1973) 'Courage and cognitive growth in children and scientists', in M. Schwebel and J. Raph (eds) *Piaget in the Classroom*, New York: Basic Books, also 1974 London: Routledge & Keagan Paul.

—— (1981) *Darwin on Man: A psychological study of scientific creativity*, 2nd edn, London: University of Chicago Press.

Gurr, T.R. (1970) *Why Men Rebel*. Princeton, NJ: Princeton University Press.

Hagstrom, W.O. (1965) *The Scientific Community*, New York: Basic Books.

Hamilton, D.L. (ed.) (1981) *Cognitive Processes in Stereotyping and Intergroup Behaviour*, Hillsdale, NJ: Erlbaum.

Harré, R. (1979) *Social Being: A theory for social psychology*, Oxford: Blackwell.

—— (1984) 'Some reflections on the concept of "social representation"', *Social Research* 51(4), 927–38.

—— (1985) Review of R.M. Farr and S. Moscovici (eds) *Social Representations*, Cambridge: Cambridge University Press, *British Journal of Psychology* 76, 138–40.

Harré, R. and Secord, P.F. (1972) *The Explanation of Social Behaviour*, Oxford: Blackwell.

Hastorf, A.H., Richardson, S.A. and Dornbusch, S.M. (1958) 'The problem of relevance in the study of person perception', in R. Taguiri and L. Petrullo (eds) *Person Perception and Interpersonal Behaviour*, Stanford: Stanford University Press.

Hawking, S. (1988) *A Brief History of Time: From the big bang to black holes*, London: Bantam.

Hearnshaw, L.S. (1986) *The Shaping of Modern Psychology*, London: Routledge & Kegan Paul.

Hegel, G. (1990) Preface and introduction to L.S. Stepelevich (ed.), *The Phenomenology of Mind*, New York: Macmillan.

Henriques, J., Hollweg, W., Urvin, C., Venn, C. and Walkerdine, V. (1984) *Changing the Subject: Psychology, social regulations and subjectivity*, London: Methuen.

Herzlich, C. (1972) 'La Représentation sociale', in S.Moscovici (ed.) *Introduction à la psychologie sociale* (vol. 1), Paris: Librairie Larousse.

—— (1973) *Health and Illness: A social–psychological analysis*, London: Academic Press.

Hewstone, M. (1989) *Causal Attribution: From cognitive process to collective beliefs*, Oxford: Blackwell.

Hewstone, M. and Brown, R.J. (eds) (1986) *Contact and Conflict in Intergroup Encounters*, Oxford: Blackwell.

Hewstone, M. and Jaspars, J.M.F. (1984) 'Social dimensions of attribution', in H. Tajfel (ed.) *The Social Dimension: European Developments in Social Psychology*, Cambridge: Cambridge University Press.

Hewstone, M., Jaspars, J. and Lalljee, M. (1982) 'Social representations, social attribution and social identity: The intergroup images of "public" and "comprehensive" schoolboys', *European Journal of Social Psychology* 12, 241–69.

Hewstone, M., Stroebe, W., Codol, J.P. and Stephenson, G. (1988) *Introduction to Social Psychology*, Oxford: Blackwell.

Hilton, D.J. (ed.) (1988) *Contemporary Science and Natural Explanation: Commonsense conceptions of causality*, Brighton: Harvester Press.

Himmelveit, H.T. (1990) 'Societal psychology: Implications and scope', in H.T. Himmelveit and G. Gaskell (eds) *Societal Psychology*, Beverly Hills, Calif.: Sage.

Himmelveit, H.T. and Gaskell, G. (eds) (1990) *Societal Psychology*, Calif.: Sage.

Hirschman, A.O. (1970; 2nd edn 1972) *Exit, Voice and Loyalty: Responses to decline in firms, organizations and states*, Cambridge, Mass.: Harvard University.

Hochberg, J.E. (1957) 'Psychophysics and stereotyping in social perception', in M. Sherif and O. Wilson (eds) *Emerging Problems in Social Psychology*, 130, Oklahoma: University Book Exchange.

Hogg, M.A. and Abrams, D. (1988) *Social Identifications*, London and New York: Routledge.

Hollway, W. (1989) *Subjectivity and Method: Psychology Gender, Meaning and Science*, London: Sage.

Hovland, I. and Sherif, M. (1952) 'Judgmental phenomena and scales of attitude measurement: Item displacement in Thurstone scale', *Journal of Abnormal and Social Psychology* 47, 822–32.

Howitt, S., Billig, M., Cramer, D., Edwards, D., Kniveton, B., Potter, J. and Radley, A. (1989) *Social Psychology: Conflicts and continuities*, Milton Keynes: Open University Press.

Israel, J. and Tajfel, H. (eds) (1972) *The Context of Social Psychology: A critical assessment*, London: Academic Press. *European Monographs in Social Psychology*, no. 2.

Jaegar, M.E. and Rosnow, R.L. (1988) 'Contextualism and its implications for psychological inquiry', *British Journal of Psychology* 79, 63–75.

Jahoda, G. (1988) 'Critical notes and reflections on social representations', *European Journal of Social Psychology* 18, 195–209.

Jaspars, J. and Fraser, C. (1984) 'Attitudes and social representations', in R.M. Farr and S. Moscovici (eds) *Social Representations*, 101–23, Cambridge: Cambridge University Press.

Jaspars, J. and Hewstone, M. (1990) 'Social categorization, collective beliefs and causal attribution', in C. Fraser and G. Gaskell (eds) *Attitudes, Opinions and Representations: Social psychological analyses of widespread beliefs*, Oxford: Oxford University Press.

Jaspars, J.M., Van de Geer, J.P., Tajfel, H. and Johnson, N.B. (1972) 'On the development of national attitudes in children', *European Journal of Social Psychology* 2(4), 347–69.

Jodelet, D. (1984a) 'The representation of the body and its transformations', in R.M. Farr and S. Moscovici (eds) *Social Representations*, 211–38, Cambridge: Cambridge University Press.

—— (1984b) 'Représentacion sociale: Phenomenes, concepts et theorie', in S. Moscovici (ed.) *Psychologie Sociale*, Paris: Presses Universitaires de France.

—— (1986) 'Fou et folie dans un milieu rural Francais: Une approche mono-graphique', in W. Doise and A. Palmonari (eds) *L'Etude des Representations Sociales*, Norchatel: Delachaux and Niestlé.

—— (1991) *Madness and Social Representations* (trans. Tim Pownall, ed. Gerard Duveen), Hemel Hempstead: Harvester Wheatsheaf.

Jodelet, D. and Moscovici, S. (1975) *La Représentation sociale du corps*, Paris: Mimeo.

Jodelet, D. and Milgram, S. (1977) *Cartes mentales et images sociales de Paris*, Paris: Mimeo.

Johnson, N.B., Middleton, M.B. and Tajfel, H. (1970) 'The relationship between children's preferences for and knowledge about other nations', *British Journal of Social and Clinical Psychology* 9, 232–40.

Kelley, G.A. and Thibaut, J.W. (1969) 'Group problem solving', in G. Lindzey and E. Aronson (eds) *Handbook of Social Psychology* (vol. 4), Reading, Mass.: Addison-Wesley.

Kelley, H.H. and Thibaut, J.W. (1954) 'Experimental studies of group problem-solving and process', in G. Lindzey (ed.) *Handbook of Social Psychology* (vol. 2), Reading, Mass.: Addison-Wesley.

Kelman, H.C. (1968) *A Time to Speak: On human values and social research*, San Francisco: Jossey-Bass.

Kerlinger, F.N. (1986) *Foundations of Behavioural Research*, New York: Holt, Rinehart & Winston.

Klein, G.S., Schlesinger, H.E. and Meister, D.E. (1951) 'The effect of values on perception: An experimental critique', *Psychological Review* 58, 96–112.

Knorr-Cetina, K.D. and Mulkay, M. (eds) (1983) *Science Observed: Perspectives on the social study of a science*, London: Sage.

Koch, S. (1959) Epilogue, S. Koch (ed.) *Psychology: A study of a science* (vol. III), 729–88, New York: McGraw-Hill.

—— (1985) 'The nature and limits of psychological knowledge: Lessons of a century qua science', in S.Koch and D.E. Leary (eds) *A Century of Psychology as a Science*, New York: McGraw-Hill.

Kon, I.S. (1984) 'The self as a historical–cultural and ethno-psychological phenomenon', in L.H. Strickland (ed.) *Directions in Social Psychology*, New York: Springer-Verlag.

van Krippenberg, A.F.M. (1984) 'Intergroup differences in group perceptions', in H. Tajfel (ed.) *The Social Dimension: European developments in social psychology* (vol. 2), Cambridge: Cambridge University Press.

Kuhn, T.S. (1962; 2nd edn 1970) *The Structure of Scientific Revolutions*, Chicago, Ill.: University of Chicago Press.

—— (1974) 'Logic of discovery or psychology of research?' in I. Lakatos and A. Musgrave (eds) *Criticism and the Growth of Knowledge*, Cambridge: Cambridge University Press.

—— (1982) 'Normal measurement and reasonable agreement', in B. Barnes and D. Edge (eds) *Science in Context*, Open University Press.

—— (1988) *Regaining the Past*, Lecture Series: London University.

Lakatos, I. (1974) 'Falsification and the methodology of scientific research programmes', in I. Lakatos and A. Musgrave (eds) *Criticism and the Growth of Knowledge*, Cambridge: Cambridge University Press.

Lakatos, I. and Musgrave, A. (1974) *Criticism and the Growth of Knowledge*, Cambridge: Cambridge University Press.

Lambert, W., Solomon, R.L. and Watson, P.D. (1949) 'Reinforcement and extinction as factors in size estimation', *Journal of Experimental Psychology* 39, 637–41.

Lambert, W. and Klineberg, O. (1959) 'A pilot study of the origin and development of national stereotypes', *International Social Science Journal* 11, 221–38.

—— (1967) *Children's Views of Foreign Peoples: A cross-national study*, New York: Appleton.

Latour, B. and Woolgar, S. (1979) *Laboratory Life: The social construction of scientific facts*, London: Sage.

Lewin, K. (1935) 'Psychosocial problems of minority groups', *Character and Personality* 3, 175–87.

—— (1948) *Resolving Social Conflicts*, New York: Harper & Row.

Lincoln, Y.S. and Guba, E.G. (1985) *Naturalistic Inquiry*, Beverly Hills, Calif.: Sage.

Lindzey, G. and Aronson, E. (eds) (1969) *Handbook of Social Psychology*, 2nd edn, (vol. 4), *Group Psychology and Phenomena of Interaction*, Reading, Mass.: Addison-Wesley.

—— (1985) *Handbook of Social Psychology*, 3rd edn, New York: Random House.

Lloyd, B. and Duveen, G. (1990) 'A semitic analysis of the development of social representations of gender', in G. Duveen and B. Lloyd (eds) *Social Representations and the Development of Knowledge*, Cambridge: Cambridge University Press.

Lukes, S. (1973) *Individualism*, Oxford: Blackwell.

—— (1973) in A.R. Luria and G. Lindzey (eds) *A History of Psychology in Autobiography* (vol. VI), San Francisco: W.H. Freeman.

Luria, A.R. (1976) in M. Cole (ed.) *Cognitive Development: Its cultural and social foundations* (trans. M. Lopez-Morillas and L.Solotaroff), Cambridge, Mass.: Harvard University Press.

McCurdy, H.G. (1956) 'Coin perception studies and the concept of schemata', *Psychology Review* 63, 211–50.

McDougall, W. (1908) *Introduction to Social Psychology*, London: Methuen.

—— (1920) *The Group Mind: A sketch of the principles of collective psychology with some attempt to apply them to the interpretation of national life and character*, Cambridge: Cambridge University Press.

McGuire, W.J. (1983) 'A contextualist theory of knowledge: Its implications for innovations and reform in psychological research', in L. Berkowitz (ed.) *Advances in Experimental Social Psychology* (vol. 16), New York: Academic Press.

—— (1986) 'The vicissitudes of attitudes and similar representational constructs in twentieth century psychology', *European Journal of Social Psychology* 16, 89–130.

Mackenzie, B. (1976) 'Darwinism and positivism as methodological influences on the development of psychology', *Journal of the History of the Behavioural Sciences* 12, 330–7.

—— (1977) *Behaviourism and the Limits of Scientific Method*, London: Routledge and Kegan Paul.

MacKenzie, D.A. (1981) *Statistics in Britain, 1865–1930: The social construction of scientific knowledge*, Edinburgh: Edinburgh University Press.

McKinlay, A. and Potter, J. (1987) 'Social representations: A conceptual critique', *Journal for the Theory of Social Behaviour* 17(4), 471–88.

Manis, M. (1960) 'The interpretation of opinion statements as a function of recipient attitude', *Journal of Social Psychology* 60, 340–4.

Manstead, A.S.R. and Semin, G.R. (1988) 'Methodology in social psychology: Turning ideas into actions', in M. Hewstone, W. Stroebe, J.P. Codol and G.M. Stephenson (eds) *Introduction to Social Psychology*, Oxford: Blackwell.

Margolis, J., Manicas, P.T., Harré, R. and Secord, P. (1986) *Psychology: Designing the discipline*, Oxford: Blackwell.

Markova, I. (1982) *Paradigms, Thought and Language*, Chichester: Wiley.

—— (1983) 'The origin of the social psychology of language in German expressivism', *British Journal of Social Psychology* 22, 315–26.

—— (1987) *Human Awareness: Its social development*, London: Hutchinson.

Markova, I. and Wilkie, P. (1987) 'Representations, concepts and social change: The phenomenon of AIDS', *Journal for the Theory of Social Behaviour* 17(4), 389–410.

Martin, B. (1970) *The Bias of Science*, Canberra, Australia: Southwood Press.

Mead, G.H. (1934) in C.W. Morris (ed.) *Mind, Self and Society: From the standpoint of a social behaviourist*, Chicago, Ill.: University of Chicago Press.

—— (1956) in A. Strauss (ed.) *The Social Psychology of George Herbert Mead*, Chicago, Ill.: Chicago University Press.

190

Meehl, P.E. (1978) 'Theoretical risks and tubular asterisks: Sir Karl, Sir Roland, and the slow progress of the soft psychology', *Journal of Consulting and Clinical Psychology* 26, 806–34.

Merton, R.K. (1957) *Social Theory and Social Structure*, New York: Free Press.

Middleton, M.R., Tajfel, H. and Johnson, N.B. (1970) 'Cognitive and affective aspects of children's national attitudes', *British Journal of Social Psychology* 9(2), 122.

Milgram, S. (1974) *Obedience to Authority: An experimental review*. New York: Harper and Row.

—— (1984) 'Cities as social representations', in R.M. Farr and S. Moscovici (eds) *Social Representations*, Cambridge: Cambridge University Press.

Miller, A.G. (1986) *The Obedience Experiments: A case study of controversy in social psychology*, New York: Praeger.

Miller, G.A. (1966) *Psychology: The science of mental life*, Harmondsworth: Pelican.

Mixon, D. (1972) 'Instead of deception', *Journal for the Theory of Social Behaviour* 2, 145–77.

Morland, J.K. (1966) 'A comparison of race awareness in northern and southern children', *American Journal of Orthopsychiatry* 36, 22.

Moscovici, S. (1961; 2nd edn 1976) *La Psychanalyse: son image et son public. Etude sur la représentation sociale de la psychanalyse*, Paris: Presses Universitaires de France.

—— (1963) 'Attitudes and opinions', *Annual Review of Psychology* 231–60.

—— (1972) 'Society and theory in social psychology', in J. Israel and H. Tajfel (eds) *The Context of Social Psychology: A critical assessment*, London: Academic Press.

—— (1973) Foreword, in C. Herzlich, *Health and Illness: A social psychological analysis*, London: Academic Press.

—— (1976) *Social Influence and Social Change*, London: Academic Press.

—— (1981) 'On social representations', in J.P. Forgas (ed.) *Social Cognition: Perspectives on everyday understanding*, 181–209, London: Academic Press.

—— (1982) 'The coming era of social representations', in J.P. Codol and J.P. Leyens (eds) *Cognitive Approaches to Social Behaviour*, The Hague: Nijhoff.

—— (1984a) 'The myth of the lonely paradigm: A rejoinder', *Social Research* 51(4), 939–67.

—— (1984b) 'The phenomenon of social representations', in R.M. Farr and S. Moscovici (eds) *Social Representations*, pp. 3–69, Cambridge: Cambridge University Press.

—— (1985a) *The Age of the Crowd: A historical treatise on mass psychology*, Cambridge: Cambridge University Press.

—— (1985b) 'Comment on Potter and Litton', *British Journal of Social Psychology*, 24, 91–2.

—— (1985c) 'Social influence and conformity', in G. Lindzey and E. Aronson (eds) *Handbook of Social Psychology*, 3rd edn (vol. 2), New York: Random House.

—— (1987) 'Answers and questions', *Journal for the Theory of Social Behaviour* 17(4), 513–29.

—— (1988) 'Notes towards a description of social representations', *European Journal of Social Psychology* 18, 211–50.

—— (1990) 'The generalized self and mass society', in H.T. Himmelveit and G. Gaskell (eds) *Societal Psychology*, Beverly Hills, Calif.: Sage.

191

Moscovici, S. and Hewstone, M. (1983) 'Social representations and social explanations: From the "naive" to the "amateur" scientist', in M. Hewstone (ed.) *Attribution Theory: Social and functional extensions*, Oxford: Blackwell.

Moscovici, S. Laga, E. and Naffrechaux, H. (1969) 'Influence of a consistent minority on the response of a majority in a color perception task', *Sociometry* 32, 365–79.

Moscovici, S., Mugny, G. and Van Avernaet, E. (eds) (1985) *Perspectives on Minority Influence*, Cambridge: Cambridge University Press.

Mugny, G. (1982) *The Power of Minorities*, London: Academic Press.

Mugny, G. and Carugati, F. (1989) *Social Representations of Intelligence*, Cambridge: Cambridge University Press.

Mulkay, H.J. (1972) *The Social Process of Innovation*, London: Macmillan Press.

Mullins, N.C. (1972) 'The development of a scientific speciality: The Phage Group and the origins of molecular biology', *Minerva* 10, 51–82.

Murchison, C. (ed.) (1935) *Handbook of Social Psychology*, New York: Russel & Russel.

Nersessian, N.J. (1987a) 'A cognitive-historical approach to meaning in scientific theories', in N.J. Nersessian (ed.) *The Process of Science*, Dordrecht: Martinus Nijhoff.

—— (ed.) (1987b) *The Process of Science: Contemporary philosophical approaches to understanding scientific practice*, Dordrecht: Martinus Nijhoff.

Ng, S.H. (1982) 'Power and intergroup discrimination', in H. Tajfel (ed.) *Social Identity and Intergroup Relations*, Cambridge: Cambridge University Press.

—— (1984) 'Equity and social categorization effects on intergroup allocation of rewards', *British Journal of Social Psychology* 23, 165–72.

O'Donnell, J.M. (1979) 'The origins of behaviourism', *American Psychology, 1870–1920*, New York: New York University Press.

Oldroyd, D.R. (1980) *Darwinian Impacts: An introduction to the Darwinian revolution*, Milton Keynes: Open University Press.

Orne, M. (1962) 'On the social psychology of the psychological experiment: With particular reference to demand characteristics and their implications', *American Psychologist* 17, 776–83.

Palmonari, A. (1988) Preface to Spanish edition of R.M. Farr and S. Moscovici (eds) *Social Representations*, Bologna: Il Molino.

Parker, I. (1987) 'Social representations: Social psychology's (mis)use of socio-logy', *Journal for the Theory of Social Behaviour* 17(4), 447–7.

—— (1989) *The Crisis in Modern Social Psychology: And How to End it*, London: Routledge.

Pepitone, A. (1981) 'Lessons from the history of social psychology', *American Psychologist* 36, 972–85.

Peters, R.S. and Tajfel, H. (1957) 'Hobbes and Hull – metaphysicians of behaviour', *British Journal for the Philosophy of Science* 8(29), 30–44.

Pettigrew, T.F. (1989) *Modern Racism: American black-white relations since the 1960s*, Cambridge, Mass.: Harvard University Press.

Pettigrew, T.F., Allport, G.W. and Barnett, E.O. (1958) 'Binocular resolution and perception of race in South Africa', *British Journal of Psychology* 49, 265–78.

Piaget, J. (1932) *The Moral Judgment of the Child*, London: Routledge and Kegan Paul.

—— (1974) Foreword to H.E. Gruber *Darwin on Man: A psychological study of scientific creativity*, London: Wildwood House.

Popper, Karl (1968) *The Logic of Scientific Discovery*, London: Hutchinson.
—— (1969) *Conjectures and Refutations*, London: Routledge & Kegan Paul.
Potter, J. and Litton, I. (1985) 'Some problems underlying the theory of social representations', *British Journal of Psychology* 24, 81–90.
Potter, J. and Mulkay, M. (1982) 'Scientists' interview talk: Interviews as a technique for revealing participants' interpretative practices', in M. Brenner, J. Brown and D. Canter (eds) *The Research Interview: Uses and approaches*, London: Academic Press.
Potter, J. and Wetherell, M. (1987) *Discourse and Social Psychology*: Beyond attitudes and behaviour, London: Sage.
Purkhardt, S.C. and Stockdale, J. (1993) 'Multidimensional scaling as a technique for the exploration and description of a social representation', G. Breakwell and D. Canter (eds) *Empirical Approaches to Social Representations*, Oxford: Oxford University Press.
Pye, L.W. (1961) 'Personal identity and political ideology', in D. Marvick (ed.) *Political Decision-makers*, Glencoe, Ill.: Free Press.
—— (1962) *Politics, Personality and Nation-building: Burma's search for identity*, New Haven, Conn.: Yale University Press.
Quine, W.V. (1976) *The Ways of Paradox, and other essays*, Cambridge, Mass.: Harvard University Press.
Rabbie, J.M. and Horwitz, M. (1969) 'Arousal of ingroup–outgroup bias by a chance win or loss, *Journal of Personality and Social Psychology* 13, 269–77.
Rabbie, J.M. and Wilkens, G. (1968) 'Intergroup competition and its effect on intra- and intergroup relations'. Unpublished report, University of Utrecht.
—— (1971) 'Intergroup competition and its effect on intragroup and intergroup relations', *European Journal of Social Psychology* 1, 215–34.
Razran, G. (1950) 'Ethnic dislikes and stereotypes: A laboratory study', *Journal of Abnormal and Social Psychology* 45: 7–27.
Restivo, S. (1984) 'Representation and the sociology of mathematical knowledge', in C. Belisle and B. Schiele (eds) *Les Savoirs dans les Pratiques Quotidiennes: Recherches sur les représentations*, Paris: C.N.R.S.
Rijsman, J. and Stroebe, W. (eds) (1989) 'Controversies in the social explanation of psychological behaviour', *European Journal of Social Psychology*, special edn, 19, 2, 339–440.
Ring, K.E. (1967) 'Experimental social psychology: Some sober questions about some frivolous values', *Journal of Experimental Social Psychology* 34, 641–53.
Roiser, M. (1987) 'Commonsense, science and public opinion', *Journal for the Theory of Social Behaviour* 17, 411–32.
Rommetveit, R. (1984) 'The role of language in the creation and transmission of social representations', in R.M. Farr and S. Moscovici, (eds) *Social Representations*, Cambridge: Cambridge University Press.
Rosenthal, R. (1966) *Experimenter Effects in Behavioural Research*, New York: Appleton.
Secord, P.F., Bevan, W. and Katz, B. (1956) 'The negro stereotype and perceptual accentuation', *Journal of Abnormal and Social Psychology* 53, 78–83.
Semin, G.R. (1985) 'The phenomenon of social representations: A comment on Potter and Litton', *British Journal of Social Psychology* 24, 93–4.
—— (1986) 'The individual, the social, and the social individual', *British Journal of Social Psychology* 25, 177–80.

Semin, G. and Gergen, K.J. (eds) (1990) *Everyday Understanding: Social and scientific implications* (*Inquiries in Social Construction* series), London: Sage.

Shapero, D. (1987) 'Method in the philosophy of science and epistemology: How to inquire about inquiry and knowledge', in N.J. Nersessian (ed.) *The Process of Science*, Dordrecht: Martinus Nijhoff.

Sherif, M. (1966) *In Common Predicament: Social psychology of intergroup conflict and cooperation*, Boston: Houghton-Mifflin.

—— (1967) *Group Conflict and Cooperation: Their social psychology*, London: Routledge & Kegan Paul.

Sherif, M. and Hovland, C.I. (1961) *Social Judgment: Assimilation and contrast effects in communication and attitude change*, New Haven: Yale University Press.

Sherif, M. and Sherif, C.W. (1953) *Groups in Harmony and Tension*, New York: Harper.

—— (1969) *Social Psychology*, New York: Harper & Row.

Sherif, M. and Wilson, M.O. (1953) *Group Relations at the Crossroads*, New York: Harper and Bros.

Sherif, M., Harvey, O.J., White, B.J., Hood, W.R. and Sherif, C.W. (1961) *Intergroup Conflict and Cooperation: The robbers' cave experiment*, Norman, Oklahoma: University of Oklahoma Book Exchange.

Shotter (1975) *Images of Man in Psychological Research*, London: Methuen.

Simon, M.D., Tajfel, H. and Johnson, N. (1967) 'An investigation of prejudice in Viennese children', *Koshner Zeitschrift für Sociologie und Sozialpsychologie* 19(3), 511–37.

Singer, P. (1983) *Hegel*, Oxford: Oxford University Press.

Smith, F.V., Vernon, P.E. and Tajfel, H. (1968) 'Obituary of Allport, G.W.', *British Journal of Psychology* 59(2), 99.

Smith, M.B. (1972) 'Is experimental social psychology advancing?', *Journal of Experimental and Social Psychology* 8, 86–96.

Steiner, I.D. (1974) 'Whatever happened to the group in social psychology?', *Journal of Experimental Social Psychology* 10, 94–108.

Stephan, W.G. (1985) 'Intergroup relations', in G. Lindzey and E. Aronson (eds) *Handbook of Social Psychology*, 3rd edn (vol. 2), New York: Random House.

Strickland, L.H. (ed.) (1984) *Directions in Soviet Psychology* (trans. E. Lockwood, N. Thurston and I. Gavlin), New York: Springer-Verlag.

Strickland, L.H., Aboud, F.E. and Gergen, K.J. (eds) (1976a) *Social Psychology in Transition*, New York: Plenum Press.

Strickland, L.H., Aboud, F.E., Gergen, K.J., Tajfel, H. and Jahoda, G. (1976b) 'Power structure in social psychology', *Representative Research in Social Psychology* 7(1), 76–86.

Strickland, L.H., Aboud, F., Gergen, K.J., Jahoda, G., Tajfel, H., Deutsch, M., Gergen, M., Jaspars, J., Kiesler, C., Lanzetta, J., Schonbach, P., Thorngate, W., Triandis, H., Zajonc, R. and Rommetveit, R. (1976c) 'General theory in social psychology', *Personality and Social Psychology, Bulletin* 2(2), 148–53.

Stroebe, W. (1979) 'The level of social psychological analysis: A plea for a more social social psychology', in L.H. Strickland (ed.) *Soviet and Western Perspectives in Social Psychology*, Oxford: Pergamon Press.

Tajfel, H. (1956) 'The role of value in the formation of a scale of judgment', *Bulletin of British Social Psychology* 29, 14 (Abstract).

—— (1957) 'Value and the perceptual judgment of magnitude', *Psychological Review of 1957* 64, 192–204.

—— (1959a) 'Quantitative judgement in social perception', *British Journal of Psychology* 50, 16–29.

—— (1959b) 'The anchoring effects of value in a scale of judgments', *British Journal of Psychology* 50, 294–304.

—— (1959c) 'A note on Lambert's "Evaluation Reactions to Spoken Languages"', *Canadian Journal of Psychology* 4, 86–92.

—— (1969a) 'Cognitive aspects of prejudice', in G.A. Harrison and J. Peel (eds) *Biosocial Aspects of Race*, Oxford and Edinburgh: Blackwell. Reprinted, *Journal of Biosocial Sciences* Supplement no. 1, 173–91 and *Journal of Social Issues* 25, 79–97.

—— (1969b) 'Social and cultural factors in perception', in G. Lindzey and E. Aronson (eds) *Handbook of Social Psychology*, 2nd edn (vol. 3), Reading, Mass.: Addison-Wesley.

—— (1969c) 'The formation of national attitudes: A socio-psychological perspective', in M. Sherif (ed.) *Interdisciplinary Relationships in the Social Sciences*, Chicago, Ill.: Aldine.

—— (1970a) 'Experiments in intergroup discrimination', *Scientific American* 223(5), 96–102.

—— (1970b) 'Aspects of national and ethnic loyalty', *Social Science Information* 9(3), 119–44.

—— (1972a) 'Experiments in a vacuum', in J. Israel and H. Tajfel (eds) *The Context of Social Psychology: A critical assessment*, London: Academic Press.

—— (1972b) 'La categorisation sociale', in S. Moscovici (ed.) *Introduction à la psychologie sociale*, Paris: Larousse.

—— (1972c) 'Some developments in European social psychology', *European Journal of Social Psychology* 2, 307–22.

—— (1972d) 'Social psychology of race relations', L. Bloom, Sociology-Book review, *The Journal of the British Sociological Association* 6(3), 463–4.

—— (1974a) 'Intergroup behaviour, social comparisons and social change'. Unpublished, Katz-Newcomb Lectures, University of Michigan, Ann Arbor (Carmen Huici).

—— (1974b) 'Social identity and intergroup behaviour', *Social Science Information* 13(2), 65–93.

—— (1975) 'The exit of social mobility and the voice of social change: Notes on the social psychology of intergroup relations', *Social Science Information* 14(2), 101–18.

—— (1976a) 'Exit and voice in intergroup relations', in L.H. Strickland, F.E. Aboud, and K.J. Gergen (eds) *Social Psychology in Transition*, New York: Plenum Press.

—— (1976b) 'Social psychology and social process', *Giornale Italiano di Psicologia* 3(2), 189–221.

—— (1976c) 'Against biologism', *New Society* 37, 240–2.

—— (1976d) 'Growing Points in Ethology – P.P.G. Bateson and R.A. Hinde', *New Society* 38, 737, 373–4.

—— (1977) 'Social psychology and social reality', *New Society* 39, 653–4.

—— (ed.) (1978a) *Differentiation Between Social Groups: Studies in the social psychology of intergroup relations*, European Monographs in Social Psychology (14) London: Academic Press.

Tajfel, H. (1978b) 'Preface and Introduction', in H. Tajfel (ed.) *Differentiation Between Social Groups: Studies in the social psychology of intergroup relations*, European Monographs in Social Psychology (14), London: Academic Press.

—— (1978c) 'Interindividual behaviour and intergroup behaviour', in H. Tajfel (ed.) *Differentiation Between Social Groups: Studies in the social psychology of intergroup relations*, European Monographs in Social Psychology (14), London: Academic Press.

—— (1978d) 'Social categorisation, social identity and social comparison', in H. Tajfel (ed.) *Differentiation Between Social Groups: Studies in the social psychology of intergroup relations*, European Monographs in Social Psychology (14), London: Academic Press.

—— (1978e) 'The achievement of group differentiation', in H. Tajfel (ed.) *Differentiation Between Social Groups: Studies in the social psychology of intergroup relations*, European Monographs in Social Psychology (14), London: Academic Press.

—— (1978f) 'The structure of our views about society', in H. Tajfel, and C. Fraser (eds) *Introducing Social Psychology*, Harmondsworth: Penguin.

—— (1978g) 'Intergroup behaviour I: Individualistic perspectives', in H. Tajfel, and C. Fraser (eds) *Introducing Social Psychology*, Harmondsworth: Penguin.

—— (1978h) 'Intergroup behaviour II: Group perspectives', in H. Tajfel and C. Fraser (eds) *Introducing Social Psychology*, Harmondsworth: Penguin.

—— (1978i) *The Social Psychology of Minorities*, London: Minority Rights Group.

—— (1978j) 'Rules of Disorder' – Marsh, P., Rosser, E. and Harré, R., *New Society* 43, 805, 555–6.

—— (1978k) 'Rules of Disorder – Reply', *New Society* 43, 806, 623–4.

—— (1978l) 'Read any good references lately?', *Bulletin of the British Psychological Society* 31 (February): 58.

—— (1979a) 'Individuals and groups in social psychology', *British Journal of Social and Clinical Psychology* 18, 173–9 and 183–90.

—— (1979b) 'Anti-Semitism', *New Society* 47(854), 373.

—— (1979c) 'Social-Psychology', *New Society* 48(863), 160.

—— (1979d) 'In defence of experimental social psychology – personal view', *Bulletin of the British Psychological Society* 32, 220–1. Abstract.

—— (1979e) 'Psychological Basis of Ideology – H.J. Eyesenck and G.D. Wilson, Book review', *British Journal of Psychiatry* 134: 443.

—— (1979f) 'The exit of social mobility and the voice of social change: Notes on the social psychology of intergroup relations', *Przeglad Psychologiciny* 22(1), 17–38.

—— (1979g) 'Human intergroup conflict: Useful and less useful forms of analysis', in M. von Cranach, K. Foppa, W. Lepenies, F. Ploag (eds) *Human Ethology: The claims and limits of a new discipline*, Cambridge: Cambridge University Press.

—— (1980a) 'The "New Look" and social differentiations: A semi-Brunerian perspective', in D. Olson (ed.) *The Social Foundations of Language and Thought: Essays in honor of J.S. Bruner*, New York: Norton.

—— (1980b) 'Experimental studies of intergroup behaviour', in M. Jeeves (ed.) *Psychology Survey* (vol. 3), London: Allen & Unwin.

Tajfel, H. (1981a) *Human Groups and Social Categories: Studies in social psychology*, Cambridge: Cambridge University Press.

—— (ed.) (1981b) 'Social stereotypes and social groups', in J.C. Turner and H. Giles (eds) *Intergroup Behaviours*, Oxford: Blackwell.

—— (1982a) 'Social psychology of intergroup relations', *Annual Review of Psychology* 33, Palo Alto, California: Annual Reviews Inc: 1–30.

—— (1982b) 'Stereotype spoleczne i grupy spoleczne (Social stereotypes and social groups)', *Studies Psychology Gizczne* 20(2), 5–25.

—— (ed.) (1982c) 'Social identity and intergroup relations', *European Studies in Social Psychology*, Cambridge: Cambridge University Press.

—— (1982d) 'Instrumentality, identity and social comparisons', in Tajfel, H. (ed.) *Social Identity and Intergroup Relations*, Cambridge: Cambridge University Press.

—— (1982e) 'Psychological conception of equity: The present and the future', in P. Fraisse (ed.) *Psychologie de demain*, Paris: Presse Universitaire de France.

—— (1984a) 'Intergroup relations, social myths, and social justice in social psychology', in H. Tajfel (ed.) *The Social Dimension: European Developments in Social Psychology*, Cambridge: Cambridge University Press.

—— (ed.) (1984b) *The Social Dimension: European developments in social psychology*, Cambridge: Cambridge University Press, and Paris: Editions de la Maison des Sciences de L'Homme (vols 1 and 2).

Tajfel, H. and Billig, M. (1974) 'Familiarity and categorisation in intergroup behaviour', *Journal of Experimental Psychology* 10, 159–70.

Tajfel, H. and Bruner, J.S. (1966) 'The relation between breadth of category and decision time', *British Journal of Psychology* 57(1–2), 71–5.

Tajfel, H. and Cawasjee, S.D. (1959) 'Value and the accentuation of judged differences: A confirmation', *Journal of Abnormal and Social Psychology* 59, 436–9.

Tajfel, H. and Dawson, J. (eds) (1965) *Disappointed Guests*, Oxford: Oxford University Press.

Tajfel, H. and Fraser, C. (eds) (1978a) *Introducing Social Psychology*, Harmondsworth: Penguin.

—— (1978b) 'Social psychology as social science', in H. Tajfel and C. Fraser (eds) *Introducing Social Psychology*, Harmondsworth: Penguin.

Tajfel, H. and Jahoda, G. (1966) 'Development in children of concepts and attitudes about their own and other nations: A cross-national study', *Proceedings of XVIIIth International Congress in Psychology*, Moscow Symposium 36, 17–33.

—— (1967) 'Children's development of concepts and attitudes about their own and other nations: A cross-national study', *Cteskoslovenskai Psychologie* 11(5), 437–44.

Tajfel, H. and Moscovici, S. (1976) 'Renaissance of old myths in social psychology: Peculiar misnomers', *Zeitschrift für Sozial Psychologie* 7(3), 292–7.

Tajfel, H. and Turner, J.C. (1979) 'An integrative theory of intergroup conflict', in W.G. Austin and S. Worchel (eds) *The Social Psychology of Intergroup Relations*, Monterey, Calif.: Brooks/Cole.

Tajfel, H. and Wilkes, A.L. (1963a) 'Classification and quantitative judgment', *British Journal of Psychology* 54, 101–14.

—— (1963b) 'Salience of attributes and commitment to extreme judgements in the perception of people', *British Journal of Social and Clinical Psychology* 3(1), 40–9.

Tajfel, H., Richardson, A. and Everstine, L. (1964a) 'Individual consistencies in categorizing: A study of judgmental behaviour', *Journal of Personality* 32(1), 90–108.

—— (1964b) 'Individual judgment consistencies in conditions of risk taking', *Journal of Personality* 32(4), 550–65.

Tajfel, H., Sheikh, A.A. and Gardner, R.C. (1964c) 'Content of stereotypes and the inference of similarity between members of stereotyped groups', *Acta Psychologica* 22, 191–201.

Tajfel, H., Flament, C., Billig, M. and Bundy, R. (1971) 'Social categorisation and intergroup behaviour', *European Journal of Social Psychology* I, 149–78.

Tajfel, H., Nemeth, C., Jahoda, G., Campbell, J.D. and Johnson, N.B. (1970) 'The development of children's preference for their own country: A cross-national study', *International Journal of Psychology* 5, 245–53.

Tajfel, H., Jahoda, G., Nemeth, C., Rim, Y. and Johnson, N.B. (1972) 'Devaluation by children of their own national and ethnic group: Two case studies', *British Journal of Social and Clinical Psychology* 11, 235–43.

Thibaut, J.W. and Kelley, H.H. (1959) *The Social Psychology of Groups*, New York: Wiley.

Thompson, K. (1985) *Readings from Emile Durkheim*, Tavistock and Ellis Horwood.

Traweek, P. (1984) 'Nature in the age of its mechanical reproduction: The reproduction of nature and physicists in the high energy physics community', in C. Belisle and B. Schiele (eds) *Les Savoirs dans les Pratiques Quotidiennes: Recherches sur les représentations*, Paris: Centre National des Recherches Scientifiqué.

Turner, J.C. (1975) 'Social comparison and social identity: Some prospects for intergroup behaviour', *European Journal of Social Psychology* 5, 5–34.

—— (with Hogg, M.A., Oakes, P.J., Reicher, S.D. and Wetherell, M.S.) (1987) *Rediscovering the Social Group: A self-categorization theory*, Oxford: Blackwell.

Turner, J.C. and Giles H. (eds) (1981) *Integroup Behaviour*, Oxford: Blackwell.

Turner, J.C., Brown, K.J. and Tajfel, H. (1979) 'Social comparison and group interest in ingroup favouritism', *European Journal of Social Psychology* 9(2), 187–204.

Vaughan, G.M. (1964) 'The development of ethnic attitudes in New Zealand school children', *Genetic Psychology Monographs*, 70, 135.

Vaughan, G.M., Tajfel, H. and Williams, J. (1981) 'Bias in reward allocation in an intergroup and an interpersonal context', *Social Psychology Quarterly* 44(1), 37–42.

Vygotsky, L.S. (1962) *Thought and Language* (ed. and trans. E. Hanfmann and G. Vaker), Cambridge, Mass.: Massachusetts Institute of Technology Press and Wiley.

—— (1978) *Mind in Society: The development of higher psychological processes* (ed. M. Cole, V. John-Steiner, S. Scribner and E. Souberman), Cambridge, Mass.: Harvard University Press.

Webb, E.J., Campbell, D.T., Schwartz, R.D., *et al.* (1981; 1st edn 1966) 'Nonreactive measures in the social sciences', *Unobstrusive Measures: Nonreactive research in the social sciences*, Boston: Houghton-Mifflin.

Weber, R.P. (1985) *Basic Content Analysis*, London: Sage.

Wells, A. (1987) 'Social representations and the world of science', *Journal for the Theory of Social Behaviour* 17, 433–46.

Wertsch, T.V. (1985) *Vygotsky and the Social Formation of Mind*, Cambridge, Mass.: Harvard University Press.

Wilder, D.A. (1986) 'Social categorization: Implications for creation and reduction of intergroup bias', in L. Berkowitz (ed.) *Advances in Experimental Social Psychology* (vol. 19), 291–355.

Wilkes, A.L. and Tajfel, H. (1966) 'Types of classification and importance of relative contrast', *Bulletin of CERP* 15(1), 71–81.

Wundt, W. (1900–20) *Voelkerpsychologie: Eine Untersuchung der Entwicklungsgesetze von Sprache, Mythus und Sitte* (10 vols), Leipzig: Engelmann.

Zukier, H. (1986) 'The paradigmatic and narrative modes in goal-guided inference', in R.M. Sorrentino and E.T. Higgins (eds) *Handbook of Motivation and Cognition*, New York: Guilford Press.

AUTHOR INDEX

SUBJECT INDEX